Learning Difficulties

AND

Sexual Vulnerability

of related interest

Disability and Child Sexual Abuse
Lessons from Survivors' Narratives for Effective Protection, Prevention and
Treatment
Martina Higgins and John Swain
ISBN 978 1 84310 563 3

Good Practice in Safeguarding Adults
Working Effectively in Adult Protection
Edited by Jacki Pritchard
ISBN 978 1 84310 699 9
Good Practice in Health, Social Care and Criminal Justice Series

Good Practice in Assessing Risk
Current Knowledge, Issues and Approaches
Edited by Hazel Kemshall and Bernadette Wilkinson
ISBN 978 1 84905 059 3
Good Practice in Health, Social Care and Criminal Justice Series

Supporting Relationships and Friendships
A Workbook for Social Care Workers
Suzan Collins
ISBN 978 1 84905 072 2
Knowledge and Skills for Social Care Workers Series

**Caring for the Physical and Mental Health of People with Learning
Disabilities**
David Perry, Louise Hammond, Geoff Marston, Sherryl Gaskell and James Eva
Foreword by Dr Anthony Kearns
ISBN 978 1 84905 131 6

Working with Adult Abuse
A Training Manual for Working with Vulnerable Adults
Jacki Pritchard
ISBN 978 1 84310 509 1

Disabled Children and the Law
Research and Good Practice
2nd edition
Janet Read, Luke Clements and David Ruebain
ISBN 978 1 84310 280 9

Learning Difficulties
AND
Sexual Vulnerability

A SOCIAL APPROACH

ANDREA HOLLOMOTZ

Jessica Kingsley *Publishers*
London and Philadelphia

First published in 2011
by Jessica Kingsley Publishers
116 Pentonville Road
London N1 9JB, UK
and
400 Market Street, Suite 400
Philadelphia, PA 19106, USA

www.jkp.com

Library of Congress Cataloging in Publication Data
Hollomotz, Andrea, 1982-
  Learning difficulties and sexual vulnerability : a social approach / Andrea Hollomotz.
    p. cm.
  Includes bibliographical references and index.
  ISBN 978-1-84905-167-5 (alk. paper)
  1. Developmentally disabled--Abuse of. 2. Developmentally disabled--Sexual
behavior. 3. Learning disabled--Abuse of. 4. Learning disabled--Sexual behavior. 5.
Sex crimes--Prevention. I. Title.
  HV1570.H65 2011
  362.3--dc22
                                    2010037542

British Library Cataloguing in Publication Data
A CIP catalogue record for this book is available from the British Library

ISBN 978 1 84905 167 5

Printed and bound in Great Britain

Contents

List of Tables and Figures

Acknowledgements

I would like to thank the research advisory committee for their keen interest and support throughout this study. Moreover, I would like to thank Colin Barnes and Mark Priestley for their ongoing outstanding guidance and encouragement, as well as Pete Coia, Felicity Armstrong and Nick Ellison for their thoughtful comments, staff and professionals at the research locations for their assistance, the editorial team at JKP for all their help and, most importantly, the respondents for sharing their stories and Andy for his patience.

Chapter 1

Introduction

People with learning difficulties are considerably more likely to experience sexual violence than non-disabled people. Explanations are often sought within the individual, who is subsequently labelled as 'vulnerable'. This label implies a causal link between learning difficulties and risk. In the UK and elsewhere a growing awareness of violence against adults has led to changes in the law and social policy, in order to facilitate better protection. These are positive developments, which are outlined in detail in Chapter 2. However, this book suggests that an exclusive focus on an individual's 'vulnerability' can become oppressive. Undue protection from risks and opportunities associated with everyday life may disable individuals from becoming competent social and sexual actors and from accessing information and services that have the potential to reduce sexual 'vulnerability'.

This book puts forward an ecological approach to conceptualising risk of sexual violence, which is underpinned by the social model of disability. It is argued that sexual 'vulnerability' is not inherent to individuals, but that it instead arises from particular social contexts. This book consequently aims to draw a holistic picture of the social processes that are involved in its creation. A range of disabling and enabling factors in the everyday lives of adults with learning difficulties are identified. The discussion includes examples about risk creation as a result of inadequate sex education, segregation, interactions with staff and limited opportunities for choice-making. Suggestions for future practice with a view to reducing risk of sexual violence are made.

This chapter begins by explaining how my interest in the subject area at hand arose from my experiences of conducting adult protection work. Next, the social model of disability, which underpins this research, is outlined. A discussion of methods and methodology that were used in the research that underpins this book follows. Finally an overview of the structure of this book is presented.

THE PROTECTION OF 'VULNERABLE' ADULTS: A PERSONAL ACCOUNT

I had my first encounter with adult protection work while I conducted a work placement at a sexual health agency as a social work student. Amongst others we delivered sex and relationship education to people with learning difficulties. One day a young woman who attended this course disclosed to me that she had been sexually violated by her maternal uncle. She was clear from the start that she wanted this issue to be dealt with confidentially, as she did not want her family to find out about it. She did not want to press charges and merely asked me for advice on ways in which she could prevent future incidents.

Working with 'vulnerable' adults was new to my agency. My manager expressed concerns about professional accountability and responsibility. We consequently consulted the applicable adult protection policy at the time, *No Secrets*. As the title of the document indicates, the policy adopts the philosophy that 'there can be no secrets and no hiding place when it comes to exposing the abuse of vulnerable adults' (Department of Health 2000, p.2). However, Dunn, Clare and Holland (2008) point out that protective interventions that are guided by the assumption of an adult's 'vulnerability' can on occasion take priority over the need to respect decision-making autonomy, which is what ultimately happened in this case. We decided to overrule the woman's wish for confidentiality, in order to be seen to be adhering to *No Secrets* 'whistle blowing' principles: support workers and social services agencies were informed and the police became involved. However, when she was pressured to press charges the young woman denied she had ever made an allegation. This appeared to be her only way out, as more and more professionals became involved to advocate on her behalf. We had failed to provide the assistance she had asked for; mere advice on means of self-protection. Instead we were eager to do the protecting for her, which she experienced as invasive.

When I later worked as a qualified social worker I remained unable to shake off the impression that my interference was not always helpful, even though a revised adult protection policy, *Safeguarding Adults* (Association of Directors of Social Services 2005, p.4), was implemented. These guidelines, too, focus on active professionals helping passive 'adults who may be in need of community care services' to be protected from violence and exploitation. I was involved in holding adult protection case conferences about individuals who were not even aware that these meetings were being held.

One case involved discussing the intimate sexual behaviour of two adults who resided in a small group establishment. Concerns were raised after a social worker visited and observed the couple in their living room. They had both been fully dressed when the man put his head between the woman's breasts. The social worker immediately resorted to 'whistle blowing'. She felt that the woman had been sexually exploited. She did not listen to the support staff, who confirmed that this relationship had been ongoing for many years, with what they believed to be mutual consent. For the social worker it was unthinkable that the woman could have a sexual relationship, as she was labelled to have a 'mental age of five'. She handed the case over to me with the words: 'I would not allow my five-year-old to have sex.'

It took months of invasive professional assessments and discussions before the case was dropped. I had to observe the couple and confirm that I witnessed signs of mutual consent, such as the woman becoming excited when her partner came home from the day centre, both of them seeking each other's company, her kissing him back when he approached her and her giggles when he put his head between her breasts. This procedure was invasive and unnecessary. Support workers who knew the couple well had observed nothing different than I had, but their accounts were overruled by the social worker who initiated the adult protection procedure, which is not in line with the principles of inter-agency partnership working that are encouraged by adult protection policies (Association of Directors of Social Services 2005; Department of Health 2000). Rather, this reflects the hierarchical structures that exist amongst professionals in health and personal social services (Perkin 1989), whereby those who are less skilled are equated with a lower status and their judgements are consequently seen to be of less value. Moreover, it appears that adult protection has become such a central topic for social services departments that professionals have become exceedingly sensitive when they encounter any type of sexual behaviours.

When I began to plan the research upon which this book is based I was initially interested in investigating how adults with learning difficulties could be supported to lead safe sexual relationships, but my continuous encounter with the notion of 'vulnerability' made me realise that this concept acts as a barrier to sexual autonomy, because the rights of a person who is assumed to be 'vulnerable' can be overwritten in the interest of their protection, as the above case studies demonstrate.

DEFINING DISABILITY

The research upon which this book is based is underpinned by the social model of disability. This section defines the core concepts of the social model and contrasts this with the individual model. Then it is discussed whether the social model has relevance to people with learning difficulties. Finally it is explained why this book uses the term 'people with learning difficulties'.

Models of disability

Individualising approaches to disability view the problems experienced by disabled people as a direct consequence of their impairment. Disability is seen as caused by personal deficiency (Oliver 1983). The assumption that 'vulnerability' is an inherent characteristic of disabled people is such an individualising concept. If impairments are the cause for the problems disabled people experience, the recommended solutions are 'cure' and 'care' (Finkelstein 1991). The solution for 'vulnerability' is protection. This makes individuals dependent on professionals who can provide these interventions.

On the other hand, the social model of disability focuses on social processes when explaining disabled people's disadvantages. It makes a distinction between disability and impairment, which was first suggested by the Union of the Physically Impaired Against Segregation (1976, pp.3–4):

> *Impairment:* lacking part of or all of a limb, or having a defective limb, organism or mechanism of the body.

> *Disability:* the disadvantage or restriction of activity caused by a contemporary social organisation which takes no or little account of people who have physical impairments and thus excludes them from the mainstream of social activities.

Disability activists, such as Morris (1991) and Zola (1982), promote the view that impairment should be celebrated as individual difference in a diverse society. In this way individuals subvert negative valuations. 'The importance of this social model of disability is that it no longer sees disabled people as having something wrong with them – it rejects the individual pathology model' (Oliver 1983, p.27).

However, Chappell (1998) argues that the social model of disability has not been utilised effectively for people with learning difficulties. She states that past emancipatory disability analysis of our society tended to focus predominantly on barriers to the inclusion of people with physical and sensory impairments, but neglected an analysis of barriers that may affect people with the label 'learning difficulties'. The emancipatory paradigm Chappell refers to would confront social oppression. 'A recognition of and confrontation with power' is central to emancipation (Oliver 1992, p.110).

On the other hand, it could be argued that Oliver (1983, 2009) was explicit from the start that the social model applies to *all* people with impairments, including people with learning difficulties. Accordingly, the inability to understand complex words is an impairment, but being excluded from gaining knowledge because information is not provided in an accessible format, for example via plain language, causes disability.

Chappell (1998) asserts that, in order to fully utilise the social model of disability to benefit all disabled people, an explicit commitment must be made to include the particular barriers encountered by people with learning difficulties in our analysis. However, this is already happening. The barriers that are likely to affect people with learning difficulties, for example barriers to information, individual and collective advocacy and adequate assistance, are often discussed with reference to disabled people in general (e.g. DCODP 1986). Even though the social model is not specifically applied to this group in general discussions, this does not lead to the conclusion that such debates are not applicable to people with learning difficulties. This book will furthermore demonstrate that the social model can be a central tool in explaining the disadvantages faced by people with learning difficulties.

Further criticisms of the social model are offered by feminist authors who argue that debates about disability should include a discussion of impairment related experiences and private domains of relationships and sexuality (Morris 1991; Thomas 1999). However, as Oliver (2009) has repeatedly pointed out, the social model does not prohibit such a discussion of impairment related experiences alongside social model explorations. Nonetheless the model itself focuses on the *collective* experience of disablement, as it does not see impairment as the cause of disabled people's economic and social disadvantages, which is why social model explorations focus on the structural and cultural causes of disability. Besides, this book demonstrates that a distinct public and private divide does not exist in respect to the sexual lives of people with learning difficulties. In Chapter 2 it is highlighted how their sexuality has been subjected to public scrutiny throughout history. Chapter 3 will explore how more covert practices continue to shape the sexual experiences of individuals today. Social model conceptualisations can thus enable us to understand how social (public) processes impact on personal and very private experiences.

Others have argued that both, impairments and disability, are social constructs and that the division between the two concepts is no longer valid (Shakespeare 2006; Shakespeare and Watson 2002). These might be interesting philosophical questions, yet they have little value in informing research, policy and practice. Such debates may furthermore be seen to take the focus away from social explorations. Disability studies scholars and disabled people do not present as a united front that seeks to re-focus attention on social processes. Unsurprisingly the dominant meanings attached to disability remain firmly rooted in personal tragedy theory. Disability is still primarily regarded as a health issue, which is in part reflected in official definitions (World Health Organization 2001).

This book makes an explicit commitment to focus on disability as a social problem. It is particularly interested in highlighting the effects of disabling barriers. It consequently avoids a discussion of impairment and focuses on exploring social factors.

Labelling and terminology

Labelling categories are not fixed and conceptualisations of 'deviance' have shifted throughout history. Armstrong (2002) asserts that labels may serve to classify difference as deviance. For instance, many of those who were seen to be 'moral defectives' under the Mental Deficiency Act (1913), such as women who gave birth out of wedlock (Weeks 1989), would today be viewed as 'ordinary' citizens. Armstrong (2002), however, warns us to be cautious about viewing historic developments as uninterrupted progress. Many impairment categories were only recently created. For instance, the Education Act (1944) expanded the array of labels for 'handicapped' children, which resulted in an expansion of segregated education. New categories of deviance, such as ADHD (attention deficit hyperactivity disorder) and Asperger's Syndrome were created (Armstrong 2002).

Intelligence is measured in a multitude of ways, for example through Intelligence Quotient (IQ) testing and with reference to 'mental age' labels. Gould (1996) offers an elaborate critique of intelligence testing. For instance, he points out that tests are culturally specific and put some individuals at a disadvantage. 'Mental age' labels must be treated with additional caution, as they may serve to justify infantilisation, as was evident in the social worker's comments about a woman with a mental age label of 'five years old' quoted earlier. In this case a woman in her fifties, with the body and sexual desires of a 50-year-old, was equated with a young child. The mental age label consequently distracted the social worker from considering the needs of this adult holistically.

Impairment labels serve as administrative categories (Finkelstein 1991), which are relevant when accessing health and social services, but otherwise they are imposed, rather than chosen (Oliver and Barnes 1998). In the UK there are currently two terms in use to describe the research population; people with learning difficulties and people with learning disabilities. The term 'learning disabilities' was first introduced in the White Paper *Caring for People* (Department of Health 1989) and is casually used by professionals and in government publications (e.g. Department of Health 2001, 2009b). The UK self-advocacy movement uses the term 'learning difficulties' (e.g. People First 2010).

Oliver and Barnes (1998, p.18) assert that 'the use of the phrase "people with disabilities" is unacceptable because it blurs the crucial distinction between impairment and disability'. When a social model approach is taken the term 'disability' has specific connotations, as described earlier. Accordingly, the phrase 'people with learning *disabilities*' translates as 'people with social barriers to learning'. This makes little grammatical sense. We may talk about excluded people, but not about 'people with exclusion'. We may talk about oppressed people, but not about 'people with oppression'.

The term 'learning difficulties' has the further advantage that it emphasises that people are *able* to learn once *difficulties* in the learning process are overcome (Harris 1995; People First 2010). This book therefore adopts this term. It is used to refer solely to individuals with intellectual impairments and not to individuals with the educational label of '*specific* learning difficulties', such as Dyslexia (The Royal College of Psychiatrists 2009). Nonetheless, many individuals would prefer not to be labelled at all (e.g. Central England People First 2010). This book therefore refrains from using labels, unless they are required to contextualise the debate.

In order to indicate that 'learning difficulties' remains an imposed category, it would be most appropriate to refer to the research population as 'disabled people who are labelled with learning difficulties'. This is a rather long term, which is why this book uses the shorter terms 'disabled people' and 'people with learning difficulties'. The term 'disabled people' is used in contexts that discuss disabling barriers that could affect the whole population of people with impairments, while the term 'people with learning difficulties' is mostly used when referring to issues that are particular to individuals with this label.

RESEARCH METHODOLOGY

The research upon which this book is based explores social causes for the increased risk to adults with learning difficulties of experiencing sexual violence. It is guided by the following questions:

- What causes increased risk to sexual violence?

- To what extent can people with learning difficulties be considered to be sexually 'vulnerable'?

- How can they increase their resistance to sexual violence?

As stated in the previous section, this book is underpinned by the social model of disability, which determines the questions that are asked, which aspects of disabled people's lives are investigated (social, rather than biological factors) and also the research methods and methodology.

In the past the lives of people with learning difficulties were recorded by others, and individuals themselves had little impact on writing their own history (Atkinson 1997). Even today some researchers seek the views of more articulate persons on behalf of disabled people. For example, a recent study in Ireland involved questioning parents and staff about the impact that day services had on the quality of life of people who were labelled with 'severe' learning difficulties (Hartnett *et al.* 2008). The researchers neither observed, nor interacted with, the research subjects themselves. However, this way of investigating provides more information about the experiences and subjectivity of the substitute persons than about the individuals concerned (Lloyd, Gatherer and Kalsy 2006).

It is worth remembering that historically the suggestion that some individuals are not lucid or articulate enough to express their views has been linked to almost every disempowered group in society, including women and children (Proctor 2001). The research upon which this book is based aims to represent the voices of people with learning difficulties, without prejudice about their abilities. Disabled people are viewed as 'expert knowers' on their own lives (Stone and Priestley 1996). I therefore value their version of the 'truth' over that of others. Consequently, it was of particular importance to design questions that people with learning difficulties could answer, without putting them in the difficult situation of having to respond to queries that did not apply to their lives. Sexuality is a central theme of the research. Yet, great effort had to be made to phrase questions about this subject in a sensitive manner, in a way that was as unthreatening as possible and that allowed individuals to back out of responding at any time. A brief overview follows, which describes the ways in which these issues were addressed.

A PARTICIPATORY APPROACH

This work included some aspects of participatory research (Zarb 1992). Such research differs from traditional approaches, as disabled people have some control over the research process. It seeks to be accountable to disabled people. This project involved a group of self-advocates as consultants. The advisory group consisted of 15 self-advocates (eight women and seven men) who met weekly at an independent self-advocacy agency. In the first phase of the consultation I translated current adult protection policies and the law, as it applies to people with learning difficulties and sexual rights, into plain language. This made these accessible for the group. The advisors noted a discrepancy between how they wanted to be seen (judged by their abilities, rather than their inabilities) and the way in which adult protection guidance portrayed them as dependent and powerless. They were therefore keen to explore the issue of assumed 'vulnerability' further.

We spent some time thinking about questions that should be asked and designing the research schedule. Group members corrected me when I was using words they did not understand. They critically examined the picture cards I designed to accompany question categories and commented on whether they thought the pictures made sense. The group also helped to write and produce three risk perception vignettes (both methods are explained later on). I then piloted the questionnaire with three self-advocates, who gave valuable feedback on this experience. During the data analysis stage group members commented on respondents' accounts and they discussed general themes, such as whether people with learning difficulties have the right to lead sexual relationships. These discussions enabled me to identify which issues people with learning difficulties consider to be of particular importance, which also assisted with data reduction.

Making interviews accessible

Interviewing relies heavily on the cognition, recall, intellectual abilities and expressive language skills of respondents. For people with learning difficulties some or all of these skills may differ from those of non-disabled people (World Health Organization 2001). This had to be taken into account throughout the data collection process.

I conducted participant observations at most of the research locations prior to the interviews. This enabled me to get to know respondents before the interviews commenced, as recommended by Arksey and Knight (1999) and to familiarise myself with part of their daily routine. I was therefore able to tailor the conceptual level of the questions during the interviews to suit an individual's communication needs and to ask more concrete questions. I was aware that respondents might not be able to concentrate for lengthy periods of time. To make interviews less demanding we stopped when the respondent became tired of talking. Most interviews were conducted in two parts. Each part normally lasted between 30 minutes and an hour.

As stated earlier, the research consultants ensured that the interviewing schedule did not include complex grammatical structures or concepts (Finlay and Lyons 2001). Instead, short sentences and simple words were used. Questions were relatively direct and specific and they concentrated on one point at a time (Arksey and Knight 1999). Many people with learning difficulties use a more concrete, rather than an abstract frame of reference (Booth and Booth 1994). This means that they may find it difficult to generalise from, or evaluate the significance of, past events. To accommodate for this way of thinking, most of the questions enquired about actual events in the respondent's life. Moreover, pictures and vignettes were used as concrete referencing tools (Rodgers 1999).

The research advisors and I developed three risk perception vignettes, to make talking about risk less abstract. Each vignette was made up of a simple story line about a person who was subjected to an unsought potentially sexual or risky approach. The story was illustrated by eight photographs. By the end of each vignette respondents were asked to advise the individual who had been approached about the way they should respond. (Findings and more detail are presented in Chapter 5.)

In addition, 36 picture cards accompanied the other 23 question categories. For example, when talking about food preparation and household chores a picture card displaying photographs of a person engaging in diverse activities, such as chopping vegetables, hoovering, washing dishes and handling an oven, was shown. Although such questions are not directly related to sexuality, they gave respondents a concrete discussion space to explore choice-making. As discussed in Chapter 2, the ability to make independent choices is an important self-defence skill. However, the abstract question: 'To what extent are you able to make choices in your daily life?' would return few responses from less articulate individuals. This is why questions about choice-making were broken down into concrete subject categories, like the above. These categories were chosen by the research advisors, who decided which choices they believed to be of importance in their daily lives.

Respondents engaged keenly with these questions. They often used the pictures as starting points for talking about routine activities they did and did not engage in. For instance, when looking at the picture of the oven some respondents told me that they were 'not allowed' to use this, because it is 'dangerous' (as discussed in Chapter 4). Without the picture as a concrete prompt they may not have thought of this limitation to their daily choices.

The respondents

The research was conducted at two statutory day centres and one independent day service provider, a centre for independent living for people with learning difficulties and a self-advocacy agency. In all of these locations I conducted participant observations prior to the research interviews, with the exception of the independent day service. Ethical approval for conducting the study had been granted by the relevant local authority departments.

I interviewed 12 men and 17 women who had labels of 'mild' to 'moderate' learning disabilities (World Health Organization 1996). All of them used speech as a primary means of communication. Individuals with 'severe' or 'profound' learning difficulties were not included in this study. This is due to the fact that interviewing requires respondents to be fairly articulate. Although I aimed to make the interviews as accessible as possible, my choice of method did nonetheless limit the range of respondents who could be included in the study.

Respondents were between 22 and 68 years old. Twelve of the respondents were under 30 years old. About half of the sample had additional impairment labels. With the exception of Michael, whose ethnicity is Pakistani, all of the respondents are White British. Attempts to include a more diverse sample have been made, yet the services that were approached for the research were often attended by few or no representatives of ethnic minority groups. This is likely to be due to the disadvantages that ethnic minority populations face in accessing services (e.g. Chamba *et al.* 1999). About half of the respondents lived with their parents or other family members. About a quarter lived in residential group settings and another quarter lived independently. Table 1.1 gives an overview of some of the personal characteristics of respondents.

Table 1.1 The respondents

Name	Age group	Sex	Living arrangement	Additional impairment label
Ann	40–49	F	3	
Bart	20–29	M	3	Yes
Bill	50–59	M	2	Yes
Bob	20–29	M	3	Yes
Britney	20–29	F	4	
Chantal	20–29	F	1	
Emma	30–39	F	3/4	Yes
Gemma	20–29	F	4	Yes
Georgina	20–29	F	1	
Jasmine	50–59	F	3	Yes
Josie	60–69	F	4	Yes
Kathy	20–29	F	3	
Leanne	20–29	F	3	Yes
Lee	20–29	M	3	
Liz	40–49	F	2	
Martha	30–39	F	4	
Mary	50–59	F	3	
Michael	20–29	M	3	
Norman	30–39	M	3	Yes
Paul	40–49	M	3	Yes
Peter	50–59	M	3	Yes
Rachel	30–39	F	4	
Richard	50–59	M	2	
Rose	40–49	F	3	
Ryan	20–29	M	4	
Salina	60–69	F	2	

Sam	50–59	M	3	Yes
Sue	50–59	F	4	Yes
Tyler	20–29	M	1	Yes

Names: Note that all names that are used throughout this book are pseudonyms

Sex: M = male, F = female

Living arrangement: 1 = independent, 2 = independent with support (not 24 hours a day, except Liz), 3 = living with family/parents, 4 = staffed 24 hours a day

This book is concerned with exploring *risk factors*, in order to make suggestions for future preventative work. It does not focus on exploring actual incidents of violence. The research upon which this book is based therefore draws on a general sample of adults with learning difficulties. It does not specifically target survivors of sexual violence. However, due to the high incidence of violence against this population it was to be expected that some respondents had experienced sexual violence and would wish to talk about it, possibly for the first time. As part of my ethical agreement I was obliged to report any first time disclosures to a named person at the research locations. The accounts of respondents who chose to talk about past violent experiences are presented in Chapter 3, with a particular focus on aiming to understand the processes that created increased risk.

Specific ethical concerns

The research that led to this book gave rise to a number of specific ethical concerns, because it involved talking to participants with learning difficulties about sensitive issues. Enabling individuals to make an informed choice about their participation was crucial. I generally introduced the research to focus groups of about six people, in order to take pressure off respondents to partake. I also provided a plain language research information booklet and consent form. If individuals expressed an interest in participating we agreed that I would visit them again, usually within the next week, to commence the interview. Before and during the interview I kept reminding respondents of their right not to answer questions. Interviews were always conducted in privacy, but with support staff close by, for example in a different room of the same building. This gave respondents the option to walk out of the interview to seek support from a member of staff at any point. None of the respondents chose this option.

I always ensured that I asked questions about sexuality last, after rapport was built with respondents. I made it clear that I would now start asking questions about this subject and I gave respondents the option not to continue with the interview. Sue chose this option, while Salina opted out half way through this section. Bart seemed nervous when I asked questions about sex. His body language changed: he moved further away on the sofa, slouched and started fiddling with some beads. I therefore stopped asking questions about this topic. As this was the last section of the interview I wanted to make sure that he left feeling more relaxed. I therefore ended the interview by asking random questions about things he had previously enjoyed talking about. I found this technique useful to overcome possible embarrassment after talking about sexuality and applied this to all subsequent respondents.

Birch and Miller (2000) assert that qualitative interviews can create a space in which individuals can reflect on, re-order and give new meaning to past and difficult experiences. While I did not consciously intend to create such a space, the interviews did have this effect on many of the respondents. For instance, Tyler told me that the interview felt like I was 'kind of a therapist' and he could 'unload' with me. Birch and Miller (2000), too, compare the research interview with a therapeutic interaction. Rachel enjoyed the 'chat' we were having. She particularly enjoyed having a confidential talk about sexual activity and sexual desires.

It became evident that talking about sensitive issues can be enjoyable, helpful and cathartic for people with learning difficulties. Yet, as with non-disabled people, it can also cause difficulties and distress: Josie started crying when I asked her about people who are important to her. She said that she misses her mother, who passed away a long time ago. Michael was equally upset when my questions reminded him of his dad, who had recently died. In both cases I interrupted the interview to comfort the respondent.

As qualitative interviews invite intimacy, disengagement in a sensitive way can be challenging. The fact that I conducted participant observations, as well as interviews, at most of the research locations had the advantage that I did not withdraw contact immediately after the interviews. Respondents were able to continue to approach me. Yet, ultimately, I left the research location entirely. I was always clear that this would be happening and that I had to 'go back to university'. Many respondents were familiar with this concept, because they were used to students attending work placements at their service settings. When I ceased to come to, for example, the day centres respondents understood that I was 'back at university'.

STRUCTURE OF THE BOOK

The remainder of this book is organised into five further chapters, which seek to explore the nature and causes of the alleged sexual 'vulnerability' of adults with learning difficulties, as well as potentially preventative mechanisms. Chapter 2 begins by outlining the historic and policy context of the work. Next it outlines which individual and social factors are assumed to cause sexual 'vulnerability'. These factors are summarised as part of a new ecological model, which illustrates how they are closely interlinked and in constant interaction with one another. Chapters 3 to 6 investigate how these processes operate in the lives of 29 adults with learning difficulties.

Chapter 3 explores the sexual competences and experiences of people with learning difficulties. It examines whether the information about sex and sexuality that was provided to respondents was useful to them, whether they are able to access information on their own terms and to make informed decisions, and how the advice they received affects their understanding. It is furthermore summarised how individuals experience sexuality and privacy. This exploration takes a particular focus on the learning and development opportunities that arise from such experiences. The impact that these may have on an individual's sense of self and self-awareness is also examined. Finally, sexual invasions are explored. Incidents of sexual violence are first described, before the causal mechanisms that allowed the attacks to succeed are highlighted. Then it is explained why the routine prescription of contraceptives to women with learning difficulties, as well as sexism, must be seen as further harmful invasions, which increase risk to sexual violence.

This book suggests that increased risk is, in large part, socially created. Chapter 4 seeks to substantiate this claim by discussing how a reduced ability to self-defend is caused by the differential treatment that labelled individuals receive. The focus will be on everyday social processes, which impact on a person's self-determination skills and on the creation of situational risk. It is outlined how fear and othering, as well as segregated support structures, influence individuals' sense of self and their social life. It is also explained how bullying and segregation affect the relational networks of individuals. Next, the barriers and support structures that enable or disable individuals from establishing and maintaining friendships are described. This is followed by an examination of relationships with support workers and of the particular risks that may arise from them. Finally, the extent to which individuals have the opportunity to exercise self-determination in their everyday life is explored with reference to individual's choices about clothes, daytime activities and residential services.

So far the discussion is focused on mostly disabling social processes in the lives of people with learning difficulties. Chapter 5 explores the way in which individuals nonetheless interact as assertive social actors. It seeks to make explicit the enabling processes and the potential that people with learning difficulties have to protect themselves. At first it is discussed how the label 'learning difficulties' affects the sense of self of individuals. The benefits of self-advocacy for identity formation are highlighted. Next, it is shown how independent living and inter-dependencies within the immediate family allow individuals to increase their autonomy and to take on responsibilities for themselves or others. The potential of real-life, consenting sexual encounters to pose as learning opportunities and to enable an individual to develop and enforce their assertiveness skills is furthermore highlighted. Finally, respondents' actual sexual assertiveness and risk perception skills are examined. It is also shown how some respondents have successfully dealt with the threat of violence in their real lives. These accounts contest assumptions of incompetence and passivity.

Overall, this book aims to suggest ways in which people with learning difficulties can increase their ability to defend against sexual violence. It outlines the disabling social processes that hinder them from developing their full potential and provides evidence of resistance skills. The final chapter summarises these processes and makes recommendations for future practice and research.

Chapter 2

Developing an Alternative Approach to Risk

This chapter provides the theoretical grounding and context for this book. It begins by outlining the recent history of people with learning difficulties, from institutionalisation to normalisation, to *Valuing People* (Department of Health 2001, 2009b). Next, the incidence of sexual violence is discussed. Legal and policy guidelines that are set out to manage risk will be outlined. The second half of this chapter suggests an ecological approach to explaining risk of sexual violence. This conceptual framework offers a tool for explaining the creation and construction of sexual 'vulnerability'. These concepts are broadly derived from Priestley's (1998) definitions of the creation and construction of disability. Consequently, this book will illustrate that the notion of 'vulnerability' can have disabling consequences in two ways: the process of social *creation* refers to the making of actual 'vulnerability', while *construction* refers to assumptions and beliefs.

CONTEXT OF THE STUDY

In order to fully appreciate the situation of people with learning difficulties living in the UK today it is useful to consider their historic standing in society and particularly their recent history. This poses challenges in itself. As stated earlier, people with learning difficulties have until recently been unable to document their own history. Ryan and Thomas (1987, p.85) assert that 'what history they do have is not so much theirs as the history of others acting either on their behalf, or against them'. Over the last 15 years there has been an increasing commitment to avert this trend and to engage people with learning difficulties in life history research (Atkinson 2004). Recent examples of individuals telling their own stories include some contributions in a special issue of the *British Journal of Learning Disabilities* (2010, *Volume 38*, 2).

Although most of the big residential institutions for people with learning difficulties have closed down by now, some people are still affected by their recent past. Furthermore, the way in which services are run today inevitably arises out of the recent history and subsequent policy changes. This book will highlight that some elements of institutional practice continue to affect some people who now live in smaller establishments in the community. Understanding past practices is therefore crucial for understanding the present. This section briefly outlines more recent historic developments in service provisions for people with learning difficulties, leading from institutionalisation to normalisation and to social role valorisation (SRV). This is followed by a brief outline of the current UK policy context and of the philosophies that impact on service provisions today. Conceptualisations of sexuality of people with learning difficulties within the given context are briefly examined.

Overall this historic and policy discussion provides an outline for the purposes of context and orientation. The influence of different political ideologies (Barnes and Mercer 2010), as well as recent developments of Individual Budgets (Department of Health 2008a) and 'cash for care' policies, such as direct payments (e.g. Priestley *et al.* 2010), are not discussed.

Historic and policy developments: from institutionalisation to normalisation to *Valuing People*

Throughout history philosophers, scientists and medical professionals advocated for the differential treatment of disabled people. For instance, the practice of infanticide dates back to antiquity. In classical Greece people with learning difficulties were kept as slaves and fools by the aristocracy (Stainton 1994, cited in Parmenter 2001, p.269). In the early decades of the twentieth century the eugenics movement became concerned with a perceived 'drastic increase' in learning difficulties amongst the population (Braddock and Parish 2001). Eugenicists advocated the view that people with learning difficulties might reproduce excessively, threatening the national heritage of intelligence. Many countries, such as the USA, Canada, Sweden and France introduced sterilisation laws (Parmenter 2001) or prevented marriage of those deemed unfit for procreation (Haavik and Menninger 1981). While sterilisation was not officially compulsory in the UK, population control was exercised by means of segregation in residential institutions, which was legally enacted by the Mental Deficiency Act (1913) (Weeks 1989). However, this did not affect all people with learning difficulties in the UK, as the Act was patchy and did not merely focus on individuals with learning difficulties or mental health difficulties, but also applied to others who were considered to be 'moral defectives'. This allowed for some persons with learning difficulties to remain with their families (Walmsley 2005).

Institutions fulfilled two purposes: on the one hand they were seen as protecting society from individuals who were seen as deviant and dangerous. On the other hand the aim was to provide a safe and stimulating environment for them (Walmsley 2005). Goffman (1961) calls institutions for ostracised groups 'total institutions'. Such establishments are characterised by barriers to social intercourse with the outside world, such as locked doors, high walls and barbed wire. All aspects of life, such as sleeping, eating, work, education and leisure activities, are conducted within the total institution. Individuals are treated alike and conduct tightly scheduled activities in large batches. There is an immense imbalance of power between inmates and staff, who tend to express their superiority by harsh treatment of the inmates, whom they perceive to be less than human (Ryan and Thomas 1987).

The sexuality of disabled people was conceptualised through two paradoxically contrasting stereotypes. It has already been discussed that they were seen as a threat to the gene pole. They were furthermore portrayed as sexually deviant, as sexually menacing and promiscuous, as having urges that were beyond their capacity to control. They were seen as oversexed and as a potential sexual threat to others (Parmenter 2001). On the other hand they were also portrayed as 'eternal children', as innocent and asexual. To protect their 'natural innocence', information about sexuality was withheld from this population. 'Any signs of sexual interest or arousal were ignored, repressed or misunderstood' (McCarthy 1999, p.53). While sex-segregated institutions were set up with the purpose of preventing procreation of 'sexual deviants', they were then treated as 'natural innocents' while they lived in these settings. Lack of available information about sexuality, dehumanisation and ignorance about the possibility of sexual activity amongst inmates created conditions within which sexual violence was rife, as detection rates were low (e.g. Crossmaker 1991; Furey and Niesen 1994).

In the last quarter of the twentieth century the way in which services for people with 'learning difficulties' were provided in England and other advanced industrial societies changed from institutionally based provisions to predominantly community-based provisions. These changes were influenced by the 'normalisation' principle, which was enacted by professionals who were concerned about the dehumanising conditions in institutions. Nirje (1994 [1969], p.19), who pioneered this concept, defines normalisation as 'making available to the mentally retarded patterns and conditions of everyday life which are as close as possible to the norms and patterns of the mainstream of society'.

However, while Nirje's (1994 [1969]) approach acknowledged that society would have to change to create such 'normalcy' for people with learning difficulties, it was Wolfensberger's (2004 [1983]) interpretation that would shape service provision in the UK. He argued that 'the most explicit and highest goal of normalisation must be the creation, support, and defence of *valued social roles* for people who are at risk of social devaluation' (Wolfensberger 2004 [1983], p.43). In order to achieve this aim the social image and competencies of individuals should be enhanced. This approach consequently focuses on changing the individual, rather than society.

Nirje (1994 [1969]) asserts that normalisation should be characterised by individuals experiencing the same rhythm of day (e.g. bedtimes and mealtimes) and routine of life (living in one place, but accessing work, education and leisure in another) as non-disabled people. He also advocates that the mixing of the sexes 'results in better behavior and atmosphere, as more motivations are added. And the mildly retarded sometimes suffer in a loneliness that has no sense, and as others, they may be better off married' (Nirje 1994 [1969], p.21).

Although revolutionary for its time, several difficulties arose from the normalisation approach and its subsequent interpretations. First, it arose out of professionals' concerns and did not include the views and aspirations of people with learning difficulties. It did not question the roles of professionals in disabled people's lives (Chappell 1992). Second, SRV continues to view disability as an individual problem, which can be overcome if individuals 'normalise' their behaviours. It is suggested that 'if an individual is to be accepted by others, his behaviour must correspond to that which is expected of his age, sex and the culture in which he lives' (Whelan and Sparke 1979, p.111). This approach does little to challenge oppression. Instead it puts pressure on individuals to learn adaptive behaviour, as their acceptance into the community is conditional.

McCarthy and Thompson (1996, p.208) furthermore assert that arguments about women having a 'civilising effect' on the behaviour of men are based on outdated sexist stereotypes. They also maintain that some individuals prefer single-sex settings and that mixed-sex settings increase women's risk of sexual violence, as the single largest group of perpetrators of violence against women with learning difficulties are men with learning difficulties. Individuals should therefore be able to choose the type of setting they prefer, rather than having to adhere to an assumed norm.

SRV furthermore limited the sexual options of individuals, as they were encouraged to aspire towards sexual behaviour that was widely accepted as the 'norm'. Homosexual activity was consequently discouraged by support workers and professionals alike (Brown 1994).

Within the last decade government thinking shifted from the broad aim of assimilation to a new vision. The White Paper *Valuing People* (Department of Health 2001) and the delivery plan *Valuing People Now* (Department of Health 2009b) are underpinned by the principle that the rights, choices and independence of people with learning difficulties must be promoted. This includes a right to education of high quality, the right to vote, to found a family, to express one's opinions and to have one's dignity respected. *Valuing People* stipulates that the starting presumption about individuals should be one of independence and not one of dependence. Services should aim to maximise independence, while working with individuals to have a 'real say in where they live, what work they should do and who looks after them' (Department of Health 2001, p.24). *Valuing People* furthermore dictates that an effort must be made to include people with learning difficulties in mainstream social life. Moreover, *Improving the Life Chances of Disabled People* (Prime Minister's Strategy Unit 2005) outlines the government's commitment to a social model approach in order to combat discrimination and social barriers to inclusion.

These policy aims were influenced by the campaigning work of the disabled people's movement and by a growing consensus amongst families, academics, professionals and policy makers about the human status of people with learning difficulties. Yet, they were also in line with broader aims of the New Labour government, such as the move from welfare to 'workfare' and a continuation of the rhetoric of individual responsibility and consumer choices, in order to achieve 'best value'. Both approaches were initiated by the previous Conservative governments (Burton and Kagan 2006).

In respect to sexuality the UK's Human Rights Act (HMSO 1998, Article 8(1)) and The UN Convention on the Rights of Persons with Disabilities (United Nations 2006, Article 22), which the UK ratified in 2009, protect the right of disabled people to respect for private, home and family life. The UN convention furthermore directs state parties to: 'Take effective and appropriate measures to eliminate discrimination against persons with disabilities in all matters relating to marriage, family, parenthood and relationships, on an equal basis with others' (United Nations 2006, Article 23).

However, Armstrong (2002, p.441) warns that a focus on such formal documents leaves out 'the messiness, variety and unpredictability of policies as they are enacted through social practice'. It must be remembered that political, temporal and spatial contexts, as well as personal characteristics of social actors, impact on social practices. This book consequently aims to explore actual experiences of individuals. This enables an assessment of the extent to which rights-based policy rhetoric affects daily experiences.

Today most people with learning difficulties live in community-based settings. On the whole, these achieve better results in terms of quality of life and social skills (O'Brien *et al.* 2001), community participation, contact with family and friends and overall satisfaction with the service (Mansell 2006). Nonetheless, practices in these settings vary. Services often focus on incapacity and risk and they may not effectively meet all of the needs of individuals using them. *Improving the Life Chances of Disabled People* (Prime Minister's Strategy Unit 2005, p.77) admits that disabled people 'are often expected to fit into services, rather than services enabling them to be active citizens'. Physical presence in the community does not ensure inclusion within it, nor does it automatically put people in a position whereby they are in control of their own lives. J. O'Brien (2005) asserts that the 'institution trap' is a mindset. Individuals may live in community-based settings. Yet, if they continue to be treated as if they are less worthy and if their lives continue to be controlled by others, they are still living in this trap.

This book considers how changes in public policy and practice impact on individuals and their particular levels of sexual 'vulnerability'. The relationship between these forces will become clear towards the end of this chapter. However, first it is important to understand what is meant by the term 'sexual violence' and how it affects people with learning difficulties.

Sexual violence: definitions and incidence

We commonly use the term 'sexual abuse' to describe experiences of sexual violence against disabled adults (e.g. Mencap 2001), older adults (e.g. Cooper, Sellwood and Livingston 2008) and young people (e.g. Firth 2009), but 'harassment', 'assault' and 'rape' to describe the experiences of non-disabled adults (e.g. Myhill and Allen 2002). This differing terminology emphasises the perceived differences between individuals who are accredited with adult social status and those who are not: adult status is characterised by an individual's inclusion in social, political, economic and family life. Adults are expected to be self-sufficient and those who are assumed not to fit this criterion are defined by their perceived dependence on non-disabled adults (Priestley 2003). The differing terminology, 'sexual abuse' and 'sexual violence', distorts the fact that sexual violence has similar devastating consequences for disabled and non-disabled adults and for working-aged adults, young people and older adults. In this book, the more commonly used term 'sexual abuse' is therefore replaced by the term 'sexual violence'.

This book adopts a broad feminist definition of sexual violence: the term refers to unsought or unwanted contact and non-contact sexual experiences, including sexual harassment, sexual assault, pressurised and coercive sexual intercourse and rape (Kelly 1988). According to the Sexual Offences Act (HMSO 2003) a sexual experience is unwanted if a person did not consent to the experience. Consent means that a person 'agrees by choice, and has the freedom and capacity to make that choice' (section 74). A person with learning difficulties who has no or little knowledge of sex and sexuality, sexual conduct and the consequences of sexual behaviour is deemed to be lacking the 'capacity' to consent to sexual behaviour (Foundation for People with Learning Disabilities 2001, para 4.5.13).

Feminist writers view sexual violence as the enactment of power and control (e.g. Holland et al. 1992; Kelly 1988). Power is 'the probability that one actor within a social relationship will be in a position to carry out his own will despite resistance, regardless of the basis on which this probability rests' (Weber 1978 [1922], p.53). According to this conceptualisation, power legitimises the use of force and violence, often within existing relationships: only 11 per cent of all serious sexual assaults are perpetrated by strangers (Finney 2006).

Due to the marginal position they hold in society, many disabled people are exposed to additional power imbalances. Individuals often feel less able to resist violence within the context of existing relationships. They may be too afraid to challenge their violator (Mencap et al. 2001). They may feel helpless and powerless (Keilty and Connelly 2001). They may think that they do not have a choice about participation in sexual activity (McCarthy 1999) or they may be dependent on their violator to meet their everyday needs (Saxton et al. 2001, 2006). The nature of existing relationships is therefore central in the formation of risk. That is why this book takes a particular interest in exploring the power dynamics in the relationships of respondents. It will be highlighted how these processes impact upon the creation and construction of 'vulnerability'.

The British Crime Survey (BCS) 2009/10 estimates that 19.7 per cent of women and 2.3 per cent of men aged 16 to 59 have experienced at least one sexual assault, including attempted assault, in their adult lives. The prevalence of rape is 3.8 per cent for women and 0.2 per cent for men. Young women experience the highest incidence of sexual violence (Hall and Innes 2010). The heightened likelihood of disabled adults to experience a sexual assault is also of statistical significance (Finney 2006).

Mencap *et al.* (2001) assert that, within the population of disabled adults, those labelled with learning difficulties are at the highest risk. Exact figures on the prevalence of sexual violence vary. Depending on the research study, definitions and sample group, the proportion of individuals who have experienced sexual violence is estimated to range from around 10 per cent to 80 per cent (Cambridge 2007). Mencap *et al.* (2001) believe that people with learning difficulties are four times more likely to experience sexual violence than non-disabled people. Amongst this group women are at increased risk compared to men. Turk and Brown (1993) state that 83 per cent of women and 32 per cent of men with learning difficulties who participated in their incidence survey in the south-east of England have reported sexual violence at some time in their lives. McCarthy and Thompson (1997) assert that 61 per cent of women and 25 per cent of men with learning difficulties, who have been referred for sex education, had experienced sexual violence.

In England and Wales only 18 per cent of incidents of sexual violence are reported to the police (Myhill and Allen 2002). The actual incidence of violent sexual offences is therefore higher than reported figures suggest. McCarthy (2000, p.144) observes: 'What really happens in terms of what, where, who, how and why cannot be completely known because sexual abuse by its very nature is a secretive and hidden activity.'

The 'vulnerable' adult within a 'risk society'

Our vague and incomplete knowledge of the causes and circumstances within which sexual violence against people with learning difficulties occurs is often translated into an assumption of risk. We do not know exactly who has to fear what from whom in which situations, but due to the high incidence of sexual violence against this population we know that *there is something to fear*. This is expressed in the label 'vulnerability'.

Advanced modern societies are deeply concerned with the management of risk. Beck (1992) calls such societies 'risk societies'. Perceptions of risk are based on the anticipation of threatening future events. They therefore 'initially only exist in terms of the [...] *knowledge* about them. They can thus be changed, magnified, dramatised or minimised within knowledge, and to that extent they are particularly *open to social definition and construction*' (Beck 1992, p.23; original italics). In contemporary Britain risk is continually assessed, managed and monitored, for instance as directed by the adult protection procedures that are discussed later on.

However, according to Bauman (2000), risk prediction is often a fruitless undertaking. He asserts that risk management assumes predictability of events within the context of rapid change, uncertainty and randomness. Risk management is thus 'trying to turn uncertainties into probabilities' (Douglas 1986, p.42). Beck (1992, pp.20–21) argues that, whatever preventative measures we take, risk remains a 'primeval phenomenon of human action'. We may wish to predict the outcomes of actions in the social world but the haphazard nature of actual events means that there will always remain an element of risk.

The establishment of causal relationships for socially recognised risks is a common process. In this way risk is made predictable and 'brought into a social and legal context of responsibility' (Beck 1992, p.28). In contrast to cognitive risk predictions, statistics about known incidents of sexual violence could be seen to be more objective. It was outlined earlier that the incidence of sexual violence against individuals with the label 'learning difficulties' is above the norm. As a result the conclusion is often reached that there must be a causal relationship between an individual's impairment and risk. People with learning difficulties are consequently assumed to be 'vulnerable'. Now that risk has become tangible it has become possible to plan preventative interventions.

Adult protection has become an issue of central concern for service providers and policy makers. Within a five-year period UK government bodies published two adult protection guidelines for England, *No Secrets* (Department of Health 2000) and *Safeguarding Adults* (Association of Directors of Social Services 2005). Furthermore, the Sexual Offences Act (HMSO 2003) makes it possible to prosecute those who have engaged an individual who does not have the 'capacity to consent' in a sexual act. The Safeguarding Vulnerable Groups Act (HMSO 2006) brought together and strengthened existing vetting schemes of prospective employees who will work with 'vulnerable' groups, in order to ensure that those who pose a risk of harming others are barred from working with such groups. Moreover, Mansell *et al.* (2009) report that the incidence of adult protection referrals is continually increasing. An invitation to a public consultation on the review of *No Secrets* received nearly 500 long and detailed written responses. Altogether 12,000 people participated (Department of Health 2009a). This scale of public engagement with debates about adult protection indicates that there is an increased commitment to enforce the right of 'vulnerable' adults to protection from dehumanising treatment and violence.

Outcomes following the consultation process include guidance notes for NHS organisations on participating in integrated multi-agency safeguarding procedures (Department of Health 2010b). In its written response to the consultation the previous Labour government announced its plans to set up an 'Inter-Departmental Ministerial Group on Safeguarding Vulnerable Adults'. It also announced new legislation to strengthen the local governance of safeguarding. 'New, comprehensive, multi-agency guidance to set out clearly the roles and responsibilities for all those involved in safeguarding vulnerable adults' was furthermore announced (Department of Health 2010a). However, the publication, which was due in autumn 2010, has been delayed by the Coalition government.

When considering issues relating to adult protection, the following question arises: who is 'vulnerable' and thus qualifies for such interventions, and how do such individuals differ from those who are not labelled in this way? There is no clear consensus on an answer to this question. Spatial analysts do not see 'vulnerability' as specific to particular sections of society but rather as a relationship that humans have with their social environments. Their definition focuses 'attention on the totality of relationships in a given social situation which constitute a condition that, in combination with environmental forces, produces a disaster' (Bankoff, Frerks and Hilhorst 2004, p.11). 'Vulnerability' thus results from interactions with external risk factors, such as inescapable natural disasters. Risk is seen as entirely situational.

Dunn et al. (2008) believe that 'vulnerability' can be both, inherent and situational, while Beckett (2006, p.3) points out that it is inherent to the human condition. To her 'vulnerability' describes the 'fragile and contingent nature of personhood'. It is an integral part of some stages of the life course, such as infancy, childhood and old age. It can also affect populations that are not immediately conceptualised as 'vulnerable'. For instance, a person might be temporarily affected by an impaired judgement capacity due to illness, drug or alcohol use. In other words, we are all 'vulnerable' at some stage in our lives.

Beckett (2006) suggests that welfare states should take on a widespread understanding of the 'vulnerability' of personhood, in order to respond to the needs of its citizens in an appropriate manner. Yet, she asserts that presently the political will to foster such a model of citizenship does not exist in the UK. Society allows little room for individuals to admit to their 'vulnerability' (Zola 1982). Accordingly, some social groups continue to be singled out and labelled as particularly 'vulnerable', such as women, children, older adults and disabled people. Their condition of 'vulnerability' is contrasted with the assumed resilience of the 'able-bodied', working-aged male. Instead of acknowledging the human nature of 'vulnerability', we assume that the 'vulnerability' of those labelled as such is fundamentally different.

Practice guidance to professionals in England often conveys the impression that there is a causal link between impairment or older age and 'vulnerability', thus being labelled with learning difficulties inevitably means that an individual is also 'vulnerable'. The most commonly used definition amongst UK professionals describes a 'vulnerable' adult as someone who:

> ...is or may be in need of community care services by reason of mental or other disability, age or illness; and who is or may be unable to take care of him or herself, or unable to protect him or herself against significant harm or exploitation. (Lord Chancellor's Department 1997, p.68)

Safeguarding Adults (Association of Directors of Social Services 2005) replaced the term 'vulnerable adult', because it was recognised that the label 'vulnerability' may lead to the assumption that the cause for violence is located within the individual experiencing it. Adults who qualified for safeguarding were termed 'adults who may be eligible for community care services'. This group is defined as 'those whose independence and wellbeing would be at risk if they did not receive appropriate health and social care support. They include adults with physical, sensory and mental impairments and learning disabilities' (Association of Directors of Social Services 2005, p.4). Despite revised linguistics, individuals who are seen to be at risk continue to be defined through their assumed dependency. This linguistic change did not assert itself and more recent government publications reverted to the term 'vulnerable' adults (e.g. Department of Health 2008b; HMSO 2006), although the report from the No Secrets consultation suggests a reconsideration of the term (Department of Health 2009a). Consultation participants largely agreed that definitions of 'vulnerable adult' need to be revised and that the term should be replaced by 'person at risk'.

However, it is worth pointing out that there is also a slight discrepancy in the No Secrets consultation report (Department of Health 2009a). On one hand many professionals advocated for the introduction of safeguarding adults legislation in England, similar to that enacted in Scotland (Adult Support and Protection (Scotland) Act 2007) and to that applicable to children (HMSO 1989, 2004). The previous Labour government was planning to respond to this, as outlined earlier. Participants to whom the guidance applies, however, assert that 'safeguarding adults is not like child protection' (Department of Health 2009a, p.6). Some of the consultants asserted that new legislative powers could extend the government's power over people's lives in a dangerous way. Amongst participants who could be seen as 'adults at risk' there is a general consensus that adults themselves should have more choice and control in directing their own 'safeguarding', which indicates a desire to shift away from the interventionist practices I witnessed, as described in Chapter 1. The report furthermore talks about 'empowerment' of the adult at risk. However, Oliver (1997, p.20) argues that 'empowerment is not in the gift of the powerful'. It is the process whereby the powerless resist the oppression of others. Individuals can consequently only empower themselves.

To conclude, balancing individuals' rights against the need to protect them from risks is a difficulty that is acknowledged by policy makers (Department of Health 2009b). In the past this balance has been continually unsettled in favour of protection from harm. However, earlier on in this section it was highlighted that all activities carry risks. One of the benefits that society has to offer its citizens is the right to make mistakes, and to try again (Kaeser 1992). Yet, as outlined earlier, disabled adults are often defined through their perceived dependence on non-disabled adults. As a consequence they are often excluded from exercising full citizen rights and responsibilities (Priestley 2003), such as opportunities for positive risk taking. While professionals may not be able to empower individuals, they can certainly aim to not *dis*empower them in the first place. This book highlights how and why such anti-disempowering practice can reduce risk to sexual violence.

THE ORIGIN OF RISK FACTORS OF SEXUAL VIOLENCE WITHIN AN ECOLOGICAL MODEL

The current focus on impairment as the main risk factor relating to sexual violence entails elements of an individual model approach to disability. This is too narrow a focus. This section therefore introduces an ecological approach, which enables us to take account of social factors in the creation of risk. This model was previously presented in the *British Journal of Social Work* (Hollomotz 2009). It enables us to understand how social and individual factors interact in the formation of risk of sexual violence. This allows us to focus our gaze beyond an assumption of 'vulnerability' and with this to move away from dominant explanations of individual causation.

Ecological approaches were first introduced about three decades ago, as a means of explaining violence against children (e.g. Belsky 1980). They continue to be used in that way (e.g. Garbarino and Eckenrode 1997; Guterman *et al.* 2009). The ecological model in Figure 2.1 displays similarities to a model that was put forward by Sobsey (1994), who examined the pattern of known sexual offences against people with learning difficulties. Sobsey (1994) analysed *actual* incidents of sexual violence, while Figure 2.1 is concerned with identifying *risk* factors, in order to examine opportunities for risk prevention work. While Sobsey (1994) posed the question why sexual violence had happened *in the past*, this model aims to highlight how sexual violence can be prevented *in the future*. Moreover, Thompson (2006) explains how inequalities and discrimination originate within the cultural (C) and social (S) circumstances surrounding a person (P) in his ecological PCS model. The structure of the ecological model of risk of sexual violence differs significantly from the PCS model. However, there are also some commonalities, which will be explored later on.

To sum up, there are a variety of existing ecological models. This discussion is by no means exhaustive. Nonetheless, the model presented in Figure 2.1 offers a new application by illustrating how environments react to people with the label 'learning difficulties' and how they thus shape their particular experiences. This provides the theoretical framework for this book, which will highlight the significance of these processes in the formation of risk of sexual violence.

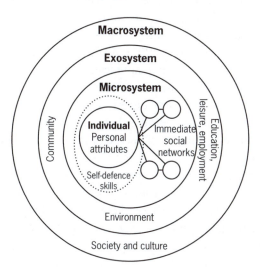

Figure 2.1 An ecological model of risk of sexual violence
Source: Hollomotz 2009, p.104

The ecological model of risk of sexual violence proposes five groups of risk factors within three systems:

- *Microsystem*: the individual (personal attributes, self-defence skills) and his or her immediate 'home' environment (e.g. family, residential services).

- *Exosystem*: neighbourhood, district, community contacts (e.g. employment, education, leisure, day services, contact with health and social services professionals, friendships, faith communities).

- *Macrosystem*: wider culture and society (e.g. England: the law and social policies, the media, normative values in industrial western societies, etc.).

In the following two sections elements of these three systems are discussed. The discussion starts at the centre of the ecological model with the individual and proceeds outwards towards the micro-, exo- and macrosystem.

Personal attributes and self-defence skills

The individual's *personal attributes* are at the centre of the ecological model. Personal attributes include age, gender, intellectual and physical impairments, ethnicity, sexuality, culture, religion, economic status, social class and so on. Age and gender are known to be major risk factors for experiencing sexual violence, with young women experiencing the highest level of risk (Myhill and Allen 2002). As outlined earlier, intellectual and physical impairments also have a significant association with risk. There is little variation in the occurrence of sexual violence amongst differing ethnic groups. Ethnicity is consequently not viewed as a particular risk factor. Economic status, on the other hand, has a high impact and those from less affluent households are at increased risk of sexual violence (Walby and Allen 2004).

Self-defence skills are a flexible part of the individual. They are shaped and developed through life and learning experiences. In this book the term 'self-defence skills' describes those characteristics that would determine whether an individual has the 'capacity' to consent to sexual activity under the Sexual Offences Act (HMSO 2003). 'Capacity' to consent is not defined by the Act, but it is assumed that an individual must possess a range of skills to be able to give informed consent to sexual activity and to effectively resist unwanted sexual approaches. The literature suggests a range of indispensable self-defence skills, which can broadly be summarised as skills relating to sexual competence and self-determination skills.

Sexual competence is an acquired skill. We are born without social awareness of sexuality and without the vocabulary to describe sexual acts. Thus, in the beginning of our lives we are all 'vulnerable' to sexual violence. Kelly (1988) interviewed non-disabled women who experienced sexual violence in their childhood. Some women stated that, at the time when the sexual violence was taking place, they did not have the words to describe their experiences. They were confused and some did not know that what was happening to them was sexual violence.

Information about sexuality is therefore crucial to increase awareness and with this it reduces risk. However, from childhood on many people with learning difficulties are socialised into an asexual role, as part of which sexual knowledge is withheld from them, as highlighted earlier. Chapter 3 will outline that this is changing for younger people in England today. Nonetheless, older generational cohorts continue to struggle with 'demystifying sexuality, developing a positive body image, mastering essential social skills, and understanding their own sexual functioning' (Rousso 1982, p.78).

Individuals who are 'protected' from sexual information become easy targets because they cannot report what they cannot say (Hingsburger 1995). Sexual competence consequently requires an individual to have the vocabulary needed to report sexual violence. Furthermore, people who require assistance with personal hygiene tasks must be able to distinguish sexual behaviours from such assistance (e.g. Foundation for People with Learning Disabilities 2001; Milligan and Neufeldt 2001). A further central feature of sexual competence is the knowledge of sexual violence. Individuals need to understand that sexual contact must be voluntary (Murphy and O'Callaghan 2004). They must know of their right to resist sexual contact (e.g. Lyden 2007) and they must have the social awareness to detect or anticipate sexually violating situations (e.g. Mencap *et al.* 2001; Murphy and O'Callaghan 2004) and they should feel in control over what is happening to their body (e.g. Hingsburger 1995; Westcott 1993). The formation of sexual competence will be examined in detail in Chapter 3. Chapter 5 will furthermore assess respondents' sexual risk perception and resistance skills.

In order to successfully self-defend against sexual violence an individual must also be able to utilise their *self-determination skills*. Self-esteem is required, as this gives individuals the confidence needed to resist an unwanted sexual approach (e.g. Hingsburger 1995; Westcott 1993). Yet, the social stigma of impairment labels may impact negatively on individuals' sense of self. The analysis of ecological systems helps to explain how self-esteem is shaped by forces in the environment (see Chapter 5).

The ability to make decisions, to say 'no' and to communicate that decision has been linked to lower levels of risk of sexual violence (Murphy and O'Callaghan 2004). Individuals should consequently make as many decisions as possible in their everyday lives to practise these skills. However, past research suggests that the way in which choice within service settings is facilitated may vary (Stancliffe, Abery and Smith 2000). Yet, recent legislative and policy changes introduced by the United Nations Convention on the Rights of Persons with Disabilities (e.g. United Nations 2006, Article 21) and the Mental Capacity Act (HMSO 2005b) encourage service providers to allow people with learning difficulties to exercise greater choice in their everyday lives and in respect to their safeguarding from harm. How these changes will influence adult protection practice is yet to be seen.

According to Wehmeyer *et al.* (1997, p.307) 'people who are self-determined act autonomously, self-regulate their behaviour, and are psychologically empowered and self-realising'. They argue that self-determination is a skill that is learned in childhood and adolescence and that age, opportunity, capacity and circumstances may impact upon it. Ecological approaches suggest that self-determination is influenced by environmental factors, such as living unit size and type, as well as broader social influences (Stancliffe *et al.* 2000). In Chapter 4 these factors are discussed in relation to fear and othering, disabled social networks and daily choice-making. Chapter 5 provides an overview of enabling processes, which can potentially increase self-determination skills, including self-advocacy and independent living.

A focus on individual attributes and self-defence skills in explaining the origin of risk of sexual violence could reflect an individual model approach to disability, unless care is taken to include social causes. This book aims to challenge individualising approaches by examining how self-defence skills result from social processes. As discussed above, they are neither fixed capacities nor inherent to the individual.

Concerns about increasing sexual self-defence skills are not limited to people with learning difficulties. In the 1980s the realisation of young women's disempowerment when faced with an unwanted sexual approach gave rise to 'Just Say No!' training for those who were considered at risk (Kidder, Boell and Moyer 1983). This approach focused on the woman who is apparently unable to say 'no' as the cause of violence. Yet, as Kitzinger and Frith (1999) have since shown, expecting individuals to 'just say no' is not particularly realistic, because refusal in everyday conversations is rarely limited to a simple 'no'. Women report that they feel 'rude' to 'just say no' and that they usually communicate refusal in more subtle ways. These actual conversation patterns are nearer to everyday conversations and involve an element of, for example, delay or apologies. Yet, these are signs that might give a potential violator the scope to argue that a person does not really mean to say 'no'. Kitzinger and Frith (1999) demonstrate that women are able to say 'no', but that the problem is that *they are not being heard.* The same may be true for people with learning difficulties, particularly those who do not use conventional means of communication.

Furthermore Hingsburger (1995) argued that it is not sufficient to merely send people with learning difficulties on sex education training where they learn that they have the right to make choices and to say 'no', if they do not have these options in their everyday life. Once individuals return to a 'home' environment in which they are disabled from making choices, from being private and being in control of their bodies, they may forget what they have learned or realise that self-determination is not relevant to their lives. Whether an individual is able to exercise self-determination is therefore very much dependent on environmental factors. A 2007 government publication (Department of Health 2007, p.77) acknowledged that services sometimes get the balance wrong between 'protecting vulnerable people and helping people have a life'. It is stipulated that positive risk taking should be a part of everyone's life. This is supported by the Mental Capacity Act (HMSO 2005b), which protects the right of people with learning difficulties to make their own decisions. This book informs this debate by examining how people with learning difficulties could be assisted to become more confident at managing risk. Social processes that disable their risk management capacities are scrutinised.

Social environments

Environments are made up of enabling and disabling factors. According to the International Classification of Functioning, Disability and Health (ICF) (World Health Organization 2001) those factors include products and technologies that may support disabled people in their lives, natural and built environments, practical and emotional support and relationships, attitudes, services, systems and policies. The physical environment is made up of naturally occurring processes and fabricated technologies, while the cultural environment incorporates social orders and ideologies. The ecological model presented in Figure 2.1 focuses on the social and cultural aspects of environments.

The individual, protected by self-defence skills, is situated within a *microsystem* – the 'home' environment. This consists of an individual's immediate social network, typically family members or paid support workers and fellow residents. According to O'Brien (1994) the term 'home' has specific connotations. It does not merely refer to any kind of residential arrangement. A 'home' must provide individuals with security of place through tenancy or ownership, control over the home and the necessary support for living there, as well as a sense of place. This includes the freedom to make choices in respect to time use, routines, possible improvements to the home and so forth, as well as taking on socially recognised roles, such as tenant or neighbour. Annison (2000) explains that a 'home' does not merely serve to meet basic needs (e.g. shelter), but that it is also central to the fulfilment of emotional and relationship needs. A 'home' can provide individuals with a sense of belonging. It gives them a means of self-expression and an opportunity to take on responsibility.

Some individuals who took part in the research lived in group arrangements they had not chosen and in which they did not have the level of control or responsibility that would allow for their residence to be classed as a 'home'. Emotional and relationship needs were not always met and individuals were not free to choose fellow residents and support staff. This is why this book attempts to avoid the use of the term 'home' when referring to residential group establishments. When it is used, it is placed in inverted commas, to indicate reservations about the applicability of this term. However, at the same time it is helpful to think of the microsystem as the 'home' environment, in the broadest sense of the term.

How others interact with an individual within this environment is crucial to the formation of self-defences. Hendey and Pascall (1998, p.424), for example, report that some young disabled adults 'felt that parents' concern for safety made a child-like and regulated existence beyond the years of childhood'. This can be conceptualised as overprotection. This term was first introduced by the psychologist Levy (1943) and refers to parental protection that is disproportionate, taking into account the developmental level and abilities of the child. It is characterised by excessive physical and social contact, prolonged infantilisation, active prevention of independent behaviour and social maturity and excessive parental control. Parents have been shown to be more protective of their disabled offsprings in comparison to their non-disabled children (e.g. Holmbeck *et al.* 2002). Overprotection may continue to affect people with learning difficulties in adulthood and is not merely executed by parents. It can be a defining feature of service structures, such as day centres and residential group settings, and it may guide staff action (Sanders 2006).

Overprotection is a hindrance to disabled people's self-determination, while it does not prevent sexual violence. Indeed, research suggests that most incidents of sexual violence take place within environments that are assumed to be 'safe', such as family and residential 'homes', day centres and educational settings (e.g. McCarthy and Thompson 1996). As outlined earlier, only 11 per cent of serious sexual assaults are committed by strangers (Finney 2006). Known social networks consequently pose a significant risk.

The risk of violence and exploitation increases within 'caring' relationships (Hendey and Pascall 1998), because of the intimacy they invite and particularly if they contain an element of dependency. Emerson *et al.* (2001) furthermore found that individuals in smaller group settings are considered to be exposed to a reduced risk of violence from co-residents in comparison with those in larger establishments. Institutionalisation has been reported to increase the risk of sexual violence, due to depersonalisation, lack of autonomy and choices and lack of communication with the outside world (Shakespeare, Gillespie-Sells and Davies 1996). Isolation and overprotection within a microsystem are consequently not effective mechanisms in the prevention of sexual violence.

The microsystem is embedded within an *exosystem* – the environment within which the 'home' is situated. This consists of the neighbourhood and community activities, such as education, leisure, employment and day services. A number of risks are known to originate from within the exosystem. Mencap (2009b, p.1) assert that individuals living independently are at a 'greater risk of befriending and abuse'. Similarly Emerson *et al.* (2001) report that, compared to individuals living in group establishments, those living within more self-sufficient contexts are exposed to an increased risk of having their home vandalised and they are considered at greater risk of exploitation. As outlined earlier, segregation within the microsystem poses risks, but so does the freedom to interact within wider social networks. Exposure to risks originating in the community (exosystem) increases with inclusion. As a consequence services need to continually weigh up risks against potential benefits. *Valuing People Now* (Department of Health 2009b, p.94) stipulates that 'positive risk taking should be a part of everyone's life'.

In order to break a cycle of violence most individuals require the support of others (Calderbank 2000). However, in the past, allegations of violence against disabled people were often met with disbelief (Calderbank 2000; Westcott and Cross 1996). In order to access help, 'someone who listens'

(Hingsburger 1995, p.61), either for signs of violence or when violence is being reported, is therefore crucial. The more friends, family members and helpers who are prepared to be attentive in this way and are present in the micro- and exosystem, the higher is the likelihood that violence can be detected and stopped.

Finally, the exosystem is embedded in the *macrosystem* – the wider society and culture. According to Thompson (2006, p.27; original italics), culture refers to 'shared ways of seeing, thinking and doing. It relates to [...] an assumed *consensus* about what is right and what is normal.' This includes 'attitudes that are observable consequences of customs, practices, ideologies, values, norms, factual beliefs and religious beliefs', which 'influence individual behaviour and social life at all levels' (World Health Organization 2001, p.190). As outlined earlier, historically people with learning difficulties have been constructed and represented as less than human (Ryan and Thomas 1987), which makes violence against this population appear to be less harmful. Westcott and Cross (1996, p.17; original italics) assert that commonly held assumptions take two extremes: people either assume that 'nobody would do *that*!', which means that warning signs are ignored and violence is allowed to continue or they assume that it does not really matter if disabled individuals are violated, as they are 'damaged/unfeeling/stupid anyway'.

Cultural values, as well as laws and policies, are central features of the macrosystem. Adult protection guidelines are an example of policy writing that affects risk by aiming to give guidance on the protection of adults. An example of a legal factor that impacts upon risk is the Sexual Offences Act (HMSO 2003), which offers particular protection to adults who are deemed to have no 'capacity' to consent to sexual activity. A further legally imposed safety factor is the vetting of staff working with 'vulnerable' groups (HMSO 2006), as discussed earlier.

Although the macrosystem is the furthest removed from individuals, which means that they have the least control and ability to influence this level, macrosystem influences will nonetheless filter down into individuals' micro- and exosystem and shape their daily experiences. The changing legal and policy frameworks within which services are obliged to operate, and popular views portrayed in the media, are just two examples of processes, which have an immediate impact.

CONCLUSION

This chapter highlighted that people with learning difficulties have historically been forced into marginal social positions and that current policy rhetoric aims to counteract this trend by asserting a commitment to increasing their inclusion and participation. An awareness of this context will enable us to appreciate the situation of respondents in this book, who are affected by past and continuing segregation and recent attempts to inclusion to varying degrees, depending on their age and social circumstances.

People with learning difficulties are disproportionably affected by sexual violence. An increasing awareness amongst practitioners and policy makers resulted in the introduction of changing adult protection guidelines. Although these changes must be celebrated as representing an increased commitment to protect 'vulnerable' adults from harm and exploitation, this chapter highlighted a range of limitations with the current approach. Most notably safeguarding interventions are guided by an assumption of individual 'vulnerability'. They are carried out by practitioners on behalf of the passive, disabled individual. However, others acting on a person's behalf will do little to equip him or her with the skills necessary to manage risk themselves. Adult protection therefore does not address disabled people's dependence on support workers and professionals. It may help with the management of a particular situational risk factor, but it does not effectively reduce the individual's level of exposure to risk in daily life, as it does not enable an increase of social and sexual competence or self-determination skills.

The assumption of inherent 'vulnerability' constitutes an individualising approach. It seeks explanations for increased risk in the individual experiencing it. This comes close to 'victim-blaming'. Individuals should never be conceptualised as the cause of risk. Instead, causes should be sought with the perpetrator and the social conditions that allowed a sexual attack to succeed. An ecological model approach can highlight environmental factors that impact upon an individual's particular level of risk. In this book it is used as a tool for retroductive research (as defined by Blaikie 2009), which enables us to start out from an observed regularity (the increased risk of sexual violence against people with learning difficulties) and to identify the underlying social processes that are responsible for producing this regularity. This book will expose how overprotection disables the individual's self-defence skills and creates conditions that can be easily exploited. It is shown that 'vulnerability' thus becomes a self-fulfilling prophecy.

Chapter 3

Sexuality

Chapter 2 highlighted that individuals need a range of skills, in order to effectively resist sexual violence. These include sexual knowledge and self-awareness. It is therefore important that a person has the opportunity to learn about the whole range of available sexual practices that may be proposed to them. Furthermore, consenting sexual experiences have the potential to enable individuals to become more aware of their sexual likes and dislikes. This chapter explores what respondents knew about sex and sexuality. It examines how individuals accessed information and whether this was useful. It also summarises how individuals experienced sexuality and privacy. The focus will be on the learning and development opportunities that arose from such experiences and on individuals' levels of control. The third part of this chapter outlines incidents of sexual violence. Social factors that assisted the perpetrator are highlighted. Next it is explained why the routine prescription of contraceptives to women with learning difficulties must be seen as problematic. Finally it is explained how gender biased assumptions about women's sexual availability can increase risk.

SEXUAL KNOWLEDGE

Understanding of sexuality is a central aspect in professional sexual consent capacity assessments (Kennedy 2003; Lyden 2007). The assumption of incapacity to sexual consent can lead to the restriction of intimate contact between individuals (Kennedy 2003). Managing risk, while balancing rights, can become problematic. When Murphy and O'Callaghan (2004) assessed the consent capacity of 60 adults with learning difficulties they found that individuals often lacked knowledge in a number of key areas, including pregnancy, masturbation, contraception, birth control, sexually transmitted infections (STIs), types of sexual relationships and legal aspects of sex. However, they argued that individuals do not need to have knowledge in all of these areas in order to consent to a proposed sexual act. They suggest lowering the criteria to a social minimum of knowledge needed to make informed decisions within a particular sexual relationship. This would enable more adults with learning difficulties to pass a test of consent capacity.

Kaeser (1992) agrees that an expectation of detailed knowledge about sexual health and the consequences of sexual behaviour is too restrictive. He suggests that individuals should merely be required to be able to consent to a proposed sexual relationship and specific sexual acts within this context, while their staff should direct their protection from harmful consequences, for example by screening partners for STIs. Instead of an expectation of detailed knowledge on sexual health and sexual practices, indicators for capacity to consent could be the fact that two individuals are content in each other's company, that they are able to communicate displeasure or alert a member of staff to help them in the event of an unwanted sexual approach and that they understand the sexual behaviour they are about to engage in. Similar principles have informed the sexual relationship policy *Making Choices Keeping Safe* (NHS Lothian 2004). (Relationship policies have been set out by some UK local authorities in line with *Valuing People* (Department of Health 2001). They seek to give guidance to staff who are working with people with learning difficulties on supporting relationship, sexual health, sex and sexuality needs.) The Mental Capacity Act (HMSO 2005b) furthermore protects the right of people with learning difficulties to make their own decisions. If a person is found to lack sexual consent capacity they should be supported to obtain the relevant skills, such as knowledge about sexuality.

This book consequently uses basic knowledge about relationships and sexual acts as benchmarks for judging 'capacity' to consent. The following sections explore the respondents' knowledge of sex and sexuality. The impact that formal sex education and other external factors had on increasing, reducing and confusing respondents' understanding is also highlighted.

Respondents' knowledge

The respondents' understanding of sex and sexuality varied. Half have experienced consenting penetrative sex. A further quarter spoke about inter-personal relationships that had a sexual element, such as kissing or cuddling. With the exception of Mary, Kathy, Paul, Norman and Ann all of the respondents had at least a basic level of knowledge on the mechanics of heterosexual intercourse. Peter, for example, explains: 'The man puts his part…into, into the woman, woman's vagina I think that's called. And that's, that's in the back. In the back, it's some part inside your bottom or… thereabouts.' He adds that reasons for having sex could be because a couple love each other or because they are married and want a family. The majority of interviewees gave similar accounts of mechanics and purpose. However, a third referred to sex merely in pragmatic terms, stating that sex has merely reproductive purposes and overlooking other reasons, such as sexual desire.

Furthermore, a third of the respondents believed that all sex is 'dirty', 'rude' or 'bad'. Their accounts are discussed later on in this chapter. Of the remaining 19 interviewees who did not conceptualise all sex in negative terms, 15 respondents made a clear distinction between consenting sex and violence. Bob, for example thinks that sex is a 'good thing if you really like someone. You're kind of, careful about, kind of…using the right method of contraception. If you don't want children.' He also states that it can be a 'bad' thing: 'If it's something like, ehm, sexual harassment, rape. … When someone touches you and you don't really want them to. … If someone kind of, like, forces having sex with someone.' Similarly, when asked whether sex is a 'good' or 'bad' thing, Leanne states: 'If, if you want it – good thing. If…not, no.' In other words, participants like Bob and Leanne can clearly distinguish a wanted from an unwanted sexual encounter.

All of the participants could name their own sexual body parts (breasts, vagina, penis), but about a quarter struggled with naming those of the opposite sex. When they named body parts they did not always use medical terms. For example, breasts were called 'tits', 'boobs' or 'boobies'. Liz calls breasts 'bust' and a vagina 'about sex'. A penis was referred to as 'willy', 'cock' or 'dick'. Nevertheless, these terms are comprehensible and would enable individuals to talk about sexual encounters. It is crucial that individuals know a term for sexual body parts of the opposite sex, regardless of their sexual orientation, as this would enable their description in case of an unsought sexual intrusion. Lack of knowledge in this area must be seen as a direct result of lack of sex education, as all respondents had demonstrated the ability to retain a descriptive term for their own sexual body part.

Moreover, most respondents did not know a term for testicles. This may not be of immediate importance for reporting sexual violence, but the fact that two thirds of the men did not know a comprehensible term may pose difficulties, should they need to report a health issue. Lack of vocabulary in this area furthermore suggests that the majority of even relatively verbal men with learning difficulties have not benefited from current UK public health campaigns, which promote self-examinations to detect prostate or testicular cancer (e.g. Everyman Campaign 2010). This indicates that some people with learning difficulties continue to be disadvantaged in their access to information that is widely available via the popular media.

About half of the interviewees stated independently that some things they do are private, like having a bath, going to the toilet, having sex and masturbating. Josie states that 'private business' is 'when you have boyfriend in bed'. Lee states when people want sex they should 'draw the curtains as well and shut the door'. When I say 'privacy' Bill immediately says: 'private parts'. Leanne says that her breasts and crotch are 'private' parts of her body and that nobody is allowed to touch them without her permission.

Participants described being allowed varying levels of privacy in their daily lives. Rachel complains that some of the staff do not knock on her bedroom door in the morning: 'Like [staff] opened the door: "Are you ready? Are you dressed smart? Are you decent?"…didn't knock on the door! They didn't! They just walk in! March in!' Other respondents, like Bob and Bart, who live with their families, state that their privacy is generally respected. Visitors to their bedrooms always knock before they enter. Being allowed privacy in that way is important, as it teaches individuals that their personal space must be respected.

Respondents' level of knowledge of STIs and the use of condoms tended to be much lower than their knowledge of the mechanics of sexual intercourse, body parts and privacy awareness. Only Emma, Tyler, Chantal, Georgina and Bob, who are all younger and more articulate, conveyed a good level of understanding. The other respondents had a blurred understanding of the causes of STIs and ways in which they could protect themselves from infections. Kathy, for example, knows that chemists sell condoms and that they 'go on the man's thing', but she thinks they are for 'having babies'. Josie believes that the Human Immunodeficiency Virus (HIV) can be spread through handshakes and Lee thinks that the flu is an STI. Martha believes that HIV means that people do not want children. Rachel, who has an otherwise excellent level of knowledge on sexual practices, believes that her ex-boyfriend used condoms for protection from his epilepsy.

As discussed earlier, fairly abstract knowledge about sexual health and contraception is not essential when it comes to distinguishing an unwanted sexual approach from a wanted one. Although it could be recommended that more accessible information on these topics is provided to people with learning difficulties, in order to benefit their sexual health, their general lack of knowledge in this area is not a contributing factor to the high incidence of sexual violence against this population. Furthermore it must be noted that young non-disabled people, too, lack knowledge in these areas.

An Australian study amongst 16- to 29-year-olds found that young people answered only an average 56 per cent of questions about STIs correctly, while many engaged in high-risk practices (Lim *et al.* 2005). Young people in the UK have also been reported to have a limited understanding of different STIs and of the fact that condoms are not merely a means of contraception (Garside *et al.* 2001). Low levels of knowledge amongst people with learning difficulties in these areas are consequently not out of the ordinary compared to the general population, but maybe this receives a different level of professional attention.

Overall the sexual knowledge of respondents varied. On the whole they were least knowledgeable about STIs and their prevention, but when it came to knowledge that would be directly relevant to identifying and reporting an unsought sexual approach their understanding was much higher. The majority could describe the mechanics of sexual intercourse. However, only half of the respondents confidently distinguished 'good' sex from 'bad' sex. This varying degree of sexual knowledge indicates that categorising the diverse research sample as sexually 'vulnerable' is not accurate. Some respondents are evidently knowledgeable. Generation and social inclusion appear to be significant factors. As the following section outlines, younger respondents who benefited from peer talk and sex education in inclusive settings had generally a better understanding.

Formal sex education

Mainstream sexual support services are often inaccessible for disabled people. For example, Civjan (2000) describes how services for survivors of sexual violence are often inadequately prepared to meet the needs of people with learning difficulties. Disabled women have been reported to frequently encounter access barriers to sexual health services, including being provided with little information about contraceptive options, not being screened for STIs and being talked to as if they were children. They also encountered inaccessible facilities and equipment (Becker, Stuifbergen and Tinkle 1997). Anderson and Kitchin (2000, p.1163) describe family planning centres as representing 'a landscape of exclusion', which deny disabled people access to services. Many individuals therefore often rely on the support of family members and specialist support agencies for information on sex and sexuality.

Sex education is a central tool in limiting 'vulnerability' to sexual violence. However, in Britain sex education in schools has been criticised for its reinforcement of institutional heteronormativity and the focus on procreation as the only 'natural' objective of sexual activity, which 'inevitably denies [young people] their immediate feelings and emotions, their pleasures or desires' (Corteen and Scraton 1997, p.85). This approach was reflected in the accounts of some of the respondents, which were presented in the previous section.

In the past many disabled young people were wholly excluded from sex education at school (e.g. Shakespeare *et al.* 1996). This has now changed, as all young people in the UK have to be taught the national curriculum (Qualifications and Curriculum Authority 1999). In addition *Valuing People* (Department of Health 2001) directs that people with learning difficulties should receive accessible sex education and information about relationships and contraception. Nonetheless Rogers (2009) recently described how a girl with learning difficulties had been excluded from a sex education event at her mainstream school. Moreover, Grieve, McClaren and Lindsay (2007) report that there continues to be a lack of suitable sex education material for people who are labelled with 'severe' learning difficulties.

The respondents in this study had varied experiences of sex education. They have accessed the education system at various points in time and the information they received was shaped by the existing policies at that time. Half of the respondents who could recall their experiences at school stated they did not receive any sex education. All of these were in the 40-plus age group. The other half, all of whom were under 40 years old, did have sex education at school. In other words, younger people have routinely received sex education, while older generations did not.

Josie, who is in her late sixties, has only learned about sex, naming body parts and 'making babies' recently, when these issues were discussed in her women's group at the day centre. Of the 24 respondents who could recall how they had learned about sex ten expressed satisfaction with the information they had received. A further six did not recall ever discussing sexuality. Eight further respondents had received partial or inaccurate sex education. Mary, for instance, has learned to name body parts and has heard about condoms, but she does not know the mechanics of sexual intercourse. Tyler, too, received incomplete information. He describes sex education at his segregated boarding school in the late 90s:

> We watched really old sex videos and learned about the human body bits. We didn't actually learn about...blow jobs or going down on a woman. Or there's, there's different positions, you know. We didn't learn that sort of thing. What we just learned was how a baby was made and it were just like, playing with bananas and a condom.

Information about different sexual practices is crucial. A person may not understand that they are being sexually violated if the violence does not take place in the heterosexual missionary position that is usually discussed at school. When Tyler was violated by a fellow pupil he did not understand what was happening because he did not know that sex between men was possible (see later on in this chapter). Being taught how to put a condom on a banana may furthermore lead some people with learning difficulties to the false conclusion that, as long as they put a condom on a banana, they are safe (Jacobs *et al.* 1989). Sex education must therefore be as concrete as possible, without such confusing demonstration aids.

Tyler picked up more relevant information during peer talk at college. Peers are often the dominant sex educators amongst young people (Elley 2008). Yet, as will be discussed in Chapter 4, many people with learning difficulties are disadvantaged in their access to peers. Emerson and McVilly (2004) report that people with learning difficulties spend little time in friendship activities and the ones they do participate in tend to take place in public places. Talk about intimate issues can consequently be difficult. Formal sex education is thus even more important for this population.

One of the research advisors, Max, who is in his early twenties, explains that two nurses once came to his day centre to deliver sex education. They told him about the family planning clinic:

Max: I've been to the sex education class before. They say something like…these family planning clinics. They give you advice and that. And they give you, like, condoms free and all that, so…

Andrea: Did you ever go to the family planning clinic?

Max: No, never.

Andrea: Why not?

Max: I just never had a chance to go. Cause the trouble is, I don't actually know where they are.

Although Max received some good information about the family planning clinic, which he retained, his educators failed to make this service accessible to him.

In contrast Georgina, one of the younger respondents, reports that she had very detailed sex education at her segregated school. She says the teacher first started the session by finding out what the students knew and then built on their existing knowledge. The subject was picked up in three consecutive years and the information became more detailed and complicated each year. Georgina says they had 'people coming in to do talks' about HIV. Her mother had also spoken to her about sex, which Georgina found helpful:

> And she says: 'If you are gonna have sex with a man, just make sure…that you get to know that person first. And make sure you use a protection.' She didn't turn around and say you couldn't have sex. She didn't say anything like that. She just made sure I was, I was careful.

Georgina's family has always given her non-judgemental advice when she asked questions about sex. For example, once, an ex-boyfriend asked her for a 'threesome'. Georgina was unsure what he meant and asked her brother about this, who explained it to her. She was then able to make the decision that 'this is not for me'. Georgina communicated this to her boyfriend. When he insisted she ended the relationship.

Knowledge about sex is shaped by the information that is available to individuals. The accounts of respondents indicate that there are barriers to accessing information at school, but these appear to be diminishing for young people today. At present the UK government is committed to enhancing sex education in schools, but these changes will not affect people who have already left the education system.

During my fieldwork I observed a women's group at a day centre. Amongst other subjects they talked about body confidence, keeping clean, having showers and using deodorant. The women in the group learned to name their own sexual body parts and about sexuality more generally. Once they went on an excursion to a lingerie department for bra fittings. Group members talked about fashion and chose the clothes they would like to wear from glossy magazines. These meetings have the potential to help the women to become more aware of and confident about their own bodies. For some of the older women this was the first time that they had an opportunity to discuss sexuality openly. This is a positive practice example, as it makes information about sexuality available to women who have already left school. However, Max's account demonstrates that sex education at the day centre is not enough. For him it would have been beneficial to be shown how to access the family planning centre, which would enable him to manage his sexual health needs independently.

Other information sources

People with learning difficulties do not live in a protected vacuum. Even when information about sexuality is withheld from them they will inevitably learn about sexuality through observing their environments, the media and direct personal experiences. For example, Mary knows that, over 30 years ago, her sister 'had to get married', because she was pregnant. She also knows that her sister used to 'go with other married men'. Yet her family never spoke directly to Mary about these issues. She learned about them by overhearing other people's conversations.

Information about sexuality has become more widely available on television, a medium that is more accessible for people with learning difficulties than written information. For example, *The Sex Education Show*, a series that captured a 'wide range of different personal experiences of sexual issues and problems, as well as offering candid advice' (Channel 4 2010) was aired in the UK in autumn 2008 (Season 1) and in spring 2010 (Season 2). Sex and relationships are also a regular feature in films, soap operas and reality TV shows. Unsurprisingly, Rose states she has learned about the mechanics of heterosexual sex through the media: 'I've seen it all before on TV and everything. And that's got me going.'

Homosexuality has rarely been discussed formally with the respondents. Yet, Bill tells me he is aware of gay relationships, because he has heard that Elton John married a man (BBC News 2005). Many respondents are aware of gay television characters, such as Craig Dean on *Hollyoaks* (Green 2008) and Debbie and Jasmine on *Emmerdale* (Hadrian 2006). Britney furthermore states that one of her best friends is gay, while Norman lives with his father and the father's same-sex partner.

Respondents' understanding was also shaped by past sexual experiences. Rachel names various places around the house, where people could have sex: 'Bed, bathroom, [laughs] on a table [laughs].' As she used to live alone with her boyfriend, all of these places were private for them. Rachel has also tried a variety of sexual positions and oral sex. She states: 'I know sixty-nine and other things in sex lives.' Rachel tells me that she enjoyed this, but that she only learned of these practices when her boyfriend showed them to her. Some respondents also described how they had learned from past sexual experiences that were not always positive. These are explored in Chapter 5.

Being exposed to unstructured sexual information in one's environment without guidance or without someone to turn to who could help to clarify issues can also cause confusion. Kathy tells me that she has seen 'horrible stuff' to do with sex on TV. What she saw frightened and disgusted her. Kathy cannot tell me whether she saw a sex or a rape scene. She is disturbed by these images and has not spoken about this to anyone.

Sex as taboo

Some respondents have learned that sex is only acceptable in certain relationships, namely those that do not apply to them. Josie, for example, believes that sex is only legitimate when a couple is married. Others were explicitly told that all sex is taboo. Ann states: 'They said to me...with sex, sex's a bit...rude.' Gemma also states that 'making love' is a 'rude' word. Some respondents have consequently voiced the belief that sex is simply 'bad'. This had a damaging impact on their understanding and often resulted in self-blame and prohibition. Overall, a third of respondents made some form of negative value judgement about all forms of sexual contact, without distinguishing wanted and unwanted sexual encounters.

For instance, Jasmine states that two people being 'on top of each other with no clothes on' is wrong. She is aware that there are special implications when people do this, but she does not distinguish wanted from unwanted sexual experiences. Norman believes that masturbation is the only acceptable way to seek sexual satisfaction and that inter-personal sexual contact is taboo. He is not the only person who has received such partial information. Some sex education programmes are explicitly based on the assumption that 'masturbation may be the only means of appropriate sexual release for those with autism' (Kempton 1998, cited in Koller 2000, p.128). Staff working with people with learning difficulties have been reported to hold liberal attitudes in respect to masturbation, yet conservative attitudes when it comes to sexual intercourse (Yool, Langdon and Garner 2003).

Rose told me that she once had to visit the doctor because it was suspected that she was pregnant. For Rose this incident marks a turning point in the way in which she perceives sex. It appears that at this point her sexual activity with her partner became known to their families. What followed was some biased sex education:

Rose: He [boyfriend] doesn't like sex. And I did. ... I make him do it... And his sister doesn't like it either. She knows, she's a nurse actually... She came here to see, she had a word with me about it, like, and that's, that's how I'd start... Cause she don't like it, that sort of thing.

Andrea: Why doesn't she like it?

Rose: Cause it knows it's rude and...it's hurting, it's hurting, [boyfriend] don't like it, so...

Andrea: Was it hurting [boyfriend]?

Rose: It was, yeah. Cause I were, I were making him, you see. So I just make him and everything. But I don't wanna get violent, really.

Hingsburger (1995) once worked with a man who had sexually offended towards children. Prior to those offences the man had a consenting sexual relationship with an adult woman, but when this was discovered the couple were punished and separated. As a consequence the man did not think that sexual offences were different from the consenting sexual relationship he had before, because he had learned that all sex was 'bad' and prohibited. Similarly, if Rose wants sex, but her boyfriend does not, teaching Rose that all sex is 'bad' does not allow Rose a positive sexual outlet. She suppresses her sexual desires because she does not want to get violent, but nobody has spoken to her about alternative options that do not involve violence (e.g. masturbation, finding a consenting partner and learning to distinguish signs of consent and refusal).

Paul, too, believes that sex is taboo. He discloses to me that he is sexually attracted to the same sex, but he immediately tells me that he does not kiss or cuddle 'boys'. By 'boys' Paul appears to mean men, as he goes on to talking about another day centre attendee, who is in his late fifties, as his 'boyfriend'. Paul says his 'boyfriend' does not know how he feels about him. To the outside observer the two men appear to be just friends. Throughout the interview Paul repeatedly mentions that sexual contact between men is not allowed. For instance, when I ask Paul how he would describe love, he replies: 'Don't kissing. Don't kiss boys... Get into bother.'

It appears that Paul had to learn that he has to keep his sexual desires secret and that he cannot act on them. Thompson (1994) confirms that, as a result of normalisation processes, most men with learning difficulties who have sex with men do not have a gay identity. Our society has become increasingly more accepting of gay people, but even if a person with learning difficulties was told a long time ago that their sexual desires are 'dirty', they may have had little opportunities to access more positive information that can contradict this in the meantime (Jones *et al.* 2004).

A recent study found that support staff are still not confident about working with gay people with learning difficulties (Abbott and Howarth 2007). Slater (2004) furthermore reports that teaching staff feel that they do not have the adequate support and information to talk about homosexuality to students. As a consequence people with learning difficulties wishing to engage in same-sex activity continue to encounter many barriers, such as lack of staff support and isolation (Abbott and Burns 2007). For this group sex remains even more of a taboo than for those seeking heterosexual encounters. According to Kinsey, Pomeroy and Martin (2003) these are not mere minority issues. He asserts that an unambiguous distinction between hetero- and homosexuality is socially constructed, as all human sexuality occurs on a continuum. In other words, he claims that the majority of the population have bisexual preferences. These are however firmly suppressed within service settings.

In summary, about half of the respondents conceptualise some aspects of consenting sexual activity as taboo. This indicates that they have received judgemental sex education. Such views restrict individuals' sexual activity to options that they believe to be acceptable. Some individuals were taught that all sex is bad. The danger with this approach is that individuals may seek violent sexual outlets if they do not feel that they have an alternative acceptable option. This has a significant impact on risk, as the single largest group of perpetrators within service settings are users of services themselves (McCarthy and Thompson 1996). The information about sexuality that is available to others using their services thus impacts on the risk of every person with learning difficulties.

Sexual knowledge: discussion

This section discussed respondents' sexual knowledge. It was shown that some knowledge is crucial to enable self-defence. This includes the ability to name sexual body parts, to recognise sexual acts and to distinguish wanted from unwanted sexual approaches. Individuals had varying levels of understanding and the claim that all of these people are 'vulnerable' to sexual violence due to a lack of knowledge would not be accurate. As sexual knowledge is socially determined, respondents' scope of knowledge is limited by the amount of information that was made accessible to them.

Respondents in the older age group (40 and over) in particular had a reduced understanding of sex and sexuality or they were more likely to see sex as taboo. Younger respondents had access to more comprehensive and positive information. This indicates that changes to social and educational policies on the macrosystem can influence processes on the exo- and microsystem. With this they can have a direct impact on an individual's level of 'vulnerability': those with an increased awareness of sex and sexuality are at reduced risk of sexual violence. However, changes to the sex education curriculum at school will not affect those who have already left the education system. Few of those who missed out on comprehensive sex education were able to access structured information or to talk about their concerns in later life. Further changes on the macrosystem that impact on information provided to adults with learning difficulties within service settings would therefore be beneficial.

For some individuals their right to privacy was disrespected at 'home', which is an invasion into their personal space and dignity that interferes with their privacy awareness. Routine invasions make it harder for a person to distinguish these from unsought sexual approaches. Lack of privacy thus increases risk.

Despite these disabling factors a significant proportion of respondents report that they have been sexually active. Their accounts are outlined in the subsequent section.

EXPERIENCING SEXUALITY

In this book the term 'sexual relationship' is used to refer to relationships that are based on mutual sexual attraction and consent. This term is used to distinguish these from other important relationships, such as friendships. In this section the accounts of respondents' sexual experiences are summarised. Some of these were shared with a sexual partner, while others were solitary experiences. Due to the limited scope of this book the discussion takes a particular focus on the way in which some experiences have enabled understanding and self-awareness. First respondents' access to sexually stimulating material is discussed. Next the positive impact that being in love had on their sense of self is outlined, with a particular focus on imaginary relationships. Finally the barriers and support structures that enabled or disabled individuals from having relationships are summarised. Further accounts by respondents who described how they have exercised assertiveness within sexual relationships are discussed in Chapter 5.

Masturbation and sexual images

One factor that can reduce risk of sexual violence is that individuals should be in touch with their bodies. They should know their sexual preferences and what feels good for them. Sexual self-awareness reduces the risk of being pressured into sexual acts that do not feel as good. This contrasts with those who have what Tolman (2001) calls a 'silent body', which means that they are not in tune with their own sexual desires and take on passive roles in sexual relationships. Sexual exploration, such as that described in this section, enables individuals to become more aware of their personal desires. In the absence of a consenting partner this can also be a safe sexual outlet.

McCarthy (1999) reports that none of the women with learning difficulties in her study readily or confidently admitted that they masturbated and that some women indicated that they did not wish to discuss this topic at all. My questionnaire did not include explicit questions about masturbation, because I did not consider the relationships I had with participants close enough to ask for intimate detail on sexual practices. Some interviewees did however volunteer this kind of information themselves. This resulted in some respondents who held liberal views discussing their sexual practices, while those who may have held negative views simply avoided talking about the subject.

Rachel ended a sexual relationship a few months ago. She states that she misses the sex. When she confided in her mother, the mother suggested exploring sexual stimulation without a partner. With a smile Rachel tells me that her mother bought her a 'thing' (vibrator) for what Rachel calls 'spots' (she could be referring to her clitoris and/or g-spot here). She describes why she uses it and how she looks after it:

> I bought it for a reason, cause eh, my mum bought it me. Me mum said to me to use it, because I've got spots. So that means I have to clean it. Morning and night. And then, if I've got any spots, put this gel onto it and then, use it. ... It's like a pear shape. It makes a funny, funny noise. ... Like, vibrator. I got one of them. ... And I can't say it in front of [fellow resident].

Rachel lives in a residential group setting. Her fellow resident does not know about the vibrator, but all the staff do. Rachel can keep her vibrator overnight, but it is locked in the medication cupboard every morning. Staff sign it in and out. In that way staff could be said to control her sexual appetite. They are furthermore inevitably aware of Rachel's private sexual activity. Nonetheless, Rachel does not seem to mind, as she appears to be able to speak openly with the all-female staff team.

Liz, who fantasises about a fictitious boyfriend (see next sub-section), states: 'When he come stay with me he go, he goes sexy. Well eh, he sometimes used to rub me.' Liz indicates that her fantasies about her 'boyfriend' include sexual desires and stimulation. Norman, who lives with his father and father's partner, had some sex education to ensure that he does not masturbate in public places:

> When outside. They're rude, cause if they do it, police could lock me up. ... That's naughty. Dad says: 'Keep a good hiding for it.' That's naughty. Should not do it outside. Do it where I do it. In a flat or house.

Norman has been taught that masturbation in private is acceptable. He can talk openly about this topic at home. When Norman wants to masturbate he tells his dad and dad's partner not to disturb him in his room.

> Norman: In house... My bedroom. Sometimes I do it. In my bedroom... Cause I've got pictures on the walls. So that's my private bits. Yeah. I do. I've got some pants, to do it in...and then they [dad or partner] wash them. And then get fresh, so it's easy.
>
> Andrea: What kind of pictures have you got in your bedroom?
>
> Norman: Everything. On the walls. Some nice people. ... I like girls, me. Grown-up ladies... I like skirts, yeah and boots.

One morning at the day centre Norman called me over to tell me that he wants to show me some 'nice girls'. He was looking through some tabloid papers that staff members had brought in and pointed to topless models and women in tight clothes. Norman told me they looked 'nice' and he liked one of them so much that he asked a member of staff whether he could take page three of *The Sun* home. The staff member looked at the picture, laughed and let him have it. Norman said he would put the picture on his bedroom wall.

Tyler tells me that he used to watch a TV programme called *Babe Station*, where he could phone up and ask the girls on the programme to show their 'tits'. Tyler also uses a phone sex line. He tells me that it only costs seven pence per minute and he explains that he can communicate with women who want phone sex and he can have what he calls a 'one handed relationship'. Although it could be argued that men like Tyler are 'vulnerable' to financial exploitation by the sex industry, he seems to retain some level of control by consciously choosing this more affordable option.

None of the respondents in this study had accessed a sex worker, but the experiences of some men with physical impairments are discussed in the literature (Sanders 2007). Some local relationship policies give guidance on access to sexually explicit material, but not about supporting individuals to access sex workers (e.g. NHS Lothian 2004). For people with learning difficulties this topic may raise concerns about 'vulnerability' and consent capacity. Access is further complicated by the fact that, in the UK, sex work is legally a grey area. However, only persistent soliciting of women for the purpose of prostitution in a street or public place, or kerb-crawling (soliciting a woman for the purpose of prostitution from within a motor vehicle), are considered to be offences under the Sexual Offences Act (HMSO 1985, sections 1–2). A support worker who assists a disabled person to arrange a visit by a sex worker, as was the case for Nick Wallis (2007), does consequently not break the law. Clear guidance for staff could enable them to understand this legal situation better. Services that aim to facilitate an equal right for people with learning difficulties to sexual expression should begin to discuss the potential dangers and benefits of such assistance.

It must be acknowledged that some respondents in this study will have held negative views about masturbation and sexual images and that only those who held liberal views about these subjects discussed their preferences. Although this data can consequently not be generalised, it does indicate that masturbation and access to sexually stimulating material can be experienced as positive by some people with learning difficulties. This enables individuals to become more aware of their sexual preferences, making it easier to distinguish positive sensations from unwanted sexual intrusions.

Being in love and imaginary relationships

Loving and being loved was an exciting and important aspect of respondents' lives. Many spoke about people they loved, such as their family, friends or partners. Half of the respondents had current sexual relationships. They expressed affectionate feelings towards their partners and stated that being in love made them happy. Some talked about making each other presents, kissing or cuddling and spending time together.

Lee said that love makes his 'heart beat fast'. To Peter love is about 'looking after someone'. Mary says it means 'not pushing yourself onto somebody'. Tyler emphasises that love is 'a commitment between two people and that's a connection-type-thing. If one feels it, the other one should feel it.' Britney explains that 'love is someone that cares for you. Don't just use you as, for a sex machine.' Chantal adds that two people who love each other might have some similar interests: 'You like each other, you get along with each other and then it turns into love, eventually.' Ryan says that people who are in love can relax with each other, 'have a laugh' and talk in confidence.

Kathy has been in a loving relationship for eight years. She laughs when she merely mentions her boyfriend: 'He loves me. Call me cute, gorgeous, sweetheart and tooth. And he's [laughs] … He's lovely! [laughs] His love makes me happy!' Lee has a fiancée. With a big smile he shows me her photograph and the text messages she has sent him, which state that she loves him and misses him when they are apart. Michael is in love with his wife: 'She fancies me [laughs]. I'm going take her out for a walk.' Michael says his wife came from Pakistan to 'look after' him. Tyler repeatedly states throughout the interview that he desires nothing more than a long-term relationship:

> I wanna be a family man in the worst way. I wanna be a dad… I've always had this dream. I'm sat on the settee with my girlfriend in my arm and my child playing at the table and I'm watching television… And I wake up with a smile on my face and a very warm feeling. I go: 'That's what I want.'

Sexual relationships have a significant impact on an individual's sense of self. They can give a feeling of worth and belonging, which is currently missing for Tyler.

Being in love was also important to respondents who were not currently in relationships. For instance, Josie, a woman in her sixties, fancies a member of staff at her day centre. She has his photo in her handbag: 'I like him. He's my madness.' The staff member himself is noticeably uncomfortable with Josie's attention and tries to avoid her as much as possible. He will ask other members of staff to work with Josie whenever this is possible. Although it has been explained to Josie that he is married and that it would be inappropriate for him to start a relationship with a service user, Josie continues to seek him out whenever she can.

Mary, who is in her fifties, supports a boy band. She has seen them in concert six times. Mary says listening to their music and watching their DVDs lifts her up when she feels down. Her favourite member has 'absolutely fantastic blue eyes' and 'a right smirk'. She has two posters of him on her bedroom wall. Mary tells me at length what he was wearing at the last concert and how attractive it made him look. She feels special when she goes to see 'the lads' and she is sure that her favourite star recognises her when he sees her in the audience and waves at her in the crowd.

Liz, who is in her late forties, states she has a boyfriend. She says he is an actor and she met him at 'the London studios': 'It's like a romance. Well that, in real life… With there being romance there. It's like being at, you know that feeling on, eh, Valentine's day.' One of Liz's support workers explained to me after the interview that Liz has a 'crush' on a soap star and will talk about him like he is her 'real' boyfriend. To Liz, however, he is real. He makes her feel happy and enjoy romance.

Julie, a woman I met at a day centre, is in a similar situation. Her 'boyfriend' is also a character in a television programme. Yet, to her all that is happening to her 'boyfriend' in the programme is real. The character he plays is married and Julie is jealous of his wife: 'He's my boyfriend!' She cries about him a lot. Staff try to discourage her and to demonstrate to her that he is not her boyfriend, but Julie will only become more upset when they say this. Julie and Liz are under the impression that they have someone who cares for them, someone who is, as Liz puts it, like 'Valentine's day'. The research advisors tell me that this is not unusual. Two advisors have friends who have similar imaginary relationships.

Imaginary companions are not unique to people with learning difficulties. For example, some young, non-disabled women have imaginary relationships with male pop idols (McRobbie 1978). Today interactive fan sites and media technologies make these relationships even more 'real' (Soukup 2006). Imaginary companions are also known to be of central importance to many children, most of whom, however, recognise the companion's 'unreality', with girls reporting more frequently that they have an imaginary companion than boys (Pearson et al. 2001). Imaginary companions in adulthood are more rare, but Bass (1983) describes the case of a non-disabled adult who relied on an imaginary companion in stressful times.

All of my respondents who reported imaginary relationships were women of the older age group (late forties and older), who relied on their companion to enable them to feel less alone. Mary states that 'the lads' have helped her through difficult times of domestic violence by her nephew (see Chapter 5). Although her social network has improved significantly (Mary now lives with a niece with whom she gets along well and she has some good friends), 'the lads' remain important to her, as they 'have always been there' for her. Similarly Josie and Liz felt lonely after the loss of their parents and their imaginary relationships filled a void in their lives.

These three women have a fantasy relationship in the absence of an actual intimate relationship. A similar case was reported by Baron, Riddell and Wilson (1999). They suggest that this can be linked to a limited understanding of how to form a real relationship. However, these fantasy relationships are significant. They give a sense of belonging and with this they increase self-awareness. As outlined previously, Liz masturbates when she thinks about her 'boyfriend'. She is, however, clear that their relationship is exclusive and that others should not touch her the way he does. This indicates a clear distinction between wanted and unwanted sexual activity. Within the context of her imaginary world Liz consequently appears to be a confident sexual actor. However, it is worth considering, on a case by case basis, whether individuals who have to retreat to a fantasy world to fulfil their emotional needs would prefer to have an actual relationship. In such cases individuals may require support to meet new people and possibly some help with understanding real relationships.

Support with establishing and maintaining sexual relationships

Some people with learning difficulties require assistance with finding a partner and maintaining a relationship, especially if they live in isolated settings that make social intercourse difficult. (These settings are discussed in Chapter 4.) However, sexual relationships of people with learning difficulties continue to be insufficiently supported (Department of Health 2007). This is confirmed by the study on which this book is based. In this section the problems and opportunities that were described by respondents are summarised.

Leanne, a woman in her mid-twenties, is desperate to find a boyfriend. She attends a day service about five times per week and spends the remainder of her time mostly with her mother. She tells me that she has no opportunity to meet new people. I know that Leanne often participates in community-based activities with her day service. I ask her whether she ever meets new people on outings, but Leanne says she does not.

Many non-disabled people meet their partners through friends or at work. Recent studies estimate that 40 per cent of American workers and a third of workers in South Africa have had relationships with colleagues (Health 24 2009). A survey by an American women's magazine found that almost 60 per cent of women had met their current partner through friends and almost 20 per cent had met their partner through work (Spethmann 2009). Yet, Leanne has no social contacts outside of the day service or her family. She does not work. These avenues to meeting a partner are consequently closed for her.

I ask her if she can think of ways in which she may be able to meet a potential partner. Leanne suggests going to night clubs. However, she has never been to a mainstream night club. She has high hopes that she may meet a partner there. According to the above quoted survey 10 per cent of non-disabled women have met their partner in this way (Spethmann 2009). Leanne is however visibly impaired. Shakespeare (1994) would argue that this would disadvantage her in an environment that puts great emphasis on physical appearance. Here she is likely to experience prejudice, as she would not conform to prevailing norms and beauty ideals.

Leanne's lack of opportunities to meet new people is not an isolated case. Many other respondents are in similar situations. Whenever they access community-based settings their movements are restricted and controlled by support workers, which means that they remain socially segregated, despite their physical presence in the community. Staff or family members often take the lead in interactions with others, as indicated in Figure 3.1.

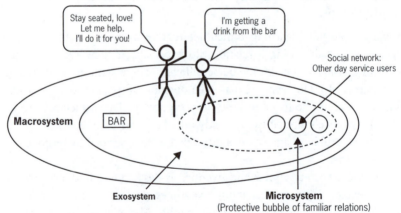

Figure 3.1 In the pub – Leanne's 'helpful' support worker

This illustrates a typical scenario in Leanne's everyday life. She described to me that, during the weekly pub outings with her day service, support workers walk up to the bar and buy her drinks, while she remains seated with a group of day service acquaintances and staff. That way she has little interaction beyond her 'protective bubble' of familiar relations. Support staff speak and act for her in an attempt to assist communication. Leanne has a speech impairment and some people may have difficulties in understanding her. Yet, by completely overtaking and communicating on her behalf staff hinder social intercourse. This is a common occurrence. Others negotiating on behalf of a disabled person who is deemed unable to speak for themselves has been referred to as the 'does he take sugar syndrome' (Brisenden 1989b; Pound and Hewitt 2003).

A potential option for meeting new people that Leanne has not identified would be to access a dating service. Concerns about 'vulnerability' and the risk of exploitation of people with learning difficulties when accessing mainstream dating agencies inspired the set-up of Stars in the Sky (2010). Individuals who choose to do so can meet other disabled people during informal social activities or formally arranged dates. Although this service is somewhat progressive, as it acknowledges that finding a partner is important, yet at times difficult for people with learning difficulties, it continues to segregate this group. Some may prefer to access mainstream services. Nonetheless, such dating agencies give individuals a further option for meeting new people.

Eight of the 14 respondents who met their partner at their day service had never made contact away from the service. This is not unusual. Relationships and friendships that were based exclusively on contact at day centres have been described by past research (e.g. Barnes 1990; Chappell 1994). Even those who were able to see their partner away from their service did not see them as frequently as they would have liked. Martha, for instance, is able to visit her boyfriend for two hours once per week. She is unsatisfied with this frequency, which amounts to a mere fraction of her free time. The visit is part of her weekly routine and staff are not made available to support her to see her boyfriend more often. However, frequency of interaction is known to impact on the strength of the tie between individuals (Feld 1997). In other words, relationships are likely to be weakened if contact is limited.

Some respondents, all of whom are in the older age group (40 and over), told me that they have never told their parents about their relationships at the day centre, because they fear they would 'get into trouble'. Social constraint causes their sexual lives to be secretive and rushed. Individuals are thus kept in a permanent state of adolescence. Peter describes to me how he would seek privacy at his day centre: 'You can go out, out there. Go outside and you can spend that, have a sexy half hour or, eh, five minutes with your girlfriend.' McCarthy (1999) observed that sexual activity of people with learning difficulties in institutional settings mostly takes place outdoors or in isolated semi-private places indoors (e.g. in unused rooms). Such rushed sexual activity allows little space for negotiations of personal boundaries. Consequently, individuals have limited time to consider whether they consent to a proposed sexual act and to communicate their decision. This places them at risk. Nonetheless, many individuals feel that they have to retreat to such isolated places.

Many respondents told me about service-based relationships, which broke down when one person stopped attending the service, even if individuals remained living within close proximity. Rose describes a more positive experience. When her day service was recently restructured the service planned to send her boyfriend to a different day service location. Rose spoke to 'the big boss' about this. He apologised and said that he did not want important relationships to break down. As a result plans were changed and the couple continued to attend the same service.

There were some further positive examples. Lee, who is in his early twenties, receives informal family support for his relationship. He has been going out with his fiancée for a couple of years. They used to go to school together, but do not currently attend the same service. Lee therefore visits her at least once per week. He has also been on a holiday with his fiancée and her family. Both families are supportive of their relationship. Lee does, however, state that he often misses his girlfriend. While around six out of ten UK adults live with a partner (National Statistics 2008), only four of 29 respondents in this study did. This option is not routinely discussed with individuals and some respondents reported that their requests were dismissed.

Ryan has sexually offended in the past. He has one-to-one support at all times, which is a customary way of providing services under such circumstances. However, this can often act as a form of informal detention (Brown and Thompson 1997). This does not appear to be the case for Ryan. He explains that he perceives his one-to-one support as enabling, rather than disabling. For example, he states that he is able to participate in more leisure activities than others who are using his service, as he always has someone with him who can take him out. Ryan is also supported to have a consenting sexual relationship with a woman with learning difficulties.

Initially he was not allowed any privacy with his girlfriend, because his 'risk management plan' prohibited this. This plan was set out by his legal guardian, the social services authority. The support service agency, Ryan's parents and his psychologist negotiated on Ryan's behalf, as they felt that risk could be managed. The revised plan stated that Ryan and his girlfriend can spend time alone in each other's bedroom, but a member of staff must knock on the door every five minutes and ask them if they are both fine. The support worker will only open the door if one person says 'no' or does not answer. Otherwise they will return five minutes later to check again. This arrangement has worked well for a number of months and the distance between intervals has gradually increased to 15 minutes. When Ryan and his girlfriend celebrated a recent anniversary, they went out for a meal.

Andrea:	Did you go out by yourself or did someone come with you?
Ryan's girlfriend:	Oh, someone came. [Support workers] came.
Andrea:	All right, so was it the four of you on a table?
Ryan's girlfriend:	Oh no...we had a table for us, me and Ryan had a table and then [support workers] had a table. But, it's like, they were watching, just watching us, you know? [pause of four seconds] I had a little bit of a privacy.

The support workers' table was some distance away from the couple, which gave them as much privacy as possible. To outside observers they looked like two different parties. These are just two examples of the creative ways in which Ryan's service ensures safety, but also allows for privacy. This can potentially reduce risk of sexual violence within service settings. As explained earlier, supporting individuals like Ryan to find legal sexual outlets can limit the risk of re-offence.

Despite many barriers, individuals who were able to sustain contact with their partner were able to experience the multifaceted nature of relationships. In some cases supportive families and services ensured that individuals were able to maintain these relationships. Accommodating factors included day services and families respecting the importance of relationships and making an explicit effort to support contact between partners.

The research advisors believe that the day centre can be a good place for meeting a new partner. Some members of the group have established successful relationships with someone they met there. However, they had been able to see each other away from the day centre to 'go on proper dates' and 'have a bit of privacy'. The advisors agree that it is important to have the opportunity to take relationships further in this way. Individuals who do not have these options are more likely to engage in rushed and risky sexual behaviour.

Experiencing sexuality: discussion

The research advisors agree that:

> It's against the law to stop a person from having a relationship. Carers, family members and friends shouldn't put their nose in what other people are doing. They should stick by you, no matter what your choice of relationship is.

As outlined in Chapter 2, people with learning difficulties have the legal and moral rights to lead sexual relationships. Loving relationships and being in love can have a positive impact on an individual's sense of self. High self-esteem has been linked to an increased ability to resist unwanted sexual approaches. Yet, some respondents did not currently have a sexual partner. In the absence of actual sexual relationships masturbation and access to sexually stimulating material enabled some of them to become more aware of their sexual preferences, making it easier to distinguish these from unwanted sexual intrusions.

While this section focused on consenting and largely positive aspects of sexuality, the remainder of this chapter will explore negative and invasive experiences.

SEXUAL INVASIONS

This section provides a discussion of factors that allowed actual sexual intrusions to succeed. Respondents' narratives are first listed without any annotations, to allow their experiences to speak for themselves. Next, the risk factors that emerge from these accounts are summarised. This is followed by a discussion of the consequences of the routine prescription of contraceptives to women with learning difficulties. Furthermore, this section discusses how sexist assumptions about women's sexual availability contribute to an increased risk of sexual violence.

Sexual violence

One person chose not to talk about sexuality at all. Two participants explicitly told me they did not wish to discuss their experiences of sexual violence. Many spoke about other forms of violence, such as intimate partner violence (see Chapter 5), bullying (see Chapter 4) and violence by family members (see Chapter 5). Five respondents spoke about experiences of sexual violence. The accounts of respondents who described the circumstances within which the violence took place are discussed below.

Tyler was sexually violated by a roommate at residential school:

> Basically what happened was: he was bi [bisexual]. I didn't know what bi was when I was at this age. And he brought a games console, cause he knew I liked games and he brought a games console in to specifically... I think the phrase is 'give me a hand job' while I was playing on the games console... I won't go down how it escalated from that. It did...and then you elbow them in the face to get them off you and they go and tell on you because they raped you. They say *you* raped *them*.

Josie tells me that her brother-in-law 'used to be a pervert'. He used to pull:

> our knickers down in front of him... He tried it with our youngest. Our [first sister]. He asked her for sex... And he asked our [second sister] and our [third sister] for it... Me mum said she's break his arm if he touched me.

Paul tells me that a woman who attends his day centre touches him in a way he perceives as sexual sometimes. Paul uses a wheelchair, while the woman is mobile. She walks up to him and he cannot get away from her. He does not like her touching him, but Paul does not know what to do about this. When I suggest that he should tell someone he states: 'It's a girl though!' Paul believes that he cannot stand up against unwanted touch from a woman. This may be due to him believing that women cannot be perpetrators.

Some members of the research committee had also experienced sexual violence and were prepared to share their stories. Below are two summaries of personal accounts, which the individuals and I have composed together:

> When I was 14 my granddad abused me. He got into my bed and tried to have sex with me. I couldn't go and tell anyone. He was a very bad man. He told me he would kill me if I told someone. I didn't think anyone would believe me. I didn't think the police would believe me that my own granddad was abusing me. I didn't think my mom would believe me. I was scared, so I didn't tell anyone.
>
> *(Nina, late forties)*

> [A member of staff] used to sexually abuse me. At first I didn't tell anyone, but then...the abuse went really bad. I told my parents and we went to the police. We took [violator] to court, but he walked away free. They said there was not enough evidence. But it did happen! This is unfair. He abused me, but he has not been punished. I felt like the police did not believe me.
>
> *(Jessica, early twenties)*

Jessica's case went to court after the Sexual Offences Act (HMSO 2003) was enforced. The increased protection that the Act offers to people with learning difficulties, as discussed in Chapter 2, did not help her, as she was unable to prove beyond 'reasonable doubt' that the sexual acts had taken place.

In order to make sense of the causes of violence it is important to take a closer look at what happened in these incidents. Figure 3.2 summarises the risk factors that can be identified in respondents' accounts.

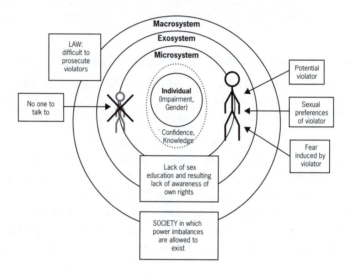

Figure 3.2 Risk factors in the ecological model

The individual's personal attributes impacted on the likelihood of sexual violence taking place. For instance, the gender of an individual will determine whether a violator is attracted to them. The fact that an individual has an impairment might mean that they are directed towards isolated or segregated settings in which dependency relations are allowed to thrive (see Chapter 4) and where information about sexuality or help are sparsely available. However, such personal attributes do not cause violence. Causes lie with the violator who is prepared to seek sexual gratification despite resistance, and with the social conditions that allowed his or her attack to succeed.

In all cases a significant factor was that the violator was a person in a position of trust, who had easy access to the individuals they violated. They were known to the victim, as they formed part of their micro- or exosystem. The violence took place within a society that accepts that some individuals can exercise power over others. Power imbalances characterised each violating experience. Tyler's violator was older than him. He had more information on sexuality and seems to have planned the attack. Paul cannot get away from a woman's unwanted touch. She is physically more mobile than he is. Nina was violated as a child by an adult relative. Jessica was violated by a person who delivered part of her daily support. Josie and her sisters were threatened by a man who was physically stronger.

Nina and Jessica report that they understood what was going on, but that they were scared to seek help. Tyler was confused about what was happening, because he did not know that sex between males was possible. Paul believes that he cannot defend himself against unwanted touch from a woman. Both men lacked information on sexuality. Jessica feels let down by a legal system that could not prosecute her violator. All of these are social factors.

All of the incidents described took place in segregated or family environments. This confirms the claim that protection by containing individuals in segregated settings is ineffective (Hingsburger 1995; McCarthy and Thompson 1996). The possibility of the presence of violators in an individual's environment can never be removed completely. The aim of this book is therefore to explore a range of alternative ways in which risk may be reduced. Positive factors that can potentially combat 'vulnerability' will be explored in Chapter 5. For now this chapter continues by outlining why the routine prescription of contraceptives to women with learning difficulties must be seen as invasive.

The routine prescription of contraceptives

As outlined in Chapter 2, past eugenic considerations have led to disabled people's sex segregation in institutions and to their sterilisation. Today's practice is more subtle but, as Block (2000) outlines, still influenced by the assumption that the sexuality and fertility of women with learning difficulties are 'dangerous'. They are frequently discouraged from falling pregnant, as they are generally perceived as being inadequate parents (Swain and Cameron 2003).

Some women are prescribed hormonal contraception, even in cases where they are not suspected to be sexually active. This is a major invasion into a person's privacy. McCarthy (1999) reports that, of 15 women in her research who used hormonal contraception, only one woman had made this decision for herself. This is mirrored in the findings of the study outlined in this book. Half the women in this research were unaware of the existence of hormonal contraception and they were unable to tell me whether they currently use any. With the exception of Kathy all of these women were in the 40-and-over age group. All the women who were aware of contraception were in their early thirties or younger. Again, this reflects the quality of sex education that was given to generational cohorts, with younger people having more detailed knowledge.

Chantal, who is in her early twenties, states that she was forced to have an implant, a long-term contraceptive that lasts for three years (Patient UK 2009), because her mother 'got worried' after she ran away from home. Chantal states: 'I didn't get a word in on what I wanted.' Martha and Rachel use hormonal contraceptives, even though they are currently not sexually active. Rachel says her mother would 'not be happy' if she came off the pill.

Nina had little control over her sterilisation about 20 years ago:

> They chose for me. I didn't have a chance. My husband's mum said once I get sterilised, nobody will try it on with me any more [try to abuse me]. My husband's mum and my social worker made the decision. They wouldn't let him marry me if I wouldn't have the operation... Every time I see babies I cry. I'd love a little boy and a girl.

Nina's 'choice' was either to marry the man she wanted to be with and to be sterilised or not to be allowed to live with her chosen partner. She was falsely informed that a sterilisation would prevent sexual violence. There is no scope to argue that her sterilisation was 'voluntary' or based on an informed and free choice. It has caused irreversible emotional damage.

Contraception and sterilisation is often used to treat health problems of women with learning difficulties, such as menstrual pains. Leanne, for example, states that she takes the pill 'for [her] hormones'. However, Rachel, Martha and Leanne are unaware of the suspected long-term side-effects of hormonal contraception, such as metabolic and cardiovascular disease (e.g. Morin-Papunen et al. 2006). They can therefore not be said to have made an informed choice about their use of contraceptives for non-contraceptive purposes.

The fact that women who use contraceptives cannot fall pregnant could furthermore serve to conceal sexual violence, as an unwanted pregnancy could be a means of detecting that rape has taken place. This happened when a young woman with severe learning difficulties who had no understanding of sexuality fell pregnant in the late 1990s and a DNA test confirmed the paternity of David Jenkins, a residential support worker. As Jenkins was nonetheless able to walk away free from court (Community Care 2000) this case has led to changes in the sex offending law. As stated earlier, the new Sexual Offences Act (HMSO 2003) makes it possible to prosecute those who have engaged an individual who does not have the 'capacity to consent' in a sexual act, as long as it can be proven that sexual activity has taken place. An unwanted pregnancy is such proof. Similar cases to the Jenkins case have led to recent successful prosecutions in the UK (Fitzgerald 2006) and the USA (*North Country Gazette* 2007). The perceived risk of an unwanted pregnancy could consequently put off a potential violator and act to protect a woman.

Two respondents had confidently chosen their contraception themselves: Emma decided she did not want any more children, as she already has two. She uses the coil, which she has chosen over the birth control pill, as she did not like having to remember to take it. Georgina chose to take the pill after she had her daughter, because she does currently not want to have another child. She states she would be protected from pregnancy, but if she met a new partner he would have to wear a condom as well, to protect her from STIs. Both, Emma and Georgina, have made an informed and free choice about their use of contraception. Like non-disabled women they were able to access information about contraception through their GP, who explained the range of available options to them. Both women accessed this service independently.

However, the women whose accounts were summarised earlier were coerced into using contraception by a family member who accompanied them to their GP and negotiated on their behalf. Information on the risks associated with hormonal contraceptives that is routinely available to non-disabled women (e.g. Womens Health Information 2009) was not made accessible for these respondents. None of these women were able to access family planning or sexual health services.

This chapter concludes by exploring a further risk factor that is particular to women. It will be highlighted why sexism increases risk.

Sexism and risk

In the following it is briefly explored how assumptions about women's sexual availability increase risk. This discussion aims to demonstrate how macrosystem forces impact on the formation of risk for the whole population, in this case the whole population of women, including disabled women. The accounts of two men who reflect sexist beliefs that have until recently been widely culturally accepted are outlined. This is followed by the narratives of two women who describe how such assumptions impact on them.

As discussed earlier on in this chapter, some people with learning difficulties have learned about sex and sexuality from TV, which can result in confusion and misunderstanding. Individuals may furthermore absorb attitudes that prevail in the social environments in which they live. When Sam, who is in his fifties, describes the mechanics of sexual intercourse, his account sounds not unlike a description of a scene from a classic James Bond film. Sam states, when a man and a woman want to have sex: 'They probably torture each other. They probably have a wrestle and just give in, lay on top and then... And pair up their arms and their legs and...if they agree to it. And...that's it.'

Bond's seduction of, for example, Solitaire in *Live and Let Die* (Fleming 1973) or that of *Octopussy* (Fleming 1983) follow a similar pattern: on both occasions Bond enters the woman's room without permission and starts sexual advances towards her, still without permission. The woman initially tries to fight Bond off and explicitly says 'no' before she 'gives in'. Sam may not have been influenced by these films at all, but this comparison seeks to demonstrate that his views have until recently been culturally normative.

It is worth locating this debate within a historic context, to explore the origin of such assumptions. Havelock Ellis, whose *Studies in the Psychology of Sex* (published between 1897 and 1928, cited in Weeks 1989) were highly influential, saw male sexuality as direct and forceful, based on the original primitive seizure of the female by the male. According to feminists Ellis's work made a significant contribution towards the eroticisation of female oppression. 'Heterosexual intercourse was essentially a re-enactment of primitive, animal courtship; the male sexual urge was essentially an urge to conquer, and the female sexual urge an urge to be conquered' (Jackson 1987, p.57). Female resistance to male sexual advances was thus 'not real' and essentially part of 'the game', designed to increase male sexual arousal. Ellis argued that female sexual pleasure and pain are closely related and that male dominance and female submission are biologically determined (Jackson 1987).

Sam feels confident about his knowledge on sex and sexuality, as he has been sexually active in the past. Yet, his views are dangerous, as they might lead to him ignoring refusal. He could find it difficult to establish whether a woman consents if he expects 'a wrestle' and to 'torture each other' to be part of sexual foreplay.

Peter tells me that he finds women in tight clothes arousing:

> You see some girls out, out in the street and they've, eh... You know, they've got really, really, really short, short skirts and short things on. And you'd say: 'Oh, I just fancy that!' And you'd, they walk past and you'd, you nearly see, you nearly see their underclothes.

To him these women are putting themselves at risk: 'If they get raped or they get...attacked or assaulted it's their fault. They're asking, you know, they ask for it...because their, their underwear is showing...or their bottom's out and that sort of thing.' Peter is not the first man to suggest that 'bad women' are to blame for sexual assault and to empathise with 'innocent' men who are unable to control their urges when confronted with a sexual key stimulus (e.g. Acock and Ireland 1983). His belief that a man has the right to act on his urges, when he 'just fancies that' and that some women 'ask for it', as well as Sam's assumptions of resistance as 'part of the game' are a product of social environments in which such beliefs may be acceptable. Yet, such assumptions may result in a higher incidence of sexual violence (e.g. Wood and Jewkes 1998). They serve to justify unsought sexual intrusions by arguing that they were provoked by the victim's behaviour.

Men with learning difficulties are known to be the single largest group of perpetrators of sexual violence against women with learning difficulties (McCarthy and Thompson 1996). When men believe they have a right to act on their sexual urges this inevitably puts the individuals with whom they share services at risk. Risk could only be effectively reduced if it became wholly socially unacceptable to hold such beliefs. To attempt to re-educate individual men would not be enough, as they merely replicate attitudes that occur in the wider society. As the origin of the problem lies with social structures in the macrosystem, universalistic change here would be much more effective and far-reaching. This is a key objective of feminist campaigns (Hester, Kelly and Radford 1996).

Georgina and Chantal, who are both attractive young women in their early twenties, were aware of the assumptions that some may make about the way they dress as indicating sexual availability.

Georgina: When I come to work I feel that I need to be careful... I remember once, I wore a new top. I wanted to wear it, because...I thought it looked nice. And one of me colleagues [a man in his twenties] thought I was wearing it to look sexy.

Andrea: Did you wear the top to work again?

Georgina: No, I didn't, because it made me feel uncomfortable... Like today, I've just worn a normal T-shirt what just comes up to your neck cause I'm frightened of wearing a top what, what's a bit lower, but people take it the wrong way and think that you're looking sexy and you're turning that man on. And it might not mean that. You might just have liked that top.

Georgina has chosen not to wear clothes that may be considered to be 'sexy'. Others' reactions to the items she wears consequently act as a means of social control. She will not wear clothes that would make her colleague state that she is trying to draw attention to herself. In Chapter 4 it will be highlighted that similar decisions about modest dress codes are often made by family members and support workers.

Chantal told me that she does not like her 'top half':

Chantal: People are always looking at...not looking at you, but looking at your top half. And it's like: 'What are you looking at?' It's so irritating all the time.

Andrea: Have you ever thought that this isn't actually your problem? That it's the people who are looking who are the problem?

Chantal: It feels like my problem, because I feel like... Have I got something on me, or do I smell or something?

Chantal believed that her breasts were too big. She felt self-conscious, because others were looking at her 'all the time'. She described that she therefore chose to wear 'frumpy' clothes. A couple of months after the interview Chantal had a breast reduction. It is worth noting that she had no other medical reasons for surgery. Chantal was able to receive NHS treatment, as a psychological assessment confirmed that the attention she received caused her emotional distress. Chantal has been sexually violated in the past. It is likely that this heightened her sensitivity to intrusive gazes.

Kelly (1988) argues that sexual intrusions towards women appear on a continuum, which reaches from more commonplace intrusions, as outlined by Georgina and Chantal, to sexual harassment and rape. She argues that the manifestation of men's gender power starts in mundane interactions and becomes routine. With this it becomes less likely to be challenged, even in respect to more 'serious' incidents. The fact that it is often seen as acceptable to gaze at their bodies and to judge them by their appearance invades the woman's personal space and makes intrusions almost customary. Within the ecological model gender is therefore linked to a variety of risk factors. Not only does the view that some women provoke rape by their appearance serve to justify sexual violence, it can also have a damaging impact on women's sense of self. This is evident in Chantal's case, who has such little respect for her body that she opts for surgery. The guilt and shame that individuals who have been subjected to an unwanted sexual intrusion often feel can furthermore lead to a reluctance to report incidents (Sable *et al.* 2006), which increases the risk that violence will be repeated. Georgina and Chantal did not challenge intrusions, but instead they blamed their bodies and the way they dress.

CONCLUSION

This chapter discussed a varied range of issues relating to sexuality. It explored the formation of sexual knowledge and positive sexual experiences. Finally negative and invasive aspects of sexuality were discussed.

People with learning difficulties have the legal and moral rights to lead sexual relationships. However, this right can be overruled when individuals are found to lack the capacity to make decisions about sexuality. The fact that we seek to protect those who are deemed unable to protect themselves indicates that we are aware of a multitude of risks and concerned about the welfare of the most 'vulnerable' members of our society. However, the discussion has pointed to a number of social processes that disable individuals from becoming competent social and sexual actors.

For instance, knowledge about sexuality must be understood as a product of social interaction, which results from the information given to an individual. Information is available in the 'home' environment (microsystem), community-based settings, such as schools and support services (exosystem) and via the popular media (macrosystem). However, people with learning difficulties continue to have limited access to mainstream community resources, confidential peer talk and written information. Many therefore continue to rely on the provision of information within their 'home', as well as within segregated educational and service settings. Some were able to pick up useful information from television, but others were confused by what they saw and had no opportunities to ask questions. For that reason individuals need to be able to talk openly about sex to a person in their immediate environment. If such an approachable person was available, they could also assist with access to sexual support services, such as family planning clinics.

It is evident that recent policy changes (macrosystem) had a positive effect on the educational experiences of younger respondents, who are overall more knowledgeable than older ones. However, particularly those in the 40-and-over age group continue to have limited opportunities to access information. This inevitably hinders their development of sexual consent capacity and it increases risk. Perhaps surprisingly, considering their construction as particularly 'vulnerable' in this respect, most participants in this study had an adequate understanding of sexuality. In many instances this was the case despite the absence of, or inferior levels of, sex education. Most respondents were able to give some descriptions of the mechanics of sexual behaviour. The accusation that all people with learning difficulties are 'vulnerable' due to their ignorance of sexuality is therefore not correct.

Nonetheless, the threat of violence guides many well-meaning family members and support workers to protect individuals from sexual experiences. Some are reportedly uncertain about the appropriateness of sexual behaviours of individuals with learning difficulties (Swango-Wilson 2009). Yet, in the absence of safe spaces, sexual activity, including violence, will take place unnoticed by those who should be available to support individuals to be safe. Consenting sexual encounters can be an opportunity to practise sexual choice-making. Positive risk taking with the appropriate safety measures in place should consequently be encouraged. For instance, if individuals were allowed privacy with their partner in their own bedroom, sexual activity would not have to take place in isolated spaces. Individuals could call for help if they needed to (Hollomotz and The Speakup Committee 2009).

The discussion furthermore highlighted that loving relationships and being in love can have a positive impact on an individual's sense of self. High self-esteem has been linked to an increased ability to resist unwanted sexual approaches and also to the ability to speak up for oneself. Individuals who had positive sexual relationships made clear distinctions between wanted sexual approaches by their chosen partner and unwanted ones by others, which indicates a heightened sense of privacy awareness.

In all of the cases of actual incidents of sexual violence that were discussed, a significant factor was that the violator was a person in a position of trust, who had easy access to the individuals they violated. Moreover, power imbalances characterised each actual incident of sexual violence. Those who understood what was happening were scared to seek help. Others had received limited information about sex and sexuality. Knowledge that is held by the violator, yet withheld from the target, is thus a form of power.

Some women were furthermore given contraceptives without the opportunity to give their full consent. In some cases this meant that inadequate information on associated health risks was provided, but in two cases the women were explicit that they did not agree to medical intervention at all. Others controlling the fertility of women with learning difficulties must be seen as a physical invasion into the woman's private sphere, which furthermore removes a protective factor. A woman's fertility could put off a potential violator, as a pregnancy would provide genetic evidence that can lead to the perpetrator's prosecution under the Sexual Offences Act (HMSO 2003).

The final section of this chapter demonstrated how assumptions about women's sexual availability further increase risk. It was shown how these can reduce women's confidence and serve to justify sexual violence. Within the ecological model gender is therefore linked to a variety of risk factors. These processes affect all women, including those with learning difficulties. This demonstrates that risk is fluid, as it can affect anyone. Therefore 'vulnerability' is not linked to a particular population. Instead an individual's level of risk arises from the interplay of social processes.

The discussion so far has focused on issues relating to sex and sexuality. An ecological approach to explaining risk of sexual violence (see Figure 2.1) requires a much broader examination. Risk is not merely influenced by factors that are directly related to sexuality and the private sphere. It is also influenced by broader social processes. Some further risk factors, such as segregation and dependency relationships, have already been mentioned. The subsequent chapter expands the discussion by examining how risk of sexual violence is negotiated in the everyday lives of people with learning difficulties. In particular, the focus will be on examining how an individual's self-defence skills are shaped and developed by differential treatment and during mundane interactions. The importance of social networks in the formation of risk is also highlighted.

Chapter 4

Risk Creation in Everyday Life

This section begins with a broad overview of the social lives of respondents. Their experiences in terms of social inclusion, employment and living arrangements are briefly examined. However, in order to maintain focus on the research questions, the discussion does not explore family networks. Respondents spoke overwhelmingly fondly of their families and they did not identify difficulties with maintaining these vital contacts.

Booth, Simons and Booth (1990, p.180) observed that the move from institutionally based settings into the community in the second half of the twentieth century has resulted in most people with learning difficulties 'making greater use of community facilities, but few developing social networks that reach out into the wider society'. Dagnan et al. (1995) confirm that, even after moving into the community, individuals' social contacts often remained limited. Two decades on from Booth et al. (1990) the research upon which this book is based reports similar findings. Many respondents found it difficult to establish and maintain significant relationships outside of segregated environments or family networks. An example of segregated social networks that were upheld throughout an episode of community presence was illustrated in Figure 3.1. Further examples are explored in relation to difficulties with maintaining friendship networks later on in this chapter.

Barriers to employment opportunities are one reason for the continuing social exclusion of disabled people. In 2009 the employment rate for working-aged adults in the UK was 77 per cent for non-disabled and 47 per cent for disabled adults (Office for National Statistics 2009). Employment rates differ further across impairment groups. Less than one in five people with learning difficulties are in employment (Office for Disability Issues 2007). The proportion of individuals in employment was even lower amongst the research sample. This is likely to be due to the fact that a high proportion of respondents were accessed through day services. Only three of the 27 participants who were of working age accessed paid employment:

Georgina worked for a self-advocacy organisation, Rachel worked part-time at a cafe and Britney worked for a disabled people's organisation for a couple of hours per week.

Around one in five respondents lived with an unrelated adult in the context of a residential service. This living arrangement continues to be unusual for the general population. In 2001 only 3 per cent of adults in the UK lived with one or more unrelated adult(s) (Walker *et al.* 2001). Voluntary group living arrangements are usually reserved for students and young professionals and associated with young adulthood. However, there was no such pattern apparent in this sample and the age of individuals living in groups varied. Furthermore, only 8 per cent of UK households comprise a parent or parents and their non-dependent children (Walker *et al.* 2001). (A dependent child is defined as a person under the age of 16 or a young person up to the age of 18 who is in full-time education.) However, about 45 per cent of the adults in this study (13 of 29) lived with a parent. One respondent lived with her sister and a further one lived with a niece.

Compared to non-disabled people, people with learning difficulties consequently continue to experience everyday life differently. Social inclusion remains a challenge, which can be directly linked to the lower employment rates that were cited earlier, as employment provides individuals with recognised, valued social roles. It will also provide financial security and with this it will enable a person to participate in leisure activities. Many adults with learning difficulties have differing social networks, because the structure of their 'home' environment is far removed from that of the general population. This chapter will point to resulting mechanisms that potentially create and reinforce a limited ability to self-defend and an increased exposure to risk.

The first section highlights how stranger-danger and fear contribute towards the spatial and social exclusion of people with learning difficulties. Segregated environments are subsequently scrutinised for their effect on an individual's self-defence skills. Next, respondents' difficulties in maintaining friendships are exposed. It will become apparent why relationships with paid support workers often fulfil a vital socio-emotional role. A discussion of additional risk factors that arise from such relationships follows. Finally, enabling and disabling forces that are responsible for the formation of self-determination skills are examined with reference to examples about clothes choices, as well as choices about daytime activities and living arrangements.

FEAR AND OTHERING

Even though the majority had experienced bullying within a segregated setting, almost all (27 of 29) of the respondents felt safe in such environments and many felt scared to leave them unaccompanied. This section explores how the notion of stranger-danger affects people with learning difficulties and contributes to their continuing co-operation with social exclusion. Next the negative effects that bullying and segregation have on the development of a person's confidence and sense of self are illustrated.

Stranger-danger and fear

Stranger-danger and fear of violence do not merely affect people with learning difficulties. Fear is also present in the general population. Women, the gay community, ethnic minority groups and disabled people have been found to be particularly fearful (Pain 2000). Fear of violence is related to a notion of risk. However, Chapter 2 explained that risk is a social construct, which initially only exists in our knowledge of it (Beck 1992). This explains why the least at risk group, older women, is the most fearful (Hollway and Jefferson 1997).

Fear of violence is a sensitive indicator of power relations that constitute social spaces (Koskela 1997). Older women may be least at risk, yet they might feel that they would lack power if they were assaulted by a younger person who is physically stronger than them. Fear often undermines the confidence of younger women as well, restricting their access to, and activity within, public space (Sheard 2010). Paradoxically men are almost twice as likely to experience violence than women and they are furthermore more than twice as likely to experience stranger violence in public spaces (Hoare and Povey 2008), yet they are comparatively less fearful.

This discrepancy between increased fear and actual risk is amplified by media representations of crime. For example, Cohen (2002) asserts that media coverage of violence against children mostly focuses on sensationally atypical cases of sexually motivated violence outside the family, thus inducing a fear of strangers. Children and young people furthermore learn to be anxious about strangers as a result of the safety advice offered by schools. However, the largest proportion of perpetrators against children are usually known to the victim (Deakin 2006). As outlined in Chapter 2, according to the British Crime Survey only 11 per cent of individuals who had been subjected to a serious sexual assault did not know their violator (Finney 2006). A fear of strangers might consequently lead individuals to seek protection with the very person who is prepared to exploit this relationship.

Although fear may exaggerate the real threat, marginalised groups are, at times, targeted with hate crime in their communities. This may include mischievous acts committed by young people, such as the persistent verbal abuse and harassment experienced by David Askew, who died of a heart attack while local youths were harassing him (Hughes 2010). Fiona Pilkington and her disabled daughter, Francecca Hardwick, had similarly experienced years of verbal abuse and assaults before Pilkington ended her life and that of her daughter (Walker 2009). Hate crime often involves a political component with consequences that far exceed the injury of the target (Boeckmann and Turpin-Petrosino 2002). For instance, Birrell (2009) points out that the use of disablist language impacts on all disabled people, beyond the person who has been addressed with an insult.

Many participants in this study altered their behaviour due to fear of strangers, which restricts their independence, although only two of the respondents have been subjected to actual crimes committed by strangers that exceeded verbal insults. A third of respondents explicitly state that they are scared to go out on their own. For instance, Sam tells me: 'I don't go out at night like I used to, because...a couple of years ago, somebody went to a night club and got knifed to death.' Analysis of the British Crime Survey 2009/10, however, suggests that violent crimes have fallen by 50 per cent since 1995 (Flatley *et al.* 2010). In other words, Sam *felt* safer when risk was higher. His current fear is amplified by the media coverage of the incident he described. This is a further example of the media reporting on selected crimes disproportionally and with this conveying a sense of volatility (Cohen 2002).

Gemma does not leave the house without the protection of others:

Andrea: Do you go outside by yourself at all?

Gemma: No. ... I always go with staff, you know.

Andrea: Why?

Gemma: Because I'm scared of, eh...people. ... God. I'm scared of people, eh, bullying me. Picking on me. You know. Do you get me?

Andrea: Mm. Has that happened before?

Gemma: No. It hasn't. Not yet. ...

Andrea: So, if it's not happened, why are you scared of it?

Gemma: I'm just scared it might. It could happen, couldn't it?

Andrea: Mm.

Gemma: Because I've got learning disabilities as well, you know.

Some respondents told me that they adjust their lives in line with other people's fears. For instance, when I asked Rose whether she would be scared to go out on her own she replies: 'No, not really. But it's my mum who'd get scared. She thinks I'm gonna, eeh, I might, you know, about getting knocked over. Or get with the teenagers and that.' I once went on an outing with Rose and I got the impression that she appears to have good road safety awareness. She walked ahead of the group and waited at each crossing or traffic light for the rest of the group to catch up with her. Although Rose does not see herself as 'vulnerable', her mother does. Parental fear restricts Rose's activities, which is an indicator of overprotection and results in a child-like and regulated lifestyle.

Two respondents in this study experienced actual incidents of theft. Ann is in her early forties. She lives with her mother and attends a day service during the week. Bill is in his late fifties. He lives independently and, like Ann, he attends a day service. The way in which they, and individuals in their environment, responded to the incidents differs. Since a group of young people stole Ann's purse when she walked home from the day centre she has not left the house unaccompanied. She now uses the Council's transport to get to the day centre. This makes her feel safe and protected. The incident distressed her and she continues to be fearful. In contrast, after a group of young people stole Bill's wheelchair, he continues to go out on his own. Bill is annoyed about the incident, but he is not frightened. He moans about 'unruly youth', but does not change his behaviour.

While Ann's mother was eager to protect her from future incidents, Bill makes repeated reference to his parents' insistence that he must learn to 'cope' on his own. He takes pride in his independence. When faced with insults and aggression from young people he feels in control, because he sees his status as an adult man as an advantage over their youth, a view that is confirmed by feminist analysis (e.g. Jónasdóttir 1988). Ann, who has experienced institutionalisation and segregation throughout her life, understands segregation to be safer than exposure to mainstream society. She is scared to go out on her own. This difference in response to similar incidents can be explained with reference to the priorities that are prevalent in their environments: protection and independence. Such different values are furthermore likely to be informed by contrasting gender role expectations, which dictate that men must be active and 'tough', while women may take on passive roles (Lindsey 2005).

Pain (2000, p.372) argues that 'crime, violence, harassment and fear have clear roles to play in the spatial and social exclusion of marginalised social groups'. Fear of crime can consequently be seen as a means of social control and governance. The effect of this can be seen in Ann's case, but also in the accounts of Sam, Gemma and Rose, who are scared by the possibility of violence and who consequently restrict their social activity. Fear has the effect that others endeavour to protect people with learning difficulties, while individuals themselves seek such protection, often in segregated environments.

Yet, as repeatedly stated, individuals are much more likely to experience violence by an individual from within their existing social networks. In this research only Ann and Bill experienced offences by strangers. As the next section will outline, about three quarters of the respondents have been bullied at school or at the day centre. Furthermore, three respondents spoke about violence within their family, two had experienced domestic violence, five had experienced violence within support service settings and two spoke about attempts of financial exploitation by acquaintances. This confirms that strangers do not appear to commit the majority of offences against people with learning difficulties. The notion of stranger-danger is therefore misleading and may give individuals a false sense of security in environments where they are most at risk.

Segregation and bullying

Segregation could be conceptualised as a form of violation, as it contradicts an individual's rights under the UN Convention on the Rights of Persons with Disabilities (United Nations 2006). It violates the Convention's general principles of 'full and effective participation and inclusion in society', 'equality of opportunity' and 'accessibility' (Article 3 (c, e, f), 19). Segregation prevents individuals from accessing the full range of opportunities that are available in the community, as discussed later on.

Almost all (27 of 29) respondents have attended segregated schools. The majority describe resulting estrangement from their local community. Chantal asserts that the stigma of going to special school prevented her from making friends in her neighbourhood:

> I have tried to meet new people and be friends with them, but because I went to a special school... Everyone where I lived used to take the mickey out of me. And call me nasty names and that. So, they don't bother with me.

Similar experiences have been extensively discussed in the literature on segregated education (e.g. D. Armstrong 2003; Shah and Priestley 2009).

McVilly et al. (2006b) assert that a shared experience of disability could be an important basis for friendship, which would suggest that segregated environments have some social benefits. This was not confirmed by this study. Some respondents even avoided other disabled people (see also

Bayley 1997). For instance, when I ask Sam how he gets on with other attendees at the day service he replies:

> I get on with, probably the odd three, because I can understand some people. I can't the other people, because of the speech, you see. It's very hard for me to, to understand them. I mean, it's embarrassing for me to go to the staff and saying: 'What's she saying? I can't, I can't, I can't hear him for words.'

Sam feels embarrassed for his lack of understanding, which is why he avoids people with speech impairments. A segregated environment that brings him together with other disabled people is not his preferred option.

Instead of the often idealised 'community spirit' amongst disabled people who 'feel happy' in the company of others who are 'like them', in a place where they 'fit in' (as advertised in a promotional video for Wiley Adult Day Care Services 2009) respondents in this study experienced stigma within segregated settings. The cultural views of the macrosystem, a society that continues to stigmatise disabled people, affected everyday life within these settings as well. Respondents who attended segregated schools report they were called names, like 'backwards, 'terminator' and 'Mongol'. Sam states that the other children at his residential school 'used to take the mickey out of me...because they thought I got a disability'. This supports claims of a 'hierarchy of impairments', even amongst disabled people (Deal 2003). The hierarchy is characterised by power imbalances between those who are considered to be 'less' and 'more' obviously impaired.

Of the 18 respondents who could remember that far back, one was a bully herself and 13 had experienced bullying at school (ten at segregated schools, two at mainstream school and one at both). Smith and Sharp (1994, p.2) describe bullying as 'the systematic abuse of power', which is carried out repeatedly and deliberately. The high figures of the prevalence of bullying that were found by this study are confirmed by Mencap (2007), who estimate that 82 per cent of young people with learning difficulties are bullied, which they claim to be twice as high as the incidence of bullying against non-disabled young people.

Georgina, who is in her early twenties, was bullied at mainstream primary school. When she moved to a segregated school she hoped that the bullying would stop:

> I thought everyone was, were treated the same. And won't pick on you and won't bully. But I did get bullied. All the advice I got was: 'Ignore them! Don't listen to them! Eventually they'll leave you alone.' And that didn't make no difference either. It, it just comes to a stage, I was that upset that I decided to stay off from school.

Most of the respondents report that teachers either did not intervene or that, even if they did, the bullying did not stop. After Georgina told her teacher why she was not attending school, her bullies were expelled for a few days. When they returned to school they continued to bully her. Mencap (2007) estimate that in four out of ten cases the bullying does not stop after the young person has informed someone. A further study suggests that in 44 per cent of reported incidents of bullying against children on the Autistic Spectrum schools have taken no action (The National Autistic Society 2006). Not being heard when reporting incidents of violence can have damaging consequences, as it teaches individuals that speaking up for themselves may have no impact. Furthermore, childhood experiences of bullying continue to affect adults, as they may lower self-esteem (Mencap 2007; The National Autistic Society 2006). Individuals may become accustomed to maltreatment and may view other incidents of violence as mere extensions on a continuum.

For most of the respondents in this study segregation continued into adulthood. Twenty-two of the 29 respondents attended day services. As highlighted earlier, this ratio does not apply to the general population of people with learning difficulties. It merely reflects how respondents were accessed: 20 were accessed through day service providers.

A day centre may be defined as a place where disabled people under retirement age meet several days per week, where personal care is available and activities are arranged. It caters primarily for those who are permanently excluded from the formal employment market (Kent, Massie and Tuckey 1984). The declared purpose of many day centres is simply to enable individuals to leave their home for a few hours, which is an important function, both for the individuals and for their families (Barnes 1990). However, there is a danger that day centres see providing respite for carers as their main objective. This concept has been criticised for implying that disabled individuals place a burden on their families (Shakespeare 2000). This has lead to a 'warehousing' model of care within day centres, whereby disabled people are seen as dependent on non-disabled helpers (Barnes 1990, adapted from Dartington, Miller and Gwynne 1981).

Day centres contravene the *Valuing People* (Department of Health 2001) core values of promoting independence and inclusion. The White Paper consequently suggests a modernisation of day services, while a follow-up consultation document suggests abolishing segregated provisions altogether (Department of Health 2007). However, Cole, Williams and Lloyd (2007) found that many local authorities are still struggling to move away from large, congregate settings. The day centre was often the only social contact individuals had outside of their home, as inclusive alternatives, such as employment, remained beyond their reach.

Some respondents describe incidents of bullying and assault at their day service. Emma reports that another user keeps invading her personal space, walking up close to her and touching her (see Chapter 5). Paul has been touched by a female service user and he did not like it (see Chapter 3). Martha complains that a man at her day service keeps calling her 'learning disability'. Peter describes how another attendee threatened him with a pair of scissors:

> He was teasing with his scissors. He says: 'I will cut your hair!' And then he came one time and put the point of the scissors in the back of my head… And then you just, you just say… 'You've been warned. Stop it!' 'Why, would I go to prison?' I says: 'You did that outside.' I says: 'You would.' I said: 'If you did anything like that to anybody in [this city] or round where you live,' I says, 'you'd be, you'd be straight into the police station or straight into, into eh…into another place.' I says: 'You wouldn't!' I says: 'They wouldn't put up with it!'

When Peter reported the incident he was told that the man who threatened him 'cannot help it'. Staff asked Peter to ignore the behaviour. Peter's account implies that people who attend day centres have fewer rights to protection from threats of violence than people 'outside', as different rules apply. His observations mirror research findings of increased levels of violence within social care settings (e.g. Healthcare Commission 2006, 2007; Strand, Benzein and Saveman 2004) and findings of some level of tolerance for violence amongst staff, who will weigh up whether they perceive an occurrence as a 'serious' incident before reporting (e.g. Jenkins, Davies and Northway 2008).

However, intimidating or violent behaviour should never be tolerated, even when it is perpetrated by a person with learning difficulties, as they, too, have a responsibility not to physically, emotionally or sexually hurt others (Cambridge 1996). Smith and Sharp (1994) assert that, in contrast to children who have to endure it at school, adults do not usually put up with bullying. While non-disabled adults are protected by bullying and harassment policies in their workplace, like that protecting NHS staff (NHS Employers 2006), such rules do not routinely apply in segregated settings.

Fear and othering: discussion

This book argues that risk is, at least in part, socially created. This section substantiated this claim by exploring the effects of stranger-danger and fear, which leads to the continuing co-operation of people with learning difficulties with segregation. Many feel 'vulnerable' in the community and seek protection in isolated environments within the micro- and exosystem where they are, paradoxically, statistically at higher risk. For instance, the fact that bullying affected the majority of respondents who attended segregated schools confirms yet again that no environment can fully protect individuals from maltreatment and violence. Bullying furthermore impacts negatively on an individual's sense of self. It must be seen as a major contributing factor towards the emerging wish to be 'normal', which was expressed by a large proportion of respondents (see Chapter 5). This reduced self-esteem and with this an individual's likelihood to stand up for themselves.

This section furthermore suggested that segregation must be seen as a form of violation, as it impacts negatively on a person's sense of self and life chances. Many of the educational, work and leisure opportunities that are available to people outside of segregated settings become unavailable. In addition, segregation impacts on the friendships and relationships of those who are affected. The permanent presence of support workers, for example, often infringes on people's privacy, which makes it difficult to form and maintain sexual relationships and friendships. The subsequent section explores the social networks of respondents in more detail.

SOCIAL NETWORKS

Isolation and exclusion from mainstream life limit the social networks of many disabled people and reduce their opportunities to meet friends or potential partners. These processes contribute to the formation of sexual 'vulnerability', as isolation can create conditions that increase risk. For instance, those who have limited social contacts have fewer opportunities to report violent incidents and fewer allies who would pick up on behavioural changes following a sexual assault. In this section it will become apparent that the social contacts of respondents were often restricted to family networks or residential and day services. Most individuals had little support to enable them to maintain friendships outside of these settings. Some respondents are therefore reliant on paid support workers to fulfil their personal support, as well as emotional needs.

Friendships

'Friendships' may be defined as voluntary personal relationships, in which individuals seek each other's company. They typically involve intimacy (e.g. Fehr 1996) and they are usually not exchange-based. That means that friends are not concerned with reciprocation of benefits (Jehn and Shah

1997). Respondents with learning difficulties in a study by McVilly *et al.* (2006b) broadly shared this view and reported that they had friends. The latter was not the case for all participants in this study on which this book is based.

Tyler states that real 'friends' are people who have 'been persistently contacting me and persistently wanting to contact me'. In his experience some of his social contacts were not making this effort and he had to 'chase' them. Tyler feels that these people do not care about him enough. Leanne adds that friends are people you can trust. Mary asserts that 'you know who your friends are when anything happens.' For instance, she states that one of her friends called her immediately after she had broken her leg. She asked Mary for support and reassurance, both of which are customary elements of a friendship. Bob says his friends regularly meet up socially, away from his college. He says that other people with whom he does not have such informal contact are not 'real' friends.

If two of the above points, meeting up informally away from structured settings and initiating contact with each other, were a benchmark, less than a third of the respondents (eight of 29) could be said to have 'friendships'. This is not to say that the remaining 17 participants did not talk about relationships that were important to them. Apart from Leanne all of the interviewees spoke about 'friends', yet, as with some romantic relationships, these contacts were often service-based.

Similarly to an example cited by Chappell (1994), none of the 14 respondents who attended council-run day services saw their friends away from the service. Such relationships are therefore extremely vulnerable to break-up. *Valuing People Now* (Department of Health 2009b) acknowledges that the way in which professionals take decisions about service delivery may ignore existing relationships and break up friendship patterns, and that insufficient consideration is often given to personal relationships in individual planning and care management processes.

Rose states that one of her friends attends a different day service venue since her day service was reorganised. She has not seen him since and she has no means of keeping in touch with him. As outlined in Chapter 3, the service ensured that she could continue to attend the same venue as her boyfriend, but it could not ensure that all friendships were maintained. This has negative consequences for the social networks of individuals who rely on their day service to facilitate contact with their friends.

Furthermore, participants of all ages told me about friends they had at school, but in most cases contact ceased as soon as they left. Gemma explains: 'I don't see them anymore. Now I moved on, you see… I still love them.' This breakdown of relationships is surprising compared to the experiences of non-disabled people, who mostly sustain some of their friendships from school into adulthood (Adams and Allan 1998). Maintaining contact could be easily facilitated for many respondents, as most remained living in the same area as their friends. However, most of them had not socialised informally with their friends while they were at school. Whereas able-bodied young people engage frequently in spontaneous social activity, such as visiting friends, this is not the case for disabled adolescents (Wiegerink *et al.* 2006). Many young disabled people are consequently more likely to socialise with people of their parents' age than with people of their own age (Barnes 1990; Stevenson, Pharoah and Stevenson 1997). Young disabled people have furthermore been reported to become less socially active and more isolated after leaving school, while the opposite is the case for their able-bodied peers (Stevens 1996).

Today many young people use social networking sites, such as Facebook, to gather and socialise with their peers (Boyd 2007). However, assistance to use them was not available to any of the participants. Only five respondents, all of whom were able to read and write independently, made use of such virtual spaces. Nonetheless, a few respondents receive some support to maintain their friendships in other ways. Overall the respondents who attended the privately run day service had more developed social networks than those in council-run services. Their service was more flexible at facilitating contact between friends. Liz, for instance, has a close friendship with a man who uses her day service. They seek each other out and spend time together. Support workers ensure that they are mostly scheduled for the same activities or that they can simply meet up at the day service base. Some individuals did not attend the service every day of the week, which gave them more time to socialise independently.

Sue lives in a small residential group setting. She does not attend a day service. Instead she engages in a range of community-based activities. Sue has a network of friends whom she has met in a variety of different places, for example while playing bingo or at the weekly coffee morning at her local community centre. Her existing friendships are supported and members of staff will help to arrange contact. For instance, they will help her to locate her friend's phone number, assist with booking a taxi to take her to an agreed meeting place or accompany her if necessary. Sue is also encouraged to meet new people by breaking her routine and engaging in new activities. For instance, at the time of the interview Sue was attending an arts and crafts course at her local community centre.

Respondents who live independently have more freedom to choose when and how they would like to spend time with their friends, provided they do not encounter any access barriers. For instance, Tyler often visits a friend who lives nearby. He also keeps in touch with his best friend from boarding school. The friend lives in a different area, quite far away, but he comes to stay with him for a few days sometimes. Similarly Mary visits a friend who lives about 35 miles away every weekend. She travels independently using buses, but she will ask for assistance in the bus station, to ensure that she boards the correct bus. These respondents were, however, fairly independent and they were therefore able to initiate contact with their friends. Those who required more support received limited help. Support with maintaining friendships like that given to Sue was the exception, rather than the rule.

Even though *Valuing People* (Department of Health 2001, p.81) stipulated that 'good services will help people with learning disabilities develop opportunities to form relationships', *Valuing People Now* (Department of Health 2009b, p.16) admits that they continue to have limited opportunities to do so. However, secure and rewarding relationships are central in determining a person's quality of life. They impact on an individual's mental health and general wellbeing (McVilly *et al.* 2006a) and, thereby, on the individual's sense of self and self-esteem. Friendships give an opportunity for social inclusion, as friends often share similar concerns or situations. Individuals have an opportunity to feel reassured in their own worth, because friendships give them an opportunity to support others, as in the situation described by Mary. Friends can furthermore rely on assistance or guidance (Bulmer 1987). Due to limited opportunities to develop friendships many people with learning difficulties rely on relationships with support workers to fulfil some of these social and emotional needs.

Relationships with support workers

The roles of 'carer' and 'personal assistant' have a psycho-emotional, as well as a functional, dimension. Many disabled individuals report that they see their personal assistants as companions (Woodin 2006; Yamaki and Yamazaki 2004). Staff in residential and day services can often become important figures in people's lives. Atkinson and Williams (1990) argue that the absence of close relationships in the lives of socially marginalised people may lead them to adopt an extended definition of friendship. They may then identify mere acquaintances as friends.

Acquaintances are characterised by limited familiarity and contact between parties. 'A strong bond, past history, and depth of mutual knowledge between the parties are lacking. The interaction between acquaintances is not necessarily voluntary or positive, as it is among friends' (Jehn and Shah 1997, p.776). Relationships with support workers fall into this category, as parties do not seek each other out voluntarily. None of the participants were using cash for care, such as *Individual Budgets* (Department of Health 2008a), to employ personal assistants of their choice. The support worker may know a wealth of intimate information about the individual they support, but they generally do not reciprocate this trust by confiding their personal issues. Power is often imbalanced, as staff tend to have social contacts outside their work environment, while the service user may have limited social intercourse and depend on this relationship.

A disabled man in Marquis and Jackson's (2000, p.416) study asserts that a good relationship with personal assistants is therefore critical to their role: 'Having someone you get along with is more important than doing the job.' Respondents in this study made similar statements. Ryan and Gemma believe that being able to talk to staff about their worries is of central importance. Over half of the respondents in this study identified some or all of their support workers as 'friends' and included me in some cases, even though they had only met me a few times. Jasmine even told me that I am her 'best friend'. (The ethical implications of forming and then terminating research relationships that become of value to respondents were discussed in Chapter 1.)

However, interactions between service user and support worker may not always turn out to the individual's satisfaction. Respondents spoke about communication difficulties: in order to have meaning communication must be a two-way process (Windahl, Signitzer and Olson 2009). When an individual introduces a topic for discussion the receiver's willingness to *listen* is as important as the individual's readiness to *talk*. Finlay, Antaki and Walton (2008a) illustrate that staff are sometimes reluctant to listen when individuals with communication impairments articulate their choices, particularly when they do this through unconventional means, such as by giving non-verbal cues. The same was true in this study. Even respondents who expressed their choices verbally encountered difficulties with being heard at times.

Gemma tells me: 'If I have any problems I always speak up about them, just tell people, you know?' Yet, Gemma's requests are often not acted upon. For example, during the interview she told me that she was unhappy about attending one of her weekly groups at the day centre, because a woman in the group kept harassing her. After the interview we spoke to Gemma's key worker. The key worker was already aware of these issues. She reminded Gemma that she likes the group activity and that she should 'simply ignore' the woman. She could not be persuaded to change Gemma's group or indeed to talk to the woman who was upsetting Gemma. When Gemma turned her back to us the key worker rolled her eyes at me. Later on she described Gemma as a 'drama queen'.

During participant observations I noticed that terms like 'drama queen' or 'challenging' were applied to a range of individuals. Similarly, Rachel tells me that staff will tell her not to 'kick off' when she is upset at times. Such reactions mark the stark difference between a friendship and a relationship with a member of staff. One party seeking to discuss their personal issues within the context of a friendship would hardly be labelled as 'attention seeking', as such behaviour is part of companionships (Fehr 1996). However, in contrast to a real friendship, relationships with staff are not balanced in this way.

It has long been acknowledged that 'challenging' behaviour can simply be a way to communicate dissatisfaction (e.g. Beukelman and Mirenda 1998). It has also been observed that individuals display less 'challenging behaviour', the more personal control they have (Stancliffe *et al.* 2000). Indeed, Wegner and Flisher's (2009) review of the literature demonstrates that 'challenging' and risk behaviour amongst non-disabled adolescents can be linked to leisure boredom. Accordingly it is worth asking why individuals have a need to express dissatisfaction through behaviour that is deemed unacceptable.

Rose tells me that she recently flushed biscuits down the toilet at her day centre because she was bored. In other words, her behaviour compensated for a lack of stimulation. Some individuals may begin to display 'challenging' behaviour as a result of violent experiences (Hingsburger 1995). Adult protection policies are explicit that support workers and professionals should look out for signs of individuals experiencing violence and be prepared to intervene (Association of Directors of Social Services 2005; Department of Health 2000). Noting changes in behaviour and questioning their causes as well as listening to individuals' concerns are therefore a vital aspect of adult protection work.

This has not become reality for many respondents. Two thirds reported incidents when their expressed wishes were overruled. For instance, Martha feels a strong sense of injustice in the way her life is controlled by staff and she consistently rebels against this. She tells me she would like to buy more revealing clothes (as discussed later on) and that she would like to attend night clubs of her choice. When we discussed these issues with her key worker after the interview she gave us a reason for every restriction. None of Martha's complaints led to any change. Britney reports that a male member of staff at her 'home' keeps flirting with her and makes suggestive comments. She feels uncomfortable with the situation. When I ask her why she has not reported him, she states that the service has not taken any of her past complaints seriously. She does not believe that they will intervene and has consequently given up on seeking help. This can have dangerous consequences, as Britney does not trust those who are employed to support and protect her.

A further and most concerning way in which relationships with staff differ from more equal relationships, such as friendships, is that, on the part of the person with learning difficulties, they may involve an element of obedience. For instance, Josie, who is in her late sixties and lives in a group 'home' for older women with learning difficulties, explains to me:

Josie: We can't go in the kitchen. ... We've been warned about going in the kitchen. ... If we get burned, staff are getting into trouble at our home.

Andrea: So you just stay out of the kitchen?

Josie: Mmh.

Andrea: Would you like to go into the kitchen?

Josie: [eyes widen, immediate response, loud] No.

Andrea: Why not?

Josie: [immediate response, loud] You mustn't get told off by the staff.

Josie was appalled when I asked her about the possibility of disobeying staff. At several points of the interview she demonstrates high levels of compliance towards staff demands. For example, Josie tells me that she is not allowed to eat at McDonald's because 'staff say so'. She also states that she cannot go out on her own to see her boyfriend because staff will not allow this: 'They're too protective of us.' Even though Josie acknowledges this, she is eager to comply with their demands every time.

The above exchange further demonstrates that people with learning difficulties are often protected from mundane hazards. For example, safety considerations about kitchen appliances were also voiced by a number of respondents who lived with relatives or in group settings. Jasmine states: 'My sister is frightened in case I get burned on the cooker.' Kathy similarly asserts that the cooker is 'dangerous'. Rose proudly informs me that she can cook lasagne, because she has learned how to do this at the day centre. Nonetheless she has never helped to cook at home. Rose states that her mother thinks: 'I'd be a bit dangerous, you know with the cooker and that.'

Many participants assessed the mundane risks they faced within a segregated environment to be more immediate than they would be for non-disabled people. They therefore accept the social construct of their increased 'vulnerability'. The resulting lack of practice in, for example, using kitchen appliances, will inevitably result in individuals developing limited (domestic) skills, which will indeed lead to an increase of risk. Social construction can thus lead to the social creation of actual 'vulnerability'. Furthermore, if individuals are not supported to judge for themselves whether a mundane hazard is safe they cannot be expected to make safety judgements on more serious matters, such as whether to participate in a proposed sexual act.

Social networks: discussion

Inter-personal relationships have a crucial impact on an individual's level of sexual 'vulnerability'. Social networks can act as enabling or disabling forces and impact on the individual's sense of self, life satisfaction, self-defence skills and situational risk. As explained in Chapter 2, in order to break a cycle of violence, most individuals require the support of others (Calderbank 2000). Families, friends and support workers play a key role in this process. Reports of individuals being referred to as 'attention seeking' by staff within service settings are therefore of concern. Some respondents found that they were not always being listened to or that their wishes were overruled and that explanations given did not satisfy them. This can impact on a person's sense of self, and they may grow to see themselves as less worthy of attention.

Moreover, the one-sided emotional attachment that some individuals form with staff has the potential to increase their dependence, which makes this relationship easily exploitable. Those with whom we have close relationships are most likely to commit acts of sexual violence towards us (see Chapter 2). Even though the importance of relationships with support workers should be acknowledged, people with learning difficulties must at the same time be supported to maintain and forge reciprocal friendships. Wider social networks would increase the number of people who could pick up on signs of violence.

The third part of this chapter explores how the development of self-determination skills is often hindered by the particular treatment that many people with learning difficulties receive within protective 'home' and social settings.

SELF-DETERMINATION IN EVERYDAY LIFE

Self-determination is a central requirement for successful self-defence against sexual violence. As outlined in Chapter 2, it is a skill that is learned and continually reinforced through practice. Yet, as the discussion towards the end of the previous section indicated, some disabled people continue to be hindered from making decisions, even in respect to small, mundane aspects of everyday life. Oliver (1996, p.48) comments that:

> many disabled adults do not have the right to decide what time to get up or go to bed, or indeed who to go to bed with, when or what to eat, how often to bath or even be in control of the times when they can empty their bladders or open their bowels.

Such lack of personal choice increases the risk that a sexual attack may succeed, as individuals become used to lacking control over what happens to their body. On the other hand, opportunities for decision-making in everyday life can counteract 'vulnerability'.

In this section the level of control permitted to respondents who were living with family members (15) and within residential services (seven) is assessed. For this purpose it is necessary to understand the process of choice-making. A choice should be an opportunity to make a selection free from coercion, which means that there should be no foreseeable consequences for a selection, other than the consequences of that selection itself (Brown and Brown 2009). Research suggests that individuals only perceive that they have choices when there are 'at least two available alternatives, either of which would meet at least some of the individual's chosen goals' (Jenkinson 1993, p.366). Choices should furthermore be active, which means that individuals' passive acceptance or compliance should not be interpreted as choice (Kishi et al. 1988). People are, moreover, 'most likely to have clear preferences in issues that are familiar, simple and directly experienced' (Jenkinson 1993, p.365).

A mere discussion of an option might therefore not be sufficient to enable an individual to fully understand it, particularly if they find abstract thought difficult. For many people with learning difficulties this means that they should have an opportunity to experience their options. For instance, in order to enable an individual to make a choice about a regular daytime activity, they should have the opportunity to try out each of the available options before deciding which one to take up. Facilitating choice-making in this way is, however, resource intensive, which is why this is not consistently implemented.

Choices can extend beyond selecting between given alternatives to control over the matter in question. The concept of personal control is closely related to self-determination (Stancliffe 2001). According to Abery (1999, p.157) self-determination 'involves a person having the degree of control over their life that they desire in those areas that they value and over which they wish to exercise control'. An argument that is used repeatedly against allowing people with learning difficulties to make their own choices is the possibility that they may make 'bad' choices (Guess, Benson and Siegel-Causey 1985). Yet, advocates of the normalisation principle have long argued that it is important for individuals to make choices, as this is expected of 'ordinary' people living in the community (e.g. Wolfensberger 1972). The Mental Capacity Act (HMSO 2005b, section 1(4)) makes the rights of people with learning difficulties to make an 'unwise' decision explicit. As discussed in Chapter 2, promoting the choices of people with learning difficulties is furthermore one of four key principles that underpin *Valuing People* (Department of Health 2001, 2009b).

However, it was also mentioned that, despite the choice-based rhetoric of current policies, institutional practices can still be prevalent in contemporary residential settings in the community (O'Brien 2005). Research has found that major life decisions about one's residence, living companions and daytime activities are substantially less available to people with learning difficulties than more routine choices (Stancliffe 2001). This will be confirmed in this section. This study found that the amount of control that individuals are allowed to have varies according to the impact that the decision to be made will have: an individual may be free to choose their food from a pre-selected range of options (e.g. food present in the 'home's' fridge), but not from all of the options that are available to them (e.g. the range of food available at the local supermarket). Individuals with learning difficulties are thus frequently presented with a restricted menu of choice. This concept can be understood literally as a menu; for example in relation to choices offered at a day centre, the menu might look like the one displayed in Figure 4.1.

Menu
Play pool
Watch TV
Arts and crafts
Yoga
Drama group
Library group
Domestic skills training
Shopping group
Jigsaws
Physiotherapy

Not on the menu
Any other leisure activity that is not offered at the day centre
Paid employment
Stay in bed all day
Go out when you feel like it, where you feel like going
Have sex
Etc.

Figure 4.1 Menu of choices at the day centre

Individuals can make a range of selections at the day centre, but at the same time their attendance of the service means that during this time an infinite list of alternative options becomes unavailable, as indicated in Figure 4.1. The options on offer are restricted and are usually pre-agreed by staff who remain in control, while an individual's selections from the menu are merely tokenistic. The following sections explain the menu of choice by drawing on case studies about women's clothes choices, as well as choices about day and residential services. In order to enable a focus on explaining the 'menu of choices' this discussion is particularly biased towards examining disabling processes. Positive examples of individuals who have more control are at times mentioned. Further positive case studies will be discussed more explicitly in Chapter 5.

Women's clothes choices

All of the women interviewed described how they opened their wardrobe every morning and selected the clothes they were going to wear that day by themselves. Women like Leanne, who require support, were always consulted about their options. However, when it came to determining which clothes they would find in their wardrobe while clothes shopping the women had less control. Only five of the 13 women, who lived with family members or in residential services, were able to choose whatever clothes they liked, even when others disagreed with this choice.

Clothes choices are an important way of expressing who we are and how we would like others to see us and also when it comes to expressing a sexual identity (Gleeson and Frith 2004). It was this sexual identity that others seemed to be eager to control:

Andrea: Have you ever been in a shop, when you wanted to buy something and the staff said: 'No, you can't have that!'

Martha: [after two seconds] You have to c...cope with it.

Andrea: You have to cope with it? ...

Martha: Like a grown-up... I have to act like a grown-up when she says 'no' to things.

Andrea: But why would she say 'no' to things?

Martha: Because if it's too –, showing all your...breast off. She won't let me have a top.

Such accounts were common amongst women who were accompanied by staff or family members when shopping for clothes. Women were advised to dress modestly or to conform to the supporter's views on 'appropriate' dress. Control in this respect was not merely restricted to younger women. During a group session at the day centre Jasmine, who is in her fifties, points at a low-cut top in a magazine and says: 'My sister wouldn't let me wear that. … Cause she don't like me in them, cause they're too low. She likes me, like, lace with, eh, all the neck.' McCarthy (1998) reports similar findings. Women in her study had a high level of control when choosing clothes out of their wardrobes, but they lacked autonomy when deciding what clothes to buy. Wardrobes do however represent a restricted menu of options.

Martha and I spoke to her key worker after the interview to clarify why Martha is not allowed to buy some of the clothes she likes. The key worker explained that, surely, Martha would not feel comfortable in more revealing clothes and that she would advise her own daughter not to wear these styles either. However, Martha will never know whether she feels comfortable in a low-cut top, if she is not given a chance to find out for herself. Moreover, Martha is an adult in her thirties and not her key worker's child. The fact that Martha believes that sometimes she has to act 'like a grown-up' suggests that she has internalised the infantilisation she is subjected to, which inevitably impacts on her sense of self.

It should be noted that staff may face a multitude of dilemmas when assisting a woman to buy clothes. They may opt for the safer option, because they are unsure whether the woman's family, other staff or managers would have objections. Stancliffe et al. (2000) observe that staff variables, such as attitudes and skills, did not result in significant variations in the level of personal control that individuals were allowed. They conclude that exo- and macrosystem influences, such as agency policies, have a more significant impact. In other words, even if a support worker thinks that a certain option would be tolerable, they may only allow individuals to opt for it if they feel it will be accepted by their agency.

Day services

The majority of the respondents who attended day services engaged in a range of activities, such as drama groups, yoga, cooking, women's and men's groups, arts and crafts, sports, self-advocacy, a library, a shopping group and so forth. They had set weekly schedules. Many liked the activities and the social aspect of coming to the day centre:

Andrea: Do you like coming to the day centre?

Kathy: Yeah, good.

Andrea: Or is there –

Kathy: It feel good.

Andrea: – is there anything –

Kathy: My friends here, my friends here. [laughs] … Good yeah.

Andrea: … Is there anything that you want to change?

Kathy: No.

Andrea: About, you know –

Kathy: No.

Andrea: – One of the groups you don't like?

Kathy: Mmh… No.

Andrea: All the groups are cool?

Kathy: Cool, yeah.

Individuals generally had some level of control when determining which activities they attended, with only five of 22 respondents stating that they could not exercise any meaningful choice. Two accounts are considered in the following.

Peter states that, when he first started attending an adult training centre (ATC) about 40 years ago, he expected to be trained to become a skilled worker, but he was disappointed: 'They called it training centre, but they weren't training us in anything.' This experience is not unusual. Brimblecomb et al. (1985) assert that ATCs 'trained' individuals until they were 65 years old. However, the work did at least keep Peter busy. When the ATC closed down he was moved to a new day service. Even though this was not what he initially wanted to do, Peter now misses the old service: 'I think they were better… Cause you could help out.' Now Peter spends most of his time in solitary activity:

> I play the organ [keyboard] for me, because, because there's eh, not a great deal of things here that, that can do really, apart from just, like, sit and watch TV all the time. Except me watch television, watch TV at home.

Peter attends the day service five days per week. He is scheduled for two weekly activities, which occupy him for two afternoons each week. He has no interest in any of the other activity groups. I discovered Peter almost by accident during participant observations, when I walked into the almost always unused room at the day centre where Peter sits all morning or sometimes all day, playing tapes or the piano and often talking to himself. Half of the time a man of a similar age who requires assistance to mobilise in his wheelchair is brought to the room by staff at his own request. He enjoys listening to Peter and Peter enjoys the company.

Bill, too, misses his former ATC:

Bill: We used to do wood work. We used to do benches and stuff. Breadboxes…and clotheshorse. … And I built it with my two hands. … It were good, woodwork. … We don't do it now no more, I miss that.

Andrea: … Are there any things that go on now that you like doing?

Bill: No, there's nothing going on now.

Andrea: So what do you do here?

Bill: Go to play pool. Cause we've got a pool table around there.

Andrea: What else do you do?

Bill: EEhm… [seven seconds pause] I do, I do my own leg on there [physiotherapy, once per week].

The ATC occupied Bill. Activities gave him some sort of achievement. However, all he is doing at his current day centre is playing pool and attending physiotherapy once per week. Most other times he is sat in the communal area talking to staff. Even so, Peter recalls that attending the ATC was not always enjoyable:

The other place where we were at before. They had, sometimes they'd do, they'd do contract work. And sometimes there wouldn't be any contract working to do. So they'd just be sat round the tables talking. There were jigsaw puzzles and books to look at and that sort of thing, but otherwise they'd be saying: 'Oh, why do, why do we come when there's nothing to do?' … You know, they were bored to tears.

It appears that this state of being has now become Peter's daily reality. Unsurprisingly he often battles with his mother about whether to get up and attend the day centre in the first place, as discussed later on. ATCs were closed down because they were exploitative and segregative (Barnes 1990). However, for Bill and Peter, who are eager to engage in some form of work, their current day centre is an even less meaningful alternative, as there is even less structure and purpose and even more free leisure time.

Even if individuals participated more keenly in the activities that were on offer and did not feel inhibited in their choices, in reality activities were chosen and run by staff. Day service attendees were never able to make choices that were not on 'the menu'. One staff member expressed her concern about the fact that individuals' choices are not reviewed regularly and that some consequently end up attending the same activity groups for many years without being encouraged to try something new. Shevin and Klein (1984) similarly observed that, without ongoing and meaningful consultation with individuals about their personal preferences, habitual behaviour can be mistaken for active choice, lack of protest for informed consent and resignation for contentment.

One occasion where this may have been the case was when I observed an activity group in which a blind man was engaged in throwing hoops at a target. We were sat in a circle and waited our turn. The man was unable to see what was going on, yet he waited meekly until it was his turn again. Nobody complained and staff later declared the morning's activity a success. When I asked a member of staff whether she thought that the visually impaired man had enjoyed the activity, she gave a positive reply and explained that he had 'enjoyed our company'.

This activity might have much more harmful consequences than mere boredom. On a different occasion a member of staff explained to me that the man is apparently frustrated with his lack of sight. This is no surprise, as the day service seems to be poorly resourced to include him. The way in which activities are facilitated often alienates him from sighted people and transforms his impairment into a disability.

Similarly Paul, who needs assistance to mobilise in his wheelchair, does not engage in the same multitude of activities as many of his physically more able peers. A staff member tells me that she observed that people with physical impairments do not go out with activity groups as often as others. She says that this is due to the fact that staff can choose whom they take out and that some find it 'too much trouble' to take out a person with a mobility impairment. This statement sums up the disempowering way in which the day service continues to be facilitated: staff and not individuals get to choose.

This is also evident in Rose's case. She described that she has been stopped from going out with the day centre's library group because she was 'naughty'. (Rose had hidden a staff member's library card while they were at the library.) I continued to visit the day centre for a couple of weeks after this incident, but Rose remained excluded from the group. The member of staff had decided that she would not take Rose out with any of her other activity groups as well. Rose was angry to start with, but after a while her attitude changed and she told me that she was never interested in the group anyway.

Leanne is entirely unsatisfied with her day service. She states that she would prefer to be with her mother, or to take up paid employment. We spoke to Leanne's key worker after the interview. The key worker stated that she knows about Leanne's ambitions to find work, but that Leanne has not yet demonstrated that she is 'determined enough', as she often loses interest half way through activities. Yet, as long as Leanne has not tried to work, she will not find out whether this would keep her interested for longer than ongoing leisure. Although Leanne is presented with a range of options of activities at her day service, she does not feel that she is in control of making real choices. As outlined earlier, individuals can only be said to have choice if they are presented with at least two options that they perceive as viable (Jenkinson 1993). Ongoing leisure does not meet Leanne's chosen goal of wanting to work. Thus, the fact that she can choose between, for example, bowling and watching TV, does not provide her with a choice that is meaningful to her.

About two thirds, 14 of the 22 individuals attending day centres, explicitly stated that they had no choice about their attendance. Peter explains:

Peter: There's many times that –, if, you know. You're in bed and you think: 'Uuh!' You don't, you don't feel like getting up to go, but, eh…you know, you have to go. You have to go if transport comes. …

Andrea: Why do you have to go?

Peter: I wish I could, but my mother said: 'Well you wouldn't stay, you wouldn't be at home all day.' Cause otherwise all I'd do, all I'll be doing is sleeping, more or less, so she said: 'Well you'd better go into, better going out'… I know there's not a great deal to do.

It appears that Peter has no access to alternative daytime activities. The day centre, inadequate as it appears to be for meeting his needs, remains 'somewhere to go' (Barnes 1990, p.192).

It is questionable whether all of the remaining eight respondents had made an informed and free choice. Bill, for example, lives independently and has a limited social network. Attending the day centre gives him an opportunity to socialise. Sam attends the day service because he has long given up on seeking paid employment in a disablist employment market. Conversely, Salina, a woman in her sixties who lives independently, tells me that sometimes she 'doesn't really feel like going'. I observed that Salina chooses to stay at home about once per week. Salina's tendency to make attendance a choice visibly annoys her key worker, who informs me that Salina ought to attend every working day. Overall only four of the 22 respondents can be said to have been similarly free to choose.

In conclusion, even though only a few of the respondents felt that they had made a choice about their attendance, the majority had an element of control in determining their activities while they were at the day service. As with selections from a pre-selected wardrobe, individuals were able to choose from a menu of options at the day service, as long as they 'behaved'. However, choosing from a limited range of options meant that individuals never experienced real control. Those who tried to make choices that were not on the menu were either ignored or labelled as 'difficult'.

This discussion demonstrated how individuals negotiate choice in their everyday lives. Salina clearly understands her right to make choices and that these will have an immediate, noticeable impact. Yet, for many of the other respondents this was not the case. Many grew accustomed to others making selections for them. Like the blind man who was throwing hoops at a target he could not see, they meekly followed other's suggestions. Rose's case demonstrates that a lack of resistance can be learned. Week by week her complaints grew quieter. She eventually stopped being angry and gave up speaking up for her right to select to attend the activity group from which she was barred. However, such learned compliance will have dangerous consequences.

Residential services

Of the decision-making categories that are discussed in this chapter, control over the 'home' environment is in many respects the most significant one. It determines an individual's immediate environment and social networks and with this opportunities for further decision-making, as the extent to which individuals are allowed to make decisions is often influenced by others in their immediate environment. Who an individual lives with is therefore decisive for decision-making in general.

Eight respondents spoke about experiences of residential group living. Mary had until recently lived in a hostel. Britney, Josie and Ryan live in registered residential 'homes' (although Ryan's 'home' houses only three men and meets many of the characteristics of supported living). Gemma, Martha, Rachel and Sue live in supported living residences. Paul and Peter furthermore spoke about their experiences of respite care. Four of these ten respondents expressed an overall satisfaction, but this did not necessarily mean that they were in full control.

The difference between supported living and residential 'homes' is that supported living residences should usually house small groups, ideally of no more than three people and they are not registered as care or nursing 'homes' (Emerson *et al.* 2001). Residents should hold their own tenancies and are thus assumed to have more control over their 'home' environments than those living in residential 'homes'. Individuals in this study who live in such establishments receive 24-hour staff support. According to the Federation of Local Supported Living Groups (CommuniGate 2010) supported living is about enabling individuals to make their own choices, to be treated as individuals, to be supported according to their needs and to be encouraged to express their own views. If these values were enforced, individuals who reside in such establishments should have an abundance of opportunities to exercise self-determination. However, this was not always the case.

According to the service manager and the philosophies that are outlined on their website, Martha's 'supported living' service prides itself on promoting choices and control. However, as the previous discussion about Martha's clothes choices has shown, this does not always work in practice. The decision that Martha's current fellow resident should move in was also made by others. Martha had clearly articulated that she did not want this, but her decision was overruled and her involvement became tokenistic. The menu of choice presented to her consisted of a range of potential fellow residents. Martha, however, wanted something that was not on the menu: to be allowed to live alone. Her key worker explains that this is not an option, as Martha's 'home' is registered as a setting for two people.

Gemma, who is in her early twenties, has recently moved to her new supported living setting with 24-hour staffing. Gemma's two fellow residents are about 20 years older than her. She did not know one of them prior to moving in together. Even though planning was long term, Gemma was not involved in choosing with whom she would live. Ryan, who is in his late twenties, gives a similar account. He wanted to live with people of a similar age, yet the men he lives with now are more than 20 years his senior. When I point this out Ryan asserts: 'Well, you can't have everything.' Although Gemma and Ryan feel happy with their current living arrangement, they seem to have settled for an option that was available to them, rather than pursuing an option that best suited their wishes. In other words, they fitted into an existing service, rather than the service being shaped to suit them. The report *Improving the Life Chances of Disabled People* (Prime Minister's Strategy Unit 2005) identifies this factor as a major barrier to independent living.

Sue is generally happy with her supported living establishment. However, at the time of the interview a new resident was living at the 'home' and Sue was very unhappy, as they did not get along. Yet, when I visited Sue a couple of weeks later the new resident had been moved, due to the residents' complaints: the three women in the 'home' did not get along. Sue's service can consequently be seen as adhering to the principles of supported living, as service user's preferences influenced service delivery.

Most of the other respondents did not have this level of control. For instance, Josie lives in a residential establishment for six older women with learning difficulties. She is scared of one of the other residents, who can become aggressive towards her. One day she attempted to attack Josie with a kitchen knife. Another day she wandered into Josie's bedroom while Josie was asleep. Staff members tell her to 'take no notice', but Josie is very upset. Her movements in her 'home' are restricted, as Josie tries to avoid being in the same room with the woman. From Josie's account it is likely that her fellow resident has dementia and receives inadequate support. This not only impacts on the woman's own quality of life, but also on that of the other residents.

To sum up, it appears that, with the exception of Sue, none of the eight people who used residential services are confidently in control of their 'home' environment. Even though Sue's wishes were respected eventually, she was also not the key decision-maker who selected the new resident in the first place. Individuals generally had to fit into services, rather than services addressing their needs. Personal attributes, such as age, their preferences and self-defined needs, were not sufficiently considered by those who made decisions. Individuals had little autonomy and their views were not sufficiently considered. There was no noticeable difference between the choices made by individuals living in residential 'homes' and those living in supported living settings.

This section concludes with the account of a young woman who highlights how her efforts to determine the course of her own life are continually blocked. Despite encountering strong opposition from professionals she continues to speak up for her wants and needs.

'It's not the right place for me': a rebel against the system

Britney is in her early twenties. She works for a disabled people's organisation and is very outspoken about her rights. However, in regards to her 'home' she appears to have little control. Britney lives in a large institutional complex and shares a unit with 14 residents, all of whom are at least 20, some 40, years her senior:

> It's not the right place for me. I'm too independent and it's the wrong age limit. They don't do fun stuff like we [young people] do. ... Before I came

> into [this place] I did all my cooking and everything myself, but now I'm in [this place] I can't do me own cooking, I can't do a bit of anything I need to do independently. I can't even manage my own money, cause they've had all that taken away from me. All me independence skills have gone out of the window.

Finlay, Walton and Antaki (2008b) claim that a reason for staff not routinely encouraging residents to participate in the preparation of their own meals can be linked to fears over food hygiene, which is a skill that staff are required to embrace (Commission for Social Care Inspection 2007, p.2). They point out that 'an unannounced visit by a relative or manager is more likely to lead to a complaint about lack of cleanliness than to a challenge over whether residents' preferences had been respected earlier in the day' (Finlay *et al.* 2008b, p.351). They argue that the preoccupation with such 'care standards' dictates staff roles and leads to individuals' choices and independence being considered of secondary importance. This might explain why it may not be seen as practical for Britney to cook her own food.

Before Britney moved to her current placement she lived in her own flat with some support. However, four years ago 'friends' had threatened to harm her in a dispute over Britney's reluctance to engage in illegal activities. Amongst others the 'friends' wanted to store stolen goods in Britney's flat and they attempted to engage her in their activities. This is not an uncommon experience. As Emerson *et al.* (2001) have pointed out, individuals in semi-sheltered accommodation are at a greater risk of exploitation from people in their local community than those living in residential 'homes'. This is precisely why Britney was moved to a more controlled environment, 30 miles away from her previous abode. Britney, however, believes that her current 'home' is not meeting her needs:

> I have to basically share a lounge with people I don't really wanna share a lounge with really...and a dining room. ... They're not my age and they always argue, no matter what. ... And it just really gets on me nerves, so I just spend most of me time in me bedroom. I don't even socialise with none of them. ... I've spent nearly two weeks in me bedroom and that's even eating in me bedroom, because I don't like it there.

Britney is eager to move out and has been trying to do so ever since I first met her (one year prior to the interview). Shortly after the interview Britney invited me to attend a care planning meeting that was held to discuss her plans to move. The meeting was attended by Britney's social worker and her manager, Britney's advocate and community nurse, two colleagues from the disabled people's organisation, Britney and I.

Initially Britney chaired the meeting. She said that she would like to move into her own flat. Her social worker and community nurse, however, asserted that they did not think Britney would be safe on her own. Main concerns included her personal safety and mental health (Britney self-harms). While the nurse voiced her concern about Britney feeling lonely, the social worker feared that Britney would 'mix with the wrong crowd' again. The social worker continued: 'There are people out there who spot a vulnerable person miles off. They will target you.' She made this assumption despite the fact that Britney is not visibly impaired.

The meeting slipped more and more out of Britney's control. Eventually she lost her role as chairperson and professionals set the agenda. They spoke about risks and what they perceived to be Britney's support 'needs'. They identified a sheltered living service, which they agreed would be 'ideal' for Britney, but she disagreed. She wants to move to a different area, to be closer to some of her new friends. The nurse and social worker insisted that Britney should consider their option nonetheless. Eventually Britney started to cry. She said that people are trying to make decisions for her all the time. Britney's advocate comforted her and tried to negotiate on her behalf. In the end the professionals convinced Britney that she should have a look at the option that was suggested by the nurse and social worker. The advocate asked what the next steps would be in case Britney does not like the service. The nurse said she would then ask for a test of mental 'capacity' to be carried out (HMSO 2005b) in order to establish whether Britney should be allowed to make decisions about her home environment. She stated that she does not think Britney would pass such a test.

For individuals to be seen as able to make a decision under the Mental Capacity Act (HMSO 2005b), they must understand the information relevant to the decision, retain that information and be able to use or weigh that information as part of the process of making the decision (section 3(1a–c)). Jenkinson (1993, p.364) observes that very few non-disabled people achieve complete rationality in everyday decision-making. Consequently she is concerned that we expect people with learning difficulties 'to become better decision makers than the rest of us'. The nurse appears to imply that Britney should only be able to make a choice if she makes choices that professionals agree with. Britney's involvement in the decision-making process consequently becomes tokenistic. The nurse threatened to use her powers as a medical professional, who can advocate for labelling individuals as lacking 'capacity', to prevent Britney from making any other selection. A year after this meeting I contacted Britney. She said she still had no concrete plans in place that would enable her to move on.

Britney's experience of working at a centre for independent living (CIL) has encouraged her to consider options that are not presented to her on a pre-selected menu. She believes that she is entitled to choose where she lives and to direct her own support by employing personal assistants and using an individual budget (Department of Health 2008a). The professionals who would have to agree to this 'package of care' are reluctant, because they would prefer to sustain their control over Britney's life by choosing the service she uses and remaining the primary care managers. As long as they are authorised to disregard her wishes, independent living will not become reality for Britney.

Britney is quite unusual. She realises that she has no real control, but she remains resilient in the face of oppression. Many of the other respondents who have been similarly disempowered have given up rebellion. For instance, as outlined earlier, Josie simply tries to avoid the co-resident who upsets her. She does not continue to insist that she does not want to share her accommodation with her. Rose flushed biscuits down the toilet at the day centre because she was bored. She later hid a staff member's library card. Rose can be said to be rebelling, but her behaviour is immediately labelled as 'challenging'. Her demand for more meaningful occupation is consequently not heard. Similarly, Britney clearly articulates her displeasure. As she tries to gain control of her own life, the power struggles that professionals are prepared to perform to counteract this become apparent. The preservation of her dependence is justified with the label 'vulnerability'.

Four years have passed since Britney had been in a dangerous situation. Her social environments and support networks have changed. She may have learned from her experience and from her work at the CIL, yet this is not considered. In Britney's case the label 'vulnerability', once acquired, hinders every new attempt to regain independence.

Self-determination in everyday life: discussion

Self-determination, an essential precondition for resistance, is an acquired behaviour (Powers *et al.* 1996). Individuals need to feel in control before they can be expected to resist sexual violence (Hingsburger 1995). Accordingly, individuals must become experts in exercising self-determination in their everyday lives. As the discussion in this section has shown, individuals are influenced by environmental factors and the behaviour of staff or family when making selections. Real choice would involve individuals choosing beyond a restricted menu. This would equip them with the skills needed to deal with unexpected and unfamiliar situations, and unsought sexual approaches fall into this category. Real choice places control with the individual. It can promote the development of a positive self-image and self-assertion (Brown and Brown 2009).

Yet, this book has shown that some people with learning difficulties continue to be disempowered in the small, routine details of everyday life. Individuals have more control in some respects than in others. Overall, they had the highest level of control when making choices about clothes from their wardrobes and about activities at the day centre. It appears that individuals had less autonomy the more significant the consequences of the selection that was to be made would be. It was demonstrated that individuals often choose from a pre-selected menu. Staff or family members did at times not respect individuals' decisions if they were not offered as part of this list of options. Respect would involve allowing an individual to make a decision that others may not perceive to be sensible (Gunn 1994). However, when Martha asserted that she wanted to buy a low-cut top, when Leanne declared that she would like to go to work or when Britney suggested independent living these preferences were dismissed. Martha's menu of choices consists of more modest clothes, while Leanne is merely allowed to consider existing activities that are on offer at her day service. Britney is given the option of choosing living arrangements that have been pre-selected by social and health services professionals.

CONCLUSION

This chapter demonstrated that for people who are labelled with learning difficulties many aspects of everyday life differ from patterns of life for non-disabled people. Fear of crime serves to justify their spatial and social exclusion. In that way it acts as a means of social control and governance. Fear is furthermore an indicator of reduced self-confidence and limited acquaintance with self-assertion, which impact negatively on an individual's likelihood to self-defend. It is also a marker of power relations, as those who have the least power are often the most fearful.

Besides limiting the social, educational, work and leisure opportunities of individuals, segregation and isolation create risks of their own. For instance, a focus on risks posed by strangers may distract individuals from assessing risks that are caused by people in their immediate environment. Segregation hinders community inclusion and, frequently, the development of close friendships and relationships. Although they lived in a range of different family homes and residential services and attended a diverse range of day services, respondents had similar experiences.

Differential treatment can consequently be seen as occurring systemically, as the causes do not lie merely within each isolated environment. They originate in the macrosystem, which dictates how people with learning difficulties should be responded to. Changes to the cultural assumptions and systems of the wider society should consequently make it possible to change the experiences of individuals. However, at the moment the UK appears to provide a macrosystem within which it is acceptable to segregate disabled people.

Due to limited friendship networks and community contacts support workers take on a vital socio-emotional role in the lives of many people with learning difficulties. They furthermore play a crucial role in the process of adult protection at the front line, as they should be available to note changes in an individual's behaviour and to listen to complaints and allegations. However, some respondents described that their support workers are not always prepared to listen to their concerns. This may eventually silence individuals, who become less likely to report their worries, including those about unsought sexual approaches.

A readiness to listen is more likely to occur in environments that have the means to enforce change. For instance, when Rose complains about boredom her concern could only be addressed if the means to enable her to engage in more stimulating activities are available. Within the margins of her day service she will always be restricted to a limited menu of options. 'Supported living homes', too, have so far not succeeded in introducing an infinite range of real choices for respondents in this study.

Within segregated settings individuals tend to be challenged less to reach their full potential. Many individuals are constructed as particularly 'vulnerable' to risks posed by mundane hazards, such as kitchen appliances. Some avoid these hazards altogether. With this they miss out on the opportunity to practise risk assessments and management. They have this done for them, which increases their dependency on the support worker's assistance. Lack of practice in managing risks will impair the development of an individual's skills, which will indeed result in increased risk. Social construction did thus lead to the social creation of actual 'vulnerability'.

Individuals were given insufficient opportunities to make choices and to exercise self-determination. Instead, they were encouraged to make tokenistic selections from a pre-arranged 'menu'. With a few exceptions, such as Britney who continues to rebel openly or Salina who does not bother attending her day service if she does not feel like it, respondents appear to be acutely aware of boundaries beyond which they cannot exercise control. Some individuals feel a strong sense of obedience to remain within those margins. This is of immediate relevance to the overall theme of this book. Individuals who distinguish available choices on their pre-selected menu from options beyond their reach are less likely to conceptualise the option of resisting an unsought sexual approach from a person who is in a more powerful position and perhaps usually entitled to present pre-selected menus to them (e.g. a member of staff) as available.

Some of these processes can be linked to overprotection. As outlined in Chapter 2, this concept refers to a kind of protection that is excessive, considering the developmental level and abilities of a person. It is characterised by excessive social contact with carers, prolonged infantilisation, and active prevention of independent behaviour and social maturity (Levy 1943). Overprotection thus hinders self-determination, which in turn makes it less likely that an individual will exercise resistance when faced with an unsought sexual approach.

To conclude, many people with learning difficulties find that their rights to make choices, to speak up for themselves, to form and maintain reciprocal friendships, to be included in mainstream society and to benefit from equal leisure, education and employment opportunities, are at times invaded. In Chapter 6 it is argued that all of these processes are part of a continuum of violence. Within this context sexual violence is seen as a mere extension of everyday invasions. Amongst others the subsequent chapter explores a range of processes that can potentially counteract such a continuum.

Chapter 5

Resistance and Self-determination

Until now the discussion focused on social processes that have predominantly negative effects on the development of an individual's resistance skills. Examples of more enabling practices were at times given. However, participants also spoke about ways in which they acted as assertive social actors, despite their exposure to disabling processes. There was evidence of resistance amongst the sample, which contradicts assumptions about their passivity and defencelessness. For instance, in the previous chapter it was outlined how Rose, Britney and Leanne rebel against their current residential and day service. They attempt to exercise self-determination. However, lack of support within their environment prevents their efforts from leading to change. For this to be possible power must shift in their favour (Dowson 1990), as was the case for Sue: when she and a fellow resident did not get along with each other their service supported the other resident to move out. This chapter provides further evidence for the resistance of people with learning difficulties. It seeks to make their capacity to protect themselves from unwanted sexual intrusions explicit. It also aims to expose potentially enabling social factors.

At first it is discussed how the label 'learning difficulties' affects the sense of self of individuals. The benefits of self-advocacy for identity formation are highlighted. Subsequently it is shown how independent living and inter-dependencies within the immediate family allow individuals to increase their autonomy and to take on responsibilities for themselves or others. The potential of sexual encounters to pose as learning opportunities and to enable an individual to develop and enforce their assertiveness skills is furthermore highlighted. Finally, respondents' sexual assertiveness and risk perception skills are outlined. Again, some of these were already touched upon. For example, all of the respondents who were subjected to bullying knew that what was happening was wrong and that they had a right not to be bullied, even when they did not receive adequate support to stop the bullying (see Chapter 4). In addition this chapter demonstrates how some respondents have successfully dealt with threats of violence, which contradicts assumptions of incompetence and passivity.

DISABILITY AND IDENTITY

Finlay *et al.* (2008b, p.350) assert that empowerment is about 'what happens between people moment by moment, in the mundane details of everyday interaction'. Policy guidance often declares an aim to empower disabled people (e.g. Department of Health 2005; Prime Minister's Strategy Unit 2005). However, as mentioned in Chapter 2, Oliver (1997, p.20) argues that 'empowerment is not in the gift of the powerful'. It is 'a collective process of transformation on which the powerless embark as part of the struggle to resist the oppression of others. [...] Central to this struggle is the recognition of the powerless that they are oppressed' (Oliver 2009, p.102).

Many disabled people report that becoming aware of the social model of disability was a deeply empowering experience. Crow (1992, p.1), for example, states that the social model enabled her 'to challenge, survive and even surmount countless situations of exclusion and discrimination'. Shakespeare (1993, p.254) asserts that 'identifying as a member of an oppressed group and organising to effect social change are critical'. Taking on the identity of a person who is labelled with learning difficulties and disabled as a consequence is vital for the success of organised self-advocacy (Finlay and Lyons 1998). Individuals will only be able to shift their gaze away from the body and onto society when they have accepted their identity as disabled persons (Hevey 1993).

However, as will be subsequently discussed, the majority of respondents in this study have either rejected their label or they battle individually against their impairment. This contrasts with those who have taken on a *political* disability identity, as cited above. Only three respondents can be said to have adopted such an identity. Their accounts are discussed in the second part of this section. Finally the role that self-advocacy can play in supporting positive identity formation is highlighted.

The wish to be 'normal'

An individual's sense of self is central to his or her ability to resist an unwanted sexual approach. A person who is confident, who is able to be private and who is aware of his or her right to refuse an invasion into their personal space will be more likely to resist an unwanted sexual act (e.g. Hingsburger 1995). However, the sense of self of individuals who are labelled with learning difficulties is often negatively affected. 'Labelling is central to the processes involved in social categorization and stratification. [...] Labels are used both to signal deviance and as organizational mechanisms for managing deviant groups' (Armstrong 2002, p.454).

As discussed in Chapter 4, the majority of the sample had to endure bullying, including impairment-specific name-calling. Most of them attended segregated education and later day services, which emphasised their difference from non-disabled people. Many individuals spoke about life 'out there' as different. Peter even observed a higher tolerance for violence within institutional settings. Many participants encountered barriers when making choices in their everyday lives and when attempting to establish sexual relationships. Being labelled with learning difficulties therefore often has a negative impact on identity formation, as individuals are forced to see themselves as different. Unsurprisingly a desire to be 'normal' was expressed by half of the respondents. Chantal, for example, asserts:

> I wish I were normal like everybody else and I wish I didn't have a learning difficulty, because I keep saying to my sisters when I do have an argument with them: 'Why can't it be them with the learning difficulty and why can't I be normal?'

Chantal explains that other people in the community do not understand people with learning difficulties. I ask whether 'the problem' with this might lie with those people, but Chantal replies: 'I feel like it's my problem, because I wish I could change myself.' Many other respondents express similar views. Gemma conceptualises her impairment in a negative way because 'me brain's not working very good'. Mary tells me that her sister 'didn't want to know' her when she was first labelled. Paul asserts that the fact that he uses a wheelchair is the reason for him not going out and being able to do most of the activities at his day centre (see Chapter 4). He appears frustrated with his wheelchair and tells me that it does not even fit into the lift at the supermarket. He directs anger at his wheelchair and not at the inaccessible lift.

For Emma, who has lived independently with a partner for over ten years, suddenly being labelled with learning difficulties came as a shock:

> I've only just been diagnosed with a learning difficulty. I've had it all my life, but ehm... Where I was living before when I was at school, they didn't know that I'd got one. They just thought I were all right.

Since the diagnosis Emma's life has changed. Her care plan states that she needs support with many things she had managed independently before, such as shopping. In other words, Emma had an impairment all her life, but she only became *disabled* when she was labelled and when services began to 'help'. Illich (1977, p.11) claims that 'disabling professionals' may impose their services on individuals who do not want them. Emma's situation appears to fit with this conceptualisation.

However, when we explored these issues further it emerged that many of the respondents who expressed a wish to be 'normal' did not want to change themselves. Instead, they merely articulated the *wish to lead a 'normal' life*. Individuals understood that a notion of 'otherness' was inflicted upon them by the differential treatment that labelled individuals receive, such as spatial segregation (F. Armstrong 2003). Paul would like to be able to access the community, without having to worry about barriers. Emma would like to be able to do things independently, as she did before she was labelled:

Emma: It upsets me cause I want to be like a normal, normal person... without having a carer or help or if you wanna call it. I just wanna do it myself. ...

Andrea: But before you found out that you had difficulties...

Emma: I didn't know that I had a difficulty and ehm, nobody told me! I just...presumed that I were born all right. ...... I'm still doing the same things as before, but ehm...now I'm having help with it and I just...it...I just don't like. I, I don't like it cause it upset, like, cause, people are helping me and I wanna do it myself.

Even Chantal asserts at a later point of the interview that the general public should be given more information about learning difficulties, as they would 'stop laughing and having a go and that'. Gemma states that other people lack an understanding of her abilities and consequently put her in situations that make her feel inadequate. She states: 'they just don't understand me'. Gemma's self-esteem suffers as a result of being asked to do things that she cannot do.

Nevertheless, none of the respondents who are cited in this section had adopted a positive disability identity and many denied that they had an impairment. Over a quarter (eight) state that they are not disabled at all, while a further fifth (six) see themselves as 'less disabled' in comparison to peers. This links back to the notion of a 'hierarchy of impairments' amongst disabled people, which was briefly discussed in the previous chapter (Deal 2003). Bill, for instance, asserts: 'I've got more brains than the others.' Britney states:

I don't really class myself as any of them, really. But, I know I've got one, and it's a learning difficulty. ... Ehm, well, I think it is. Cause I've got a, apparently I've got a mind of a younger age. ... So, but that's the only thing

> what's wrong with me. I don't think as, like people do think. But, I just don't class myself as any, really.

This is a very negative conceptualisation, which focuses on 'things that are wrong'. It should be no surprise that Britney rejects this label. Even though she attends a day centre, Salina differentiates herself from the category of 'disabled people'. To her this term refers to individuals with physical impairments. Salina says she comes to the day centre to help 'disabled people', for example by opening doors for them or bringing them cups of tea. She does not see herself as different from the staff.

Jahoda and Markova (2004) observe that comparing themselves positively with other disabled people enables individuals who are faced with the threat of stigmatisation to maintain a positive sense of self. However, by denying that they are part of this group, individuals reinforce stigmatised images of disability as implying weakness and otherness. Such accounts of denial have been extensively discussed in the literature (e.g. Watson 2002). Finlay and Lyons (1998) confirm that a third of the people they interviewed rejected the label 'learning difficulties'. Only 28 per cent of the respondents in Davies and Jenkins' (1997) study accepted the label for themselves.

Rapley, Kiernan and Antaki (1998) argue that individuals may consciously reject their socially ascribed 'toxic' identity in order to orient themselves to the need to be 'ordinary'. In other words, instead of wishing to be 'normal' these respondents simply view themselves as 'normal'. This also applies to many respondents in this study. For instance, like Salina, two thirds of the day centre attendees class their daytime activity as 'work'. Barnes (1990) made a similar observation in his study. The concept of 'going to work' provides individuals with a normative social role. They align themselves with their generational cohort and adopt the identity of a working-aged adult.

A further factor that determined how respondents saw themselves was their conceptualisation of independence. Along with the dominant views in western industrial societies, Bill associates independence 'with the ability to do things for oneself, to be self-supporting, self-reliant' (as cited by Morris 1993, p.22). Bill always uses crutches, rather than his wheelchair, to walk short distances, even when this is painful, exhausting and lengthy. He has been brought up to pride himself on his physical 'independence':

> I used to go out with me dad. ... And I fell and he won't pick me up. This woman said to me dad: 'Aren't you gonna pick your son up?' 'No. He's got to rely on his own two feet.' Is what I need. ... It's what, the hard way they did it, me parents. I had to get up meself. ... Well, you have to! ... And I did it on my own two feet, cause I'm strong enough. I do strengths.

Ryan explains that he always felt that he had to compensate for his impairment: 'I've always tried pleasing people in my life, cause that's with my difficulty, that's what I've always thought I've had to do. … I've always tried to prove that I can do things, when really I can't.' This willingness to please may put Ryan at an increased risk of sexual violence, as it may impair his resistance against those he aims to please. Both Bill's and Ryan's accounts reflect an element of felt stigma, which they wish to prevent from becoming enacted stigma by disguising their discreditable identity (Scambler 1989). Faced with the negative consequences of stigmatisation these respondents attempt to 'pass as normal' (Edgerton 1967; Goffman 1963), a process that has been described by many other disabled individuals (e.g. Lingsom 2008).

Lee openly rejects the stigma associated with his impairment label. He believes that he has simply outgrown it:

Lee: I was Down's Syndrome.

Andrea: And…are you Down's Syndrome now?

Lee: No…I'm a man.

Andrea: How is that different?

Lee: Because eh, when I was a kid I was, eh, Down's Syndrome…
          Now I am grown up.

Lee explained that, in contrast to 'Down's Syndrome', 'grown-ups' drink beer and have girlfriends. He associates Down's Syndrome with a negative educational label. As evidence for his adult status he produces his mobile phone and shows me pictures of him with a pint of beer in the pub and pictures of his girlfriend. Lee rejects the negative assumptions that are associated with his impairment label by rejecting the label *per se*, because he does not think its implications apply to his life, as he cannot identify with the image of a 'child-like' person with Down's Syndrome.

Jahoda and Markova (2004, p.725) cite a man who resided in a hospital setting who prefers to be called 'resident' rather than 'patient': 'That's wee boys patients… I'm a grown man now.' Sue, too, expresses her concern about her status by changing terminology. She rejects being called 'service user' and advocates that the term should be removed from the files at her 'home'. Similarly, Sam remembers his outrage about having to get registered 'handicapped' with the employment office in the 1970s, after his attempts to find a job failed: 'They were calling people handicapped. And I weren't handicapped. … I'm no different to anybody else. I'm classing myself like me sister. Like me mum and dad.'

In order to resist stigmatisation these respondents consequently reject their imposed labels. Lee, Sam and Sue appear to have a more positive sense of self as a consequence. However, the struggle to 'overcome' the existence of impairments, which was candidly described by Bill and Ryan, adds further to the oppression of disabled people, who will be unable to admit to requiring assistance or accommodations within this framework (Morris 1991). This means that nothing is done to remove disabling barriers. Finkelstein (1980) warns that such approaches continue to see disability as an individual problem.

Positive disability identities

While two thirds of respondents described incidents of resistance against disabling forces at some point, only three, Bob, Mary and Georgina, all of whom attend an independent self-advocacy organisation, have consciously adopted a positive disability identity.

Bob states: 'My parents have said that it's kind of, the Autism that kind of, like, makes some people, like, better at things... And I think that's why I'm good at computers.' When asked how he feels about being labelled as being on the Autistic Spectrum, Bob asserts: 'I can still do things that anyone else could do. Sometimes I'd favour it really.' When prompted further, Bob explains that he has not always been this confident. When he was younger he found it hard to talk to people, but he describes a supportive family, friends and school environment. Gradually he learned to become more confident in social interactions. At the time of the interview Bob was studying to be an IT technician in a mainstream environment.

As outlined earlier, Mary was rejected by her sister and bullied at school as a consequence of being labelled. She blamed herself at the time, but today she says: 'I've accepted it more. I've accepted the way I am.' Georgina has similarly endured bullying and segregation in the past, but today she is a confident self-advocate who is outspoken about her rights. She believes that her impairment does not hinder her from leading an inclusive life in the community. Georgina takes a sense of pride in herself and she challenges those who treat her differently. With that she clearly identifies disabling barriers in her environment. For instance, when Georgina fell pregnant, a social worker became involved:

> I felt she was only involved because with me disability, really. The midwife knew I had a learning disability and she turned around. She'd want to get a social worker involved. ... I *did* turn round and said I didn't want one, but she turned round and says: 'I know, I understand that, [Georgina], but... that is my job.' ... Then it worries you. Then it thinks: 'But... Oh no! You've

told them you've got a learning disability, then they get a social worker involved. Then will that social worker take your child away from you?'... As some people with learning disabilities have. It has happened to them.

Georgina does not view her impairment as an obstacle, but instead she is concerned with other people's attitudes.

It was suggested earlier that assessments for decision-making capacity often expect people with learning difficulties 'to become better decision makers than the rest of us' (Jenkinson 1993, p.364). In this instance Georgina was furthermore expected to be a better parent 'than the rest of us', as she was exposed to additional assessments of her parenting skills over a number of months before the social worker eventually stopped visiting. Georgina understands that she had to prove herself to the professionals, but this does not impact negatively on her sense of self. She realises that the attitudes of professionals and not her impairment pose a barrier.

Some of the other respondents, who did not articulate entirely positive views, described nonetheless how they encountered ignorance and disablement and articulated social causes. Tyler, for example, suggests that all people with learning difficulties should be valued for their personalities. He states that only 'small-minded, one-sided people' reduce them to their impairments. Ann cannot make sense of the fact that 'people outside' will not talk to her when she approaches them for a friendly chat: 'I don't know what the matter is. Why are they not talking to me? ... People mean or they're saying: "Nut!"'

In general the research advisors were more outspoken about social disablement than interview respondents. The advisors repeatedly stated that treating individuals in an unequal or disabling manner is wrong. When I presented Emma's account of how her label changed her everyday life, a lively debate broke out. In the extract below they are discussing whether Emma should be allowed to go shopping on her own:

Nina: She can!

Josh: Come on!

Betty: She should be able to do them.

Lisa: She's no different from anyone else!

Nina: No different. She should go shopping.

Josh: She should go shopping and that!

Joseph: They were just jealous that she was doing so well. That's why they are stopping her. ...

Trevor: She was all right last time. Why can't she do it this time?

Similarly, when I presented Chantal's account of how she wished she was 'normal', the advisors were critical of this concept: Lisa asked 'What's normal? It's normal to have a difficulty. Isn't it?' All of the advisors strongly disagreed with the claim that other people's lack of understanding was Chantal's personal problem:

Josh: I wouldn't say it's her problem.

Nina: Not really.

Josh: ... She should be more proud in herself that she's got difficulties. She shouldn't be hard on herself. ...

Lisa: She shouldn't wish herself normal at all, because she's no different to everybody else. ...

Josh: Stop beating yourself up!

Lisa: If you have a learning difficulty –

Josh: Be proud!

Lisa: – so what?

Josh: And be proud of it!

In other words, there was a general consensus amongst the research advisors that impairment is an aspect of human diversity. As Betty puts it: 'Some people think that other people are different to everybody else, when everybody is different. ... There's some things that other people can do. Some things that I can't do and some things I can do.' Swain and French (2000) would call such conceptualisations an affirmative social approach to disability, whereby disability can be understood as a positive social identity. Individuals thus reject the tragedy model of disability. They understand that disability is a socially created condition, but they also embrace their impairment as a positive aspect of human diversity of which they must not be ashamed.

I was surprised to find that the research advisors have much more positive attitudes towards disability, compared to the participants. Their views may be a direct consequence of their involvement in self-advocacy, as this should encourage individuals to speak up for their rights. What is more, the group discussion gave members a chance to encourage each other to see the social causes for the problems individuals experienced. I have observed some self-advocates, most notably Chantal, who were outspoken about their rights in the context of their self-advocacy group, but in individual interviews they continued to voice doubts about their rights and abilities. The group context does therefore appear to be potentially empowering. The subsequent section explores these issues further.

Self-advocacy

Self-advocacy can be defined as a very specific and individual act: 'A person assumed to have no voice, or nothing to say, speaks; and so challenges the identity they have been assigned' (Dowson 1990, p.6). Self-advocates aim to determine the course of their own lives (Goodley 2000). They speak up and take responsibility; they stand up for their rights, make choices and strive towards independence (People First Workers 1996). In short, self-advocacy is a practice that contests oppression (Dowse 2001). It can also be seen as a group activity in which members represent themselves and their immediate peers within a specific context. Or it refers more broadly to 'people with learning difficulties campaigning for people with learning difficulties as a whole' (Dowson 1990, p.6).

Some individuals who attended independent self-advocacy groups found that their involvement had benefited them personally. Georgina believes that she is only able to be a good self-advocate in her everyday life because she receives an appropriate level of support from her self-advocacy organisation. If she feels overwhelmed with a situation she knows that the disabled and non-disabled co-workers will listen to her and offer practical and emotional support.

Ryan has attended a self-advocacy group for a number of years. He states that speaking up for himself 'is just something I got used to doing. … Eh, with going to [self-advocacy group] has given me the confidence to do it.' I ask Britney, who demonstrated a high level of resistance against pressures and control in her everyday life (see Chapter 4), how she has become so confident in speaking up for herself. She replies:

> I think it's just the courage what people have built up for me. … I wouldn't have basically had the courage to speak up for my rights. But it, but because I've been working [at a disabled people's organisation] and I have been working with people to help me…build me courage up, I think that's why it is.

Tyler works for a self-advocacy organisation that is run by people with learning difficulties and non-disabled co-workers who assist individuals to utilise their skills. He suggests that self-advocacy has even more important implications for his life:

> Tyler: I pretty much would say…and I don't care how over the top this sounds…[self-advocacy agency] saved my life. … Because, before I came to [self-advocacy agency] I was on such a downer, I didn't go out at all. …
>
> Andrea: How did [self-advocacy agency] change all that?

Tyler: Because [self-advocacy agency] lets me work the hours I wanna work, uses my skills on the computers to the effect I want to be used, meet new people, socialise, network, which is what I wanna do when I... And when I gets into meeting or I get put into schemes or, whatever, it makes me feel important. It makes me feel wanted by people. ... And to me that's the most important thing in the world.

For Tyler the self-advocacy organisation is much more than just a place where he can speak up for himself. It is a place that does not judge him and that provides the flexible working conditions he needs.

Disability and identity: discussion

Some of the individuals in this study have internalised stigma. In other words they blame themselves for the differential treatment they are subjected to. This is a disabling factor that can potentially reduce self-esteem. Yet, further exploration revealed that not all of the respondents who detested their impairment label had a negative sense of self. Some of them expressed a wish to live a 'normal' life, rather than a wish to become 'normal'. Impairment labels had nonetheless a negative impact. Some respondents described how they put themselves under pressure to attempt to pass as 'normal'. This has further disabling consequences.

A positive disability identity can promote self-advocacy, as individuals are more likely to believe in their ability to make changes. Forming such a positive identity can, however, be a challenge in a social context of attitudes that devalue disabled people and in which individuals continue to be disempowered and segregated (as discussed in Chapter 4). Social environments must therefore be organised to reflect acceptance and respect for disabled people. This is, however, hard to achieve in segregated environments. Further fundamental changes in the macrosystem would therefore be necessary to affect systematic change. If the latest proposals by *Valuing People Now* (Department of Health 2009b) to move away from segregated day services and to include individuals in mainstream social activities would become reality, this could contribute to this process.

Furthermore, a social model approach to disability, self-advocacy and a positive disability identity all have the potential to significantly increase an individual's confidence and with this their readiness to resist unwanted approaches and invasions. These matters are interlinked. A social model approach, which has become part of the macrosystem in our society, highlights social barriers. The views of Bob's parents appear to be strongly influenced by this model, which in turn impacts on Bob's self-image.

Moreover, involvement in self-advocacy can introduce individuals to the social model and lead them to take pride in themselves.

RECOGNISING OPPORTUNITIES FOR AUTONOMY

Opportunities for developing autonomy are determined by environmental factors. This section begins by exploring two sets of circumstances that can potentially encourage individuals to take on responsibilities, to make decisions and to become increasingly autonomous. First, the enabling nature of independent living environments is explored. The accounts of individuals within such settings are contrasted with those of individuals who live in group establishments and with family carers. Second, it is shown that individuals who live with their relatives do at times occupy vital social roles within their family. The opportunities that arise from such arrangements are subsequently discussed. The final part of this section explores the extent to which consenting sexual encounters can pose as learning opportunities, which encourage the development of assertiveness skills.

The benefits of independent living

Services for people with learning difficulties are expected to comply with the government's recently published Independent Living Strategy (Office for Disability Issues 2008) and many are keen to advertise themselves by using independent living terminology. However, on closer inspection they focus predominantly on supporting individuals to carry out physical tasks. For example, back in 2009, Mencap (2009a) advertised independent living services as: 'help with medication, managing money, going to the supermarket or getting out for an evening to meet friends', as well as the use of home adaptations to increase physical independence. Their website featured a photograph of a woman with Down's Syndrome preparing a meal, with a support worker watching over her progress. Such approaches to independence continue to be in line with the dominant views in western industrial societies, which associate independence with physical self-reliance (as cited by Morris 1993).

Some respondents in this study use residential services that adopt a similar philosophy. Martha, for example, has learned many domestic skills, such as cleaning and cooking, since she moved to her 'supported living home'. Physically she is much more 'independent' than before, but when it comes to making choices about her sexual relationship, who to live with, her daytime and evening activities and the clothes she wears, Martha is not allowed choice beyond a restricted menu (see Chapters 3 and 4).

This research endorses the disability rights movement's definition of independent living. Accordingly, it is understood as disabled people having the same choices, control and freedom as any other citizen. 'This does not necessarily mean disabled people "doing everything for themselves," but it does mean that any practical assistance required should be under the control of disabled individuals themselves' (Brisenden 1989a, p.9). In other words, those who require support should be in control of the ways in which this is provided to them. For instance, it would not be enough to be supported to 'get out for an evening'. A person, and not the staff's shift pattern, should also be able to determine how long they will stay out for, a cause that Heavy Load (2010), a punk band made up of musicians with and without learning difficulties, are promoting with their *Stay Up Late* Campaign.

In line with this approach to independence seven of the participants can be said to live independently. In contrast to the other respondents these people have, overall, a higher level of control when determining where and with whom they live. For instance, Salina and her husband, who also has learning difficulties, live in a council-let bungalow, which they have chosen themselves:

> Me and [husband] went, had a look at it. … We looked in the bathroom: it was a walk-in shower. Then it, the room, room were big and bedroom were big and kitchen were big, so…so… [husband] just turned around, [husband] says to this lady: 'Uuh, can we have it, can we have it then, cause we like it.'

Salina did not like their previous flat, because the neighbours were noisy, but 'it's ever so quiet' where she lives now. She says there are some 'funny neighbours', but they also have some neighbours they are friendly with.

Georgina lives on her own with her child. With the help of the self-advocacy agency, which pays her a full-time wage, she got her own mortgage:

> I like living there [own house], cause it's giving me a chance to be independently… I know I've got [child], but I do feel lonely sometimes, but…I like it when me mum is happy enough to come over and sit with me for a while. … She likes to come up…like today…I'll go down to me mum's and I'll sit with me mum and me dad and me brother for a while.

Even though Georgina lives independently, she does not have to be on her own or cope by herself. She receives support from her family or the self-advocacy agency when she needs it. However, she decides for herself if she requires help.

Georgina manages her own money, but she explains that she has some difficulties with calculating the exact amount of change she will receive when she pays for something in a shop. She states that it helps her to look at receipts, which will tell her exactly how much money she should receive back. Georgina also knows that you have to be careful not to pick up too many things in a shop. She says if she only had 50 pence on her and she wanted a can of pop and a chocolate bar, she would have to put something back. She often has to tackle such issues in her everyday life. Georgina finds them difficult, but she is proud to manage them on her own.

Four of the seven respondents who live independently receive formal support services. In most cases this amounted to a few hours of support per week, but Liz, who lives in her own flat, receives a 24-hour service, because she is assessed as requiring ongoing advice and supervision. Nonetheless she feels free to do what she likes to do. For example, she describes how she likes to spend her Sunday morning:

> I…on my own. And I can do what I want to do. … Washing up, ironing and…watch telly. And the breakfast on the morning. I like my cup of tea in bed. … And, eh, sometimes I get cook.

Salina and her husband are visited by a support worker once each week:

> They help me to do the cleaning and they, like, they look in your fridge. If you've got any of that stuff what's out of date. … And then they sort me receipts when I pay, with bills and that.

Salina can also ring the support agency if she needs additional help or advice. In her everyday life she manages her money independently, but she finds it difficult to pay bills. Whenever she receives a bill she therefore calls the support agency. Like Georgina she thus directs the additional support she requires herself.

Chantal, Salina and Richard live with their partners and they support each other. Chantal states:

> Me and me partner just like, help each other out with us own house and… So like…he does one thing and I do another. And if I…if me or my partner get stuck with something, then we just help each other.

Chantal acknowledges that inter-dependency is an integral part of her relationship. Bill reports that, when he first moved into his own home, his parents were supportive: 'My dad said: "It's your choice." It isn't up to us.

We can't tell you what to do.' Tyler describes how moving into his own flat has changed the way he looks at himself:

> I've only been living in my flat since [seven months ago]. Before that I kind of had this mindset that I was living with my parents, you also had to do everything my parents told me or do everything that my parents wanted me to do. It was kind of a mindset I got into and it did affect my life a lot.

Tyler's mother used to make him buy clothes when he still lived with her, but he prefers to spend his money on video games or DVDs. Now that he lives on his own he can choose to spend his money on whatever he likes. Tyler furthermore states that he 'cannot be bothered' to cook on most days and he simply eats 'snack stuff'. He realises that some of the options he chooses are not particularly healthy.

Tyler also chooses his daytime activities himself. On many days he does not get up before lunchtime and he only goes to the self-advocacy agency, where he works on a voluntary basis, when he feels like going. Salina similarly chooses whether or not to attend the day service (see Chapter 4). Both accounts contrast with Peter's experience (see Chapter 4), who would also like to stay in bed some days instead of attending the day centre. However, his mother makes him get up and go.

Stancliffe *et al.* (2000) found that individuals who were living semi-independently in the community had higher levels of personal control than those who lived in group 'homes'. However, they also found that individuals in this group had a higher level of self-determination competencies. They suspect that individuals with a higher level of ability are more likely to live in more independent environments. On the other hand it could be argued that living in more independent environments increases self-determination competencies. This is evident from the account given by Tyler, who is now enjoying increased autonomy. Georgina furthermore spoke about carrying out tasks that she finds difficult, such as budgeting. A support worker could make this easier for her, but then she might have to share the control in the decision-making process.

In conclusion, it emerges that individuals who live independently have a higher level of choice and control compared to those who live with family guardians or in group settings. This is confirmed by past research: less restrictive environments are proven to lead to gains in self-determination (Wehmeyer and Bolding 2001), while smaller living units allow residents to have more control than larger ones (Stancliffe *et al.* 2000). Individuals with higher levels of self-determination skills may also be more likely to live independently. This living arrangement will then enable them to further develop their skills. Whether increased independence is caused by the individual's pre-existing level of skills or their environment is therefore a 'chicken or egg' scenario: it may not always be clear what came first. However, within an ecological frame of reference it can be argued that independent living environments certainly have a positive impact on self-determination. Liz's account demonstrates that independent living is realisable for individuals who require high levels of assistance. Despite drawing on ongoing 24-hour support, Liz feels in control at all times.

Inter-dependencies in the family

Some feminists have described disabled people living within their families as burdening the mostly female carer, while the disabled person is referred to as 'dependent' (e.g. Dalley 1988; Finch and Groves 1980). According to a recent report family carers continue to face disadvantages in their access to paid employment (Yeandle *et al.* 2006). A 'carer' has thus been defined as 'someone whose life is in some way restricted by the need to be responsible for the care of [a disabled or older adult]' (Pitkeathley 1989, p.11).

However, disabled writers have long argued that it is unhelpful and unrealistic to assume that there is an uncomplicated dividing line between dependency and independence. Inter-dependence is a necessary social condition, as all citizens in advanced industrial societies are dependent on the services and goods provided by others (Brisenden 1998; Oliver 1989). In other words, it makes little sense to single some groups out and to label them as particularly dependent. Furthermore, Morris (1991) asserts that the roles of 'carer' and 'cared for' are blurred and sometimes shifting. This is confirmed by this study.

A third of the respondents told me that they had lived or are currently living with a disabled relative (four cases) or a relative over 65 who requires some assistance (six cases, in two of which the relative had acquired an impairment in older age). A further five interviewees did not talk about their role as 'carers', but they were currently living, or had lived, with a family member over the age of 65. Some respondents described how their skills were utilised and that, as well as being supported by their relative, they supported them. Such relationships have also been identified by other authors (e.g. Walmsley 1996; Williams and Robinson 2001).

A similar proportion of men (3 of 12 male respondents) and women (4 of 17 female respondents) made explicit reference to their family member's reliance on their help with household chores and daily living activities. Williams and Robinson (2001) report a similar ratio. This contradicts the perhaps outdated assumption that 'caring' roles are predominantly taken on by women (Dalley 1988). Hirst (2001) observed an increase in men's involvement in care during the 1990s. A further explanation for the equal involvement of men amongst the research sample could be that people with learning difficulties who live with their parents often 'had not chosen to stay at home and they had not willingly (or even unwillingly) taken on the role of carer, but had simply always been there at home' (Williams and Robinson 2001, p.60). When their parents grew older or acquired impairments, the adult offspring with learning difficulties who had remained at home was, irrespective of gender, more readily able to help than their non-disabled siblings, who had moved out.

Peter, who is in his late fifties, helps his mother to carry the grocery shopping. Sometimes he does not want to go to the supermarket, but his mother depends on his help and she compels him to go. Peter says when he is disobedient his mother will tell him:

> If ever she passed away, she said, 'If I weren't here, you'd be in a sorry state. Cause there's be nobody to look after you and that sort of thing. You'd either have to go into a home or eh… [respite centre], or somewhere like that. You wouldn't be able to do a lot of things there that you do at home, cause, eh, you know, they wouldn't, they would have you ruled. You'd have to look after yourself' and all that sort of thing.

Although Peter's mother depends on his help, she points to his alleged dependency on her.

Rose's mother had a stroke. She remained hard of hearing afterwards and finds physical chores difficult. Rose has a lot of responsibilities in the household, including cleaning and ironing. She finds this difficult and is angry that she has more responsibilities than her non-disabled sister, who lives nearby and only helps out when she visits. Rose would like to move out, to free herself from all of these duties, but her mother and sister oppose this. In other words, Rose does not have a choice over whether or not she is providing support to her mother.

Sam's father has dementia. Sam helps him with a range of practical things, like going to the post office to collect his pension or going to the local community centre to socialise or play pool or bingo. Sam is happy to help out and feels a sense of responsibility towards his parents. The roles have shifted. He states that his parents used to 'look after' him and now he becomes increasingly involved in supporting them.

Gemma has until recently lived with her parents. Her mother has multiple sclerosis:

> I used to make her drinks. I used to do her ironing. I used to like, eh, do her dusting or something like that… But, but it was very hard to help her when she were poorly, you know.

Mary lives with her niece, who is physically impaired. While Mary requires assistance with cooking meals and understanding complex information, her niece requires assistance with some physical household chores. Mary also takes care of the dogs. She describes an inter-dependent relationship, which benefits both women: 'I'm sort of keeping an eye on her and she's keeping an eye on me, that's how it's working out at the moment.'

It becomes apparent that 'caring' relationships can be mutually supportive. Rose's mother is reliant on her help and opposes her proposal to move out, perhaps because she could not get by without Rose. Rose is unhappy with her role. The difficulties for adult offsprings who are forced to support their parents have similar causes to those faced by children who are labelled as 'young carers': their help is needed because their parents do not receive the appropriate level of support services that would enable them to cope without their offspring's help (Morris and Keith 1995).

Yet, people with learning difficulties are often fixed in their role as 'cared-for' (Williams and Robinson 2001), as Peter's mother implies. Although 'carers' often see the help they receive from their disabled offspring as vital, they perceive themselves as holding sole responsibility and being in control (for example instructing the other what to do) (Walmsley 1996). In this study only Mary stands out as an individual whose role as provider, as well as receiver, of support is recognised.

The opportunity to take on supportive responsibilities within the family can enable the development of autonomy and independence skills. It can also give a sense of purpose and it has a potentially positive effect on self-esteem. The subsequent section explores how sexual encounters acted as a further opportunity for individuals to practise autonomy and self-determination.

Sexual encounters as learning opportunities

In order to avoid the possibility of them having a negative experience, people with learning difficulties are often protected from sexual contact altogether. Rogers (2009, 2010) points out that some protection remains at times vital to make sure that individuals are not exposed to unmanageable risks, even within a rights-based framework. She is offended by the fact that mothers in particular are often accused of being overprotective and warns that some guidance with risk management is essential. These are valid claims, which will be confirmed in this section.

Chapter 3 highlighted that consenting sexual exploration can nonetheless help individuals to familiarise themselves with their likes and dislikes, which may result in increased sexual and social competence. In the following the accounts of those individuals who have had negative experiences in the context of their consenting sexual relationships are outlined. It is discussed how these experiences enabled individuals to learn from them. Accounts of respondents who have furthermore demonstrated assertiveness towards their partner are examined.

Georgina speaks about some hurtful past experiences. Several partners have 'two timed', argued often or did not care about her enough. Georgina says that she sometimes felt used:

> Sometimes I felt a bit confused. If the person really wanted to be with me or not. Cause, I also, one of the guys I went with… They didn't really wanna go out with me. They're just doing it to make an impression on their mates. To see if they could get off with a girl.

Another ex-boyfriend did not like her wearing glasses: 'He were just a funny guy. He just kind of…just won't accept *me* as *me*.' Georgina thinks that men might sometimes talk women into having sex with them:

> It's the man what normally wants the sex. Just say that woman might be watching TV. She might not be interested. And he could just go and say: 'Should we go to bed early?' They can start it off by wanting to hug you a lot or wanting to kiss you a lot. And…trying all sorts to get behind you to get you to go to bed early.

She finds this 'annoying' and states that she will not go along with a man's suggestions if she does not want to have sex. Georgina had a succession of non-disabled and disabled boyfriends in the past. She feels confident to stand up to either. As a consequence of negative experiences she had during her previous relationship, Georgina informs me that she has now positively chosen to remain single for a while.

When talking about privacy Britney explains how she had to learn how much she values it through an 'embarrassing' experience:

> I once had sex in a car with some other people that were having it as well [laughs]. Really embarrassing, but I was drunk, so I didn't realise [laughs]. Every time that me and me boyfriend did have it after, it was me bedroom at my place, where no one else where… But…then I didn't feel as embarrassed, so I were more relaxed.

In this instance Britney could be said to have gotten into a 'vulnerable' situation when she was drunk. Yet, after she had this experience, which she merely found 'embarrassing' and not exploitative, she became adamant to choose places where she felt more comfortable to have sex. Similar experiences of learning from past mistakes have also been reported by young, non-disabled women who experimented with sexual practices (Tolman 2001).

Rachel becomes disturbed whenever she speaks about her past relationship. She and her boyfriend had lived together. The couple were supported during daytime hours and allowed privacy at night. They were initially happy and Rachel particularly enjoyed their sex life (as described in Chapter 3). After about a year, however, her boyfriend became physically violent towards her: 'He was throwing money round the living room, harassing me, getting into bed. Harassing me. Swearing at me. Pushed me up the wall.' Rachel sought help from her support agency, which immediately enabled her to move out. Several months later Rachel continues to be upset by what had happened to her. She repeatedly states: 'I feel hurt.'

Unfortunately, we can never say for certain whether a relationship will remain positive or whether it may turn into an upsetting experience for those involved. However, as a self-advocate once pointed out to me: 'Some relationships work out, some don't. But the person with learning difficulties should be able to try to make it work' (Hollomotz and The Speakup Committee 2009, p.94). Individuals should be allowed to take positive risks whenever possible, with support when necessary, as this will increase their autonomy. This experience was painful for Rachel, but nobody could have predicted the changes in her boyfriend's behaviour. Rachel was able to experience her relationship, with all its positive and negative components, in the same way as a non-disabled woman would have done. At the same time she had an excellent support network in place, which enabled her to get out of a domestically violent situation as soon as she asked for help. Rachel has recently met a new boyfriend, but she tells me that she wants to 'take it a bit slower' for now.

Salina once had a boyfriend who kept asking her for money. She eventually had to end the relationship because he was so insistent. She then met a 'nice man' at a charity-run social club for people with learning difficulties. Eventually they got married and moved in together. I ask Salina what she liked about her husband when she first met him. She replies: 'Oh, it were all right. It were nice. Takes me half way, takes me out and…it was us wedding anniversary yesterday, eh, Monday. Yeah. I bought him a watch and he bought me some earrings.' Although Salina describes some areas of conflict, for example he does not understand why she buys so many bags and shoes and he spends too much money in the pub, they generally get on fine. She likes the way he respects her and never pressures her. As Salina's narrative demonstrates, her current relationship is based on give and take.

Emma previously lived with a long-term partner. He was controlling and restricted her activities. Emma had to ask him for permission when she wanted to go out and he sometimes locked her in a room. Emma states that her father eventually helped her to move out. Like Rachel she needed support to break free from this relationship. Emma has now been with a new boyfriend for a year. She states that the attributes she likes about him are: 'His looks [laughs]. Ehm…just the way he treats me. It's really sweet the way he treats me, to eh, how my ex used to, to treat me. Erm… He's loving, he's caring.'

Chantal was engaged to get married at the time of the interview. Previous boyfriends just 'did her head in' and she 'dumped them' within a short space of time. I ask her why she feels different about her fiancé. Chantal states:

> He understands me in a way. And he sticks up for me when people put me down and gives me hope and that and tells me not to worry. We do have a laugh and we do end up arguing and that all the time. But, that's probably part of relationships, isn't it?

Jasmine has a boyfriend at the day centre. They sit next to each other when they eat their packed lunches and he often calls out to me: 'Look! This is my girlfriend!' Jasmine will smile shyly and he will give her a cuddle or a kiss on her cheek. He has bought Jasmine a ring, which she keeps on her in her handbag. He continually asks her why she does not wear it and he does not like the fact that Jasmine wears a ring her sister gave her instead. But Jasmine continues to keep his ring in her bag.

> Jasmine: He had gone on his knees. He said to me: '[Jasmine], I want you to marry me.' I said: 'No.' I went home and my sister and [sister's partner] just turned and started laughing.
>
> Andrea: Why don't you want to marry him?
>
> Jasmine: I keep saying I haven't got the money. I have some upstairs, but I'm saving up for Christmas.

Jasmine did not find it unusual that her sister and partner laughed at the incident. This signifies that her family does not take her concerns seriously. Nonetheless, to Jasmine and her boyfriend, a couple in their fifties who only see each other at the day centre, this is a serious issue. This example demonstrates that Jasmine can be self-determined towards her boyfriend. She tells him that she does not want to get married, despite his persistence.

Recognising opportunities for autonomy: discussion

The discussion in this section drew attention to the potential benefits of independent living. Those are that it provides individuals with a multitude of opportunities to make decisions and to direct the ways in which support should be provided to them. Practice in everyday decision-making has the potential to increase self-determination competences. Moreover, people who live independently are not subjected to undue surveillance. They consequently have more freedom to express their sexuality and to be sexually active.

A significant proportion of the research sample could be conceptualised as 'carers' for an adult relative. This contradicts the widespread perceptions of their 'dependency'. Yet, this inter-dependence, the parent depending on the disabled adult offspring, might also result in the parent nurturing their offspring's dependence on them for their own benefit. Most of the respondents, however, enjoyed their role as supporters. Taking on valued social roles within the family has the potential to enable autonomy and independence skills, which can increase self-esteem. These are positive mechanisms, which will increase resilience.

Some of those respondents who had an opportunity to experience sexual relationships had negative experiences. While these were upsetting at the time, this did give them an opportunity to learn from their encounters and to develop their relationship skills. Some respondents demonstrated an ability to resist pressure, to take charge of their relationships and to change the aspects they did not like. In other words, they were exercising autonomy to lead their relationships in ways they felt comfortable with. Nevertheless, being able to refer to a support network was at times vital to enable individuals to protect themselves from relationships that they no longer experienced as positive.

So far this chapter has not only discussed opportunities for autonomy, but it has also demonstrated respondents' ability to take on responsibilities and to be assertive, including assertiveness within sexual relationships. The final section focuses on examining the sexual assertiveness and self-defence skills of respondents in detail.

ASSERTIVENESS AND SELF-DEFENCE SKILLS

Individuals require a range of self-defence skills in order to effectively resist an unwanted sexual approach. As outlined in Chapter 2, these can be summarised as sexual competencies and self-determination skills. The formation of sexual knowledge, including privacy awareness and the vocabulary to describe sexual acts, were discussed in Chapter 3. Chapter 4 explored social factors that impact predominantly negatively on self-determination. The previous section furthermore highlighted how individuals may increase their sexual competences and practise self-determination skills by learning from sexual and relationship experiences.

This section outlines participants' actual levels of sexual risk perception, their awareness of sexual violence and concepts of 'vulnerability'. In addition, it is outlined how some respondents have reported violent incidents and walked away from potentially violating situations. It will become apparent that a large proportion of the research sample have demonstrated a perhaps unexpectedly high level of skill in these areas.

Risk perception

Almost all of the respondents are aware of sexual violence and of their right to say 'no' to unwanted touch. Sue, for example, states: 'I don't think I would let anybody touch me. Like, when somebody from my family comes, I just give them a cuddle and that's it.' Only Michael does not appear to be aware of the distinction between wanted and unwanted sexual activity. All the other participants could tell me what they would do in the event of an unsought sexual intrusion: all of them said they would tell someone about it. All but three of them described how they would furthermore seek to defend themselves in risky situations. Kathy, for example, suggests she would tell the violator: 'Go away! Leave me alone!' Ann says she would walk away. Leanne, who has a mobility impairment, states that she would call for help.

Half of those interviewed clearly stated that they were aware that sexual violence could be perpetrated by people they know or by strangers. Sam, for example, states: 'It could be a doctor. It could be, like yourself [interviewer], couldn't it?' Britney states: 'It could even happen in our care home. ... It doesn't matter where you are, if someone does it, then someone does it.'

However, the other half of the respondents told me that only certain people would violate. Leanne believes that all violators are strangers. Kathy believes that people with authority, like staff or parents, would not violate. Yet, sometimes people's awareness was not that straightforwardly obvious from merely asking the question: 'Who could do this?' Josie initially answered that violators are 'criminals' and therefore only 'strangers', because none of the people she knows are 'criminals'. Yet, later on she tells me about her brother-in-law who 'used to be a pervert' (see Chapter 3). In other words, she might be able to identify unsought sexual approaches when they happen to her, but she does not use the same term that she uses for the more unusual stranger-crime cases she has seen on TV.

As outlined in Chapter 1, respondents were asked to comment on three risk perception vignettes. The vignettes describe potentially hazardous situations. They consist of eight photographs each and a simple story line. Vignette 1 introduces two friends and work colleagues, John and Jill. One day John gives Jill an unexpected embrace. Jill looks shocked. John tells Jill that friends are allowed to do this and that he finds her sexy. Vignette 2 shows how a support worker, Susan, strokes the leg of a service user, Liz, while telling her that she is beautiful. Afterwards Susan asks Liz for secrecy about this. Vignette 3 tells Frank's story. One day he meets a stranger in the park. They start talking and discover a common interest in music. The man invites Frank to his house. By the end of each vignette the respondents were asked to advise the individual who had been approached by the other actor what they should do.

In their responses to the vignettes there was no difference in recognising risk in the scenario that involved a stranger and in those that involved a support worker and a friend as a potential violator, even for people who had stated earlier that only strangers would sexually violate. Most respondents were clear about the actor's right to say 'no' to the unsought approach in their responses. Only Paul and Michael found the vignettes too difficult and were unable to imagine what would happen next and to articulate a response. This is a methodological limitation, as the vignettes assumed some level of abstract thought on the part of the respondent.

Bart articulated a response every time, but he did not pick up on the notion of risk that was implied in the scenarios: his comment on the first vignette is that friends are allowed to cuddle. In response to the second vignette he says that he is unsure what Liz should do, because Susan is her 'carer'. He has no concerns about Frank following the stranger home (Vignette 3), as he has just made a new friend and they are getting along well. Yet, for Bart this exercise may merely demonstrate that he finds it difficult to imagine being in someone else's situation. A further possibility is that he does indeed lack an appreciation of dangers. Nonetheless, this does not lead to the conclusion that Bart would be entirely unable to stop an unwanted sexual approach, as a real-life approach would feel different from trying to imagine a fictitious situation.

The remaining 26 of 29 respondents clearly demonstrated an ability to anticipate danger in their response to the vignettes. They advised the characters to protect themselves and demonstrated self-protective competences when assessing the situation and planning actions. For instance, in their answers to the first vignette, most respondents distinguished acceptable behaviours in friendships from sexual relationships. Emma emphasises that the two characters are 'just friends, not boyfriend and girlfriend' and that friends 'don't do that'. Richard observes that the trouble with this vignette is that he has put his arm around her without her asking him. Salina remarks that Jill does not seem to think John's approach is acceptable. Therefore Jill's view makes it 'not right'.

In the extract below Sue responds to the second vignette:

Sue: I don't think she's, should touch anybody, anybody's legs really, should you?

Andrea: Mmh.

Sue: Unless if you don't want them to, innit? Really, she shouldn't done that. That is wrong... Sue...she like they are gay. Like what used to be on the telly... Can't ya remember on, eh, *Emmerdale Farm*? [British TV soap] ... Then when she were kissing that other lady... She could, it could get like that, couldn't it?

Andrea: Yes... So what if Susan wouldn't stop touching her?

Sue: Ehm...phu! Really like, Liz could say 'I'll have another care worker.' ... She could say: 'You can have the sack!' ... Couldn't she?

Andrea: Would she tell someone that she wants to sack Susan?

Sue: Ehm... Really, I think she would first find out. Like, phone up and ask somebody else to come in place of Susan...and then that's it. Then she'll go somebody else then.

Sue then explained that she would follow these procedures in her own residential setting. This is not an unusual response. Ryan, Tyler, Georgina and Britney, for instance, drew on their own experiences of procedures at the services they use and gave similar responses.

Nonetheless, respondents did not always suggest that the characters in the risk perception vignettes should avoid all inter-personal contact. Liz states that she likes to be touched with affection by her support workers sometimes, but they never touch her like the support worker in Vignette 2 touches the woman she works for. Respondents found the most scope for interpretation in Vignette 1, where a friend gives Jill an unexpected embrace. Sue states: 'He shouldn't do that really, should he? Unless she wants that. Like, she wants to ask him to do it. That is different innit it?' Tyler similarly initially says Jill should tell John to stop, 'but if she does like it, if it's one of those unexpected things: "Uh-I-didn't-expect-that-but-I-like-you-too-type-thing", then it's OK.'

Even the third vignette, which describes how Frank meets a stranger, could be seen as an opportunity. Although almost all of the group were adamant that Frank should not follow the stranger to his home, there were three exceptions. Leanne initially suggests that Frank should not go with him, but then she asserts, if Frank wants to get to know the new person he should ask his mother whether this is safe. Ryan suggests that Frank could take some safety precautions before attempting to get to know the man:

He should get his address and get a friend round with him later, so he's not on his own. That 'let's listen to music' could lead to something else... Like on nude...eh, photos. Rather than doing it straight away, just going in, he should say: 'Oh, I'll have your address and I come in a few days. We'll listen to music.' He should take his carer with him, or somebody he relies on that can be with him, so nothing goes off.

These are excellent coping strategies. They ensure that Leanne and Ryan are safe. At the same time they are open to get to know new people and will not entirely distrust every new person they meet.

There were no significant differences between the answers of male and female respondents and those of individuals with different impairments. The majority (26 of 29) were able to anticipate risk and to plan actions to combat it. The fact that some people were able to see interactions as potential opportunities, yet only when they were wanted by both parties and only if some safety precautions were taken, demonstrates that they are able to appreciate the complexity of social relationships.

I was surprised by the sample's high levels of hypothetical risk perception, which presents a stark contrast to the assumptions of low levels of self-defence skills made by adult protection policies (Association of Directors of Social Services 2005; Department of Health 2000). By hypothetical risk perception I mean the ability to identify risk in fictitious scenarios. Individuals' responses to actual unsought sexual approaches will be different to their theoretical responses, because we do not always act as we say we would. Even some non-disabled women who are subjected to domestic violence and wish to break away from their partner can find it difficult to escape, due to the emotional impact of the violence and the power relations within which it occurs (e.g. Mullender 1996). Respondents who can identify risk in the safe and detached space of an interview may therefore not recognise it when it occurs in the context of existing relationships. Those who described how they would exercise assertiveness may find that they lack the power to do this in the event of an actual attack, in the context of an existing relationship. Nonetheless, in these cases risk would not be caused by the individual's lack of awareness. Instead it would arise from a particular social context.

The subsequent section provides further evidence for the risk management skills of respondents. The accounts of those who spoke about the ways in which they had dealt with actual threats of violence are explored.

Preventing and reporting violence

Not all of the respondents in this study have been exposed to potentially violent incidents. It is therefore difficult to quantify what proportion would be able to prevent violence in real life. This is further complicated by the fact that an individual's reaction to an unsought sexual approach is influenced by situational factors, as discussed above. Consequently, a person who has successfully protected themselves in one situation may not be able to do so in another. Nonetheless, in addition to those respondents who have described incidents of sexual violence from which they could not escape (see Chapter 3), a further 11 participants spoke about actual hazardous or violent incidents and the ways in which they have prevented and reported them.

Rachel states she would dial 999 if anyone harassed her and she has done this in the past, when her ex-partner was verbally aggressive towards her. She was alone with him when he shouted at her. She felt unsafe and called the police, much to the annoyance of the manager of her support service, who told me that the incident was not 'serious enough' for this. However, what matters is that Rachel sought help when she felt unsafe and that she could no longer control the situation. The manager's reaction may further confirm the suggestion that there is an increased tolerance for violence within service settings (Jenkins *et al.* 2008), an issue that was already touched upon in Chapter 4.

Emma feels uncomfortable when a man who uses her support agency touches her. He had done this the morning of the interview:

> He keeps coming close to me. … I feel a bit uncomfortable. … He did, he grabbed hold of…that's why I went out to [staff] [and told her about it]. … He just grabbed me sides there. … Every time I'm with him he just makes me feel uncomfortable, because I know what he's gonna do.

Emma identifies this invasion into her personal space as unwanted. She later describes that she avoids being close to this man, to protect herself. When she feels unable to deal with a situation she asks a member of staff for help.

Josie tells me that once 'a lad tried to get hold of my boobs, so I kicked him'. She goes on to explain that the 'lad' was another user of her day centre. Her intervention was effective. He did not try to touch her again. Mary tells me that one of her male friends touches her knee sometimes. She says this is OK because she likes him, but it would not be acceptable for other people to do that: 'They'd just get my elbow!' These participants are clear about their personal space and the actions they would take or have taken in case of an unwanted intrusion.

Some respondents spoke about incidents of violence in their families. This is not a unique experience for people with learning difficulties. Barnett, Miller-Perrin and Perrin (2005) outline that family violence affects individuals across the life span, from child physical, sexual and emotional violence to courtship violence and date rape, violence amongst spouses and violence against older adults. Like violence in institutional settings, violence within the family occurs behind closed doors, surrounded by 'thick walls of secrecy' (McCain 2006, p.vii). Reporting may be hindered by shame (McCain 2006), lack of access to the outside world (McCarthy and Thompson 1996), fear of the violator or dependency and disempowerment (Mencap 2001). However, some individuals have successfully overcome these barriers and prevented or reported violence and managed risk themselves.

Josie, who is in her late sixties, used to live with her sister. She says that her sister was beating her. She sought help, which resulted in her moving out:

> I told me carer at work [day centre]. And then they told me if I wanted to move I could move out of that flat... Cause it was my, on my own, my decision to move out of the flat.

Mary used to live with her nephew, who was physically and emotionally violent and exploited her financially:

> Many times I was locked in a room all day and all night. ... I had a bucket [to go to the toilet]. And...he's taken all the money off me. He wouldn't let me have any money, unless I asked him for it and he'd be watching over while I had that...

One day Mary went to tell her social worker: 'They moved me straight away. Because I think they'd actually, sensed there's something wrong.'

Mary's and Josie's self-referrals are somewhat unusual. Self-referrals have been reported to account for only 4 per cent of referrals for adult protection (Mansell *et al.* 2009). As outlined earlier, Rachel, too, reports that she called the police when her ex-boyfriend was violent towards her. Of these three incidents only Mary's case resulted in an official adult protection procedure. In other words: Rachel's and Josie's pursuit of protection would not be included in the official statistics. It is therefore possible that individuals actively seek protection themselves far more frequently than statistics suggest, which contradicts assumptions of helplessness.

This is especially true if the accounts of those who sought support informally and those who managed the threat of violence themselves are included. As stated earlier in this chapter, Salina, for example, ended a relationship with a boyfriend who tried to financially exploit her. Emma immediately approached a member of staff after the other service user touched her. Peter stopped attending an activity group because he felt threatened by another man (see Chapter 4).

Mary currently manages her relationship with her nephew on her own. She moved out from his home over seven years ago. These days she stays with him occasionally, when she visits a friend who lives in the area. I ask Mary whether she is scared that he will once more become violent towards her, but Mary states: 'I says to him: "Look, if I come and stay with you, you do not start on me! Do anything to me!" No. He hasn't! He's just been… polite.' In other words, Mary has set out her personal boundaries and she asserts some level of control. Her nephew knows that she is not issuing 'empty threats', as she has reported him in the past. Despite her negative experiences with him, Mary is keen to maintain contact. She acknowledges that her nephew is not an inherently 'bad' person. He has behaved badly in the past, but as long as she remains assertive with him she does not feel threatened.

It therefore appears that a number of people who are labelled with 'learning difficulties' can successfully manage threats of violence by themselves. Yet, we may not give them enough credit for doing so. Discussions often focus on the most severe case studies of violent attacks that resulted in adult protection procedures, which mostly apply to incidents in which individuals were unable to prevent violence themselves (e.g. Mencap *et al.* 2001).

Respondents in this study who reported or resisted violence knew of their right not to be violated or exploited. Resistance was prevalent amongst individuals from all age cohorts and amongst individuals with a range of impairments. Women spoke more readily about experiences of resistance, but the research sample was too small for generalisations to be drawn about the impact that gender has on resistance or on the willingness to talk about this topic. Overall, the above case studies contest assumptions of 'vulnerability'. It should be no surprise that many respondents subsequently revealed that this concept has little relevance to describe their daily experiences, as discussed below.

Respondents' understanding of the term 'vulnerability'

The assumption of 'vulnerability' often directs service interventions. Individuals should consequently understand what this term means in order to appreciate why the services they use are often organised around their protection. Only then will they be fully informed about the principles that underpin service delivery. However, there was much confusion amongst respondents when it came to define what 'vulnerable' means. Only eight of the interviewees were able to give a definition. The others did not know the term and were unaware that it is often applied to people with learning difficulties, with the exception of Emma:

I have heard of it, but I don't know…what it means. … [Care company manager] keeps saying that, ehm, the people with learning difficulties have got, they're vulnerable adults. I keep hearing that, but I don't know what it means.

Bill is one of the eight individuals who supplied a definition. He conceptualises 'vulnerability' as something negative and distances himself from the term. He states that it refers to 'people who are born like that'. Bob defines 'vulnerable' as 'someone who can't protect themselves easily'. He does not think that the term applies to him: 'I can take care of myself'. However, he says he was 'vulnerable' as a child, like all children, and adds that 'maybe some people with learning disabilities might need some help'. Chantal, too, conceptualises 'vulnerability' as a developmental stage she passed through:

My teachers and my mum used to tell me that I were vulnerable. Because I used to do everything what other people told me to and if, eh, a bloke come along I used to be more interested in the bloke. … I just switched off and not listen to anybody else, apart from him. I used to like, do everything what he used to tell me to do.

Chantal, who is in her early twenties now, states that she has grown out of being 'vulnerable' and that she has learned to look after herself as she has grown older. She states that she did not find it helpful to be labelled 'vulnerable' at the time and that she would have preferred her mother to talk to her about the things that were worrying her, instead of 'shouting from the top of the roofs that I was vulnerable'.

Georgina, in contrast, thinks that 'vulnerability' can be a helpful concept, because someone who cares about you can point out to you in which ways they think you are at risk. Mary initially asserts that the term 'vulnerable' only applies to a certain type of person:

Mary: Ah! I've heard of that, yeah! Cause eh, one of my friends, the girl that's Down's Syndrome…she…I don't think she'd know what's going on. Eh, I always say she's vulnerable to things happening.
      …

Andrea: What would you say if someone would say that to you?

Mary: What, that I was vulnerable?

Andrea: Yes.

Mary: In a sense…any person with learning difficulties is vulnerable… You know, if you don't want anybody to do anything…try'n get them away, but they would –, insist being, doing things to you. …

Andrea: Do you think that I am vulnerable?

Mary: If you were with, were anybody, strangers were, I think you would be vulnerable for people to...to go up and try'n touch you. ... It could actually be anybody.

On closer inspection Mary begins to recognise that 'vulnerability' can be applied to 'anybody'. In her view 'vulnerability' becomes an ordinary aspect of the human condition, as described by Beckett (2006) and Zola (1982) (see Chapter 2). Similarly Ryan described 'vulnerability' as:

somebody who is shy, not that they can't...speak up for themselves... Ehhh, old people, anybody really... It's not, it might not just be on one thing. It could be various. A new place they've gone to, where there's lots of people they've not met before: 'Who am I gonna meet? What are they gonna be like?' So you're a bit wary. ... Vulnerability is, it can cover everything really and any person.

This relates back to some of the difficulties that were discussed in Chapter 2. As 'vulnerability' is a vague concept, which is described differently by different authors, it could mean anything to anybody.

Britney was placed in a residential 'home' for her protection, because she was at immediate risk of violence and exploitation by a group of young people who had befriended her (see Chapter 4). Yet, following this incident her support system can be said to be almost 're-abusing' her by infringing her freedom and her rights to make independent choices. Britney's current 'home' environment resembles what Hingsburger (1995) would call a 'prison of protection', within which Britney is largely protected from mainstream society, relationships that may develop within it and independent decision-making. Britney is aware of the term 'vulnerability' and she has strong views about it:

It's saying that people with learning difficulties can't look after themselves and can't say: 'No.' But even people without learning difficulties might find it hard to say: 'No.' ... So really, we all should be in care. ... Why should these called-so normal people be allowed to get sexual abused and stay out in the community? If they need help they should be taken into residential care.

In other words, Britney suggests that risk of sexual violence is an inevitable risk in people's lives, no matter who they are. This is confirmed by the literature, as discussed in Chapter 2. Risk factors can consequently only be reduced and not removed. The discussions throughout this book have furthermore demonstrated that protection by containing individuals in segregated settings is ineffective. The aim of this book is therefore to explore a range of alternative ways in which risk may be reduced. Tyler suggests some solutions that would make people with learning difficulties less sexually 'vulnerable':

> I think with a person with a learning disability, I think like me, if they didn't get the proper education and stuff, they're gonna be very vulnerable. If they've got the proper education, they got told: this is a blow job. This is a, you know, they've got all the sexual phrases, you know. Blow job. Pussy. Clit. … If they knew all those things and they know what they said was right and what they said was wrong, you know, they'll be learning and they wouldn't be so vulnerable.

Tyler had limited sex education at residential school and only learned about the full variety of possible sexual practices, when he was in his early twenties. Lack of information prevented him from recognising the sexual violence he experienced as a teenager (see Chapter 3). He asserts that exposure to more precise information could therefore be an enabling factor, while protection from holistic information on sexuality leaves individuals exposed.

Assertiveness and self-defence skills: discussion

It emerges that most respondents were unaware that the term 'vulnerability' is often applied to people with learning difficulties. Most of the ones who were familiar with the term either excluded themselves from the definition or they viewed 'vulnerability' more broadly as an attribute that affects all humans. 'Vulnerability' consequently does not appear to be a relevant or helpful concept that enables these adults to understand their particular situation better. This is perhaps no surprise, as most interviewees have demonstrated that they are not entirely 'vulnerable'.

On the contrary, the accounts presented in this chapter indicate that many people with learning difficulties are indeed aware of the risk of sexual violence and that they can play an active role in directing and regaining their own protection. Yet, it was also noted that accounts of everyday resistance are hardly acknowledged by adult protection statistics, which only reflect those cases of individuals who were unable to protect themselves and who subsequently received professional interventions.

In most cases of actual unwanted sexual intrusions respondents described that risky situations are best handled by asking others for help. Josie's account of simply 'kicking' the intruder was thus unusual. However, when individuals seek to access support they may encounter barriers. As shown in Chapter 4, during everyday interactions some were labelled as 'drama queens' or 'challenging' by staff. This may mean that they cannot rely on being listened to when they need to report a problem. The resources that individuals would need in order to direct their own protection consequently become unavailable. This might be the reason why Rachel sought help outside of her segregated world when she called the police. However, when they arrived the support staff intervened. Rachel's care manager did not consider the verbal attack that Rachel had experienced to be serious enough for a police investigation. Despite the considerable distress that her ex-partner had caused, charges were never pressed. Yet, Rachel continues to be upset by what has happened to her and is unable to find closure.

CONCLUSION

Self-advocacy and adopting a positive disability identity can increase individuals' confidence and with this their readiness to be assertive. The disability movement, which operates on the exo- and macrosystem, can provoke positive change for individuals. Yet, those who remain isolated within segregated settings are less likely to benefit.

This chapter explored the potential benefits of independent living. Respondents who live independently had a higher level of choice and control compared to those who live with family guardians or in group settings. All of them received formal or informal support, but individuals themselves directed the ways in which support should be provided to them. The resulting expertise in everyday decision-making has the potential to increase self-determination competences.

It was also highlighted that people with learning difficulties are not the dependent, passive receivers of 'care' that they are often assumed to be. Individuals demonstrated their ability to take on responsibility for themselves and for others. However, the vital role that people with learning difficulties may have within their family networks should be more openly acknowledged. This could modify cultural assumptions of passivity and 'vulnerability' and enable us to recognise the potential of people with learning difficulties to exercise autonomy.

Respondents who had the opportunity to do so indicated that engaging in consenting sexual experiences enhanced their understanding of sex and sexuality. They became more confident in articulating what they wanted. When a relationship broke down they generally tended to settle for a new partner who they felt cared more for them than the previous one. Even negative experiences enabled respondents to increase their sexual self-awareness. Some did however need help to break up a relationship.

This shows that, even when individuals engage in sexual relationships independently, their support networks in the micro- and exosystem remain crucial.

This chapter demonstrated that people with learning difficulties have an unexpectedly high ability to exercise resistance and autonomy, which contrasts with commonly held assumptions about their sexual 'vulnerability' (e.g. Department of Health 2000, 2008b; Mencap *et al.* 2001). Male and female individuals of a range of ages, who live in various settings, were mostly able to identify risk, even if they lived in overly protective environments or had limited information on sex and sexuality. As outlined in Chapter 2, risk is a speculative concept. Individuals do not necessarily need to know exactly what they have to fear. Even an individual who has a limited understanding of sex and sexuality may be able to anticipate unsought intrusions and violence. Most respondents in this study thus identified unsought and unwanted touch as potentially risky features. This leads to the conclusion that these individuals understand the concept of risk.

This may not mean that individuals will identify and stop an unwanted sexual approach in real life, as they will experience actual approaches within their own social setting differently to the fictitious ones they discussed. However, this deviation is caused by complex social factors, such as power relationships, rather than individual factors. In other words, 'vulnerability' would not lie with the lack of skill of a person who is unable to defend themself, but rather with the social situation. Preventative work must therefore focus on encouraging the fictitious resistance and resilience that was demonstrated by respondents to become reality in their everyday lives.

This chapter furthermore presented evidence that demonstrated that over a third of the respondents had indeed successfully managed the risk of violence in their real lives. Yet, it was argued that such case studies receive limited attention in policy development. The accounts of those who have managed risk can inform our understanding of factors and social processes that enhanced their risk management capacity. These will be further explored in Chapter 6.

Conclusion

People with learning difficulties are often described as particularly 'vulnerable' to sexual violence. However, such constructions and representations are based on an essentialist view of 'vulnerability', which arises from categorical group membership or labelling. Rather than assuming the existence of inherent 'vulnerability', this book explored some of the mechanisms that potentially create and reinforce reduced sexual competence and a limited ability and readiness to self-defend. It was outlined how the label 'learning difficulties', or the more frequently used label 'learning disabilities', shapes the everyday experiences of 12 men and 17 women living in England. An ecological model approach was utilised to illustrate these processes.

The aim was furthermore to draw attention to the complexity of the social circumstances within which sexual violence occurs. Similarities between the routine experiences of respondents and the circumstances surrounding sexual violence were discussed. They will be further elucidated in this chapter. Moreover, it was examined to what extent the participants in the study on which this book is based can be considered to be 'vulnerable'. Their knowledge of sex and sexuality and their ability to exercise self-determination in their everyday, as well as sexual, lives was explored. Finally, the ways in which people with learning difficulties can and in fact have increased their resistance to sexual violence were discussed.

The sampling strategy of this research did not specifically target survivors of sexual violence. The prevalence of self-defence skills was assessed on a general sample of adults with learning difficulties, rather than exclusively amongst those who are known to have been unable to protect themselves in the past. This has the advantage that findings can be generalised to the whole population of people who are labelled with 'mild' to 'moderate' learning difficulties living in England, although, due to limitations to the research sample, they may not be generalised to individuals who have 'severe' or 'profound' labels (World Health Organization 1996).

It should be noted that those who have experienced sexual violence are not necessarily more 'vulnerable' than those who have not. The difference between the two groups is that the former has definitely encountered a violent assault, while the latter may have never been exposed to immediate risk. Or they have fought off such a threat. This would indeed demonstrate the presence of self-defence skills.

This study was set against a backdrop of rapid policy change. Data collection had concluded before the publication of *Valuing People Now* (Department of Health 2009b). New multi-agency guidance on safeguarding 'vulnerable' adults (Department of Health 2010a) was still in draft at the time when writing was completed. Ongoing research that evaluates the effect that such changes have on the lives of individuals is therefore crucial. Nonetheless, this book presents some important findings, which can be applied to different policy contexts in a variety of geographic locations and across time. For instance, observations about the social creation of risk, as well as recommendations for interventions to reduce it, are universally applicable.

The first part of this chapter provides an overview of the enabling and disabling processes that were identified by this study. It also summarises the extent to which respondents can be understood to be 'vulnerable'. The second part will make suggestions for future practice. It will point out how social environments would have to change in order to maximise people's ability to self-defend.

CONCEPTUALISING 'VULNERABILITY' AND RISK

Within the last decade an increasing awareness of sexual violence against people with learning difficulties prompted calls for changes to the sex offending law (e.g. Mencap *et al.* 2001), which were implemented by the new Sexual Offences Act (HMSO 2003). Professionally led adult protection work has become an issue of central concern for practitioners and UK government bodies (Association of Directors of Social Services 2005; Department of Health 2000, 2008b, 2009a). These are important processes, which reflect an increased commitment to enforce the right of people with learning difficulties to protection from dehumanising treatment and violence.

At the same time this study was undertaken against a background of increasing policy commitment to promoting the legal and civil rights, independence, choices and inclusion of people with learning difficulties (Department of Health 2001, 2009b). These two policy areas can at times contradict each other. The task to balance a person's rights to independence against an obligation to protect can become problematic.

A focus on risk may at times neglect an appraisal of the potential of individuals with learning difficulties to act autonomously and to manage hazards independently. Consequently this book aims to point to the *abilities* of people with learning difficulties and to *disabling* social processes that hinder them. This section begins with a summary of social processes that impact upon risk. Then it is shown how many of them are connected. It is explained why they can be understood as occurring systematically, as part of a continuum of violence. Finally, the extent to which respondents in this study were found to be sexually 'vulnerable' is discussed.

Utilising the ecological approach

The conceptual basis for this study involved the development of a new ecological model (see also Hollomotz 2009), which enables an appreciation of the complex interactions between individuals and their environments in the formation of risk. This makes a much broader examination of risk possible, which extends beyond assumptions of individual 'vulnerability'. The ecological model enables us to identify the underlying social processes that are involved in the formation of risk. Some of the factors that were examined in this study are summarised in Figure 6.1.

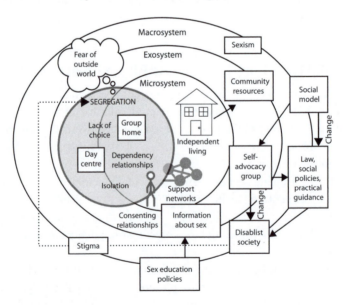

Figure 6.1 Social factors in the ecological model

The ecological model identifies three distinct systems within an individual's environment: the microsystem, which is an individual's immediate 'home' environment; the exosystem, which is the environment within which the 'home' is based, usually referred to as the community; and finally the macrosystem, the wider society and culture, including laws and social policies. The individual is situated at the centre of this model (this is not illustrated in Figure 6.1, but it is shown in Figure 2.1). Social processes in the three systems are in constant interaction with each other, as well as with the individual.

Chapter 2 presented evidence from the literature, which suggests that an individual requires a range of skills in order to defend against sexual violence. These were summarised as sexual competence and self-determination skills. The first group of skills is comprised of a good level of knowledge about sexuality, possible sexual practices and of one's own sexual preferences. This knowledge will enable individuals to identify sexual approaches and to distinguish wanted from unwanted ones. They must furthermore be aware of the possibility of sexual violence. An understanding of one's right to resist sexual pressure is also essential. The second group of skills determines whether a person will be able to resist in the event of an actual unsought sexual approach. Necessary skills include an ability to make decisions, to say 'no' and to communicate that decision, as well as a readiness to speak up for oneself and to be assertive, which is linked to self-esteem. This book has explored how these sexual self-defence skills, as well as situational risk factors, are shaped by social processes within the micro-, exo- and macrosystem. A range of patterns emerged. These are summarised below.

The formation of risk to sexual violence through constant interaction between ecological systems is not exclusive to people with learning difficulties. All individuals in a given society may be exposed to increased risk at times. Particular risk factors have also been exposed in respect to, for example, women and children (e.g. Garbarino *et al.* 1997; Kelly 1988). These risk factors also affect populations of disabled people, such as disabled children and disabled women. In order to highlight how social processes that occur in mainstream society may at times further aggravate the risks to which disabled people are exposed, this book briefly discussed a gender-related risk factor.

It was shown that assumptions about women's sexual 'availability', which may occur in societies where patriarchal power imbalances continue to exist, further increase risk. Men may feel as if they have a right to gaze at and judge women's bodies. This sense of ownership may disempower women who are subjected to such attention and cause estrangement from their bodies. Women in this study also spoke about changing the way they dress to avoid such attention. Instead of reporting the men who made sexually suggestive comments, which the women perceived as invasive, they sought the blame within themselves, with this accepting gendered power imbalances. However, self-blame can act as a barrier to reporting sexual violence (Sable *et al.* 2006).

Chapter 3 explored the formation of sexual knowledge amongst respondents. It emphasised that knowledge is a direct outcome of the information respondents have received. Lack of knowledge is therefore not solely caused by an individual's inability to comprehend or retain information. It is also a socially determined risk factor that can be reduced if people with learning difficulties are given comprehensible information in accessible formats, such as by means of plain language, concrete references and direct experience. However, particularly respondents in the older age group (40 and over) have often received no formal sex education. When they did receive information this was on occasion partially inaccurate. It was at times value-driven and indoctrinated the view that sex was 'rude'.

The fact that all of the younger people in this sample had received sex education, even though they attended a variety of schools in different exosystems, indicates that changes to sex education policies on the macrosystem have systematically affected these generational cohorts. This example illustrates that the macrosystem can have an immediate impact, even on individuals who live isolated lives in protective settings. However, most of those respondents who have received some form of sex education did not receive a comprehensive level of information. This leaves individuals at risk, because they are not adequately prepared to understand the full range of possible sexual acts that may be proposed to them.

Being in love had an affirmative impact on individuals' sense of self. Participants felt a sense of belonging, even when their relationships were fictitious. However, a number of respondents pointed out barriers that interfered with their real-life relationships. These include family members and support workers who may not accept that a person with learning difficulties has a right to experience sexual relationships. Others reported practical difficulties that hindered them from seeing their partner, such as a lack of staff to facilitate contact.

However, it was also shown that respondents' consenting relationships were not always entirely positive. This may explain why staff and family members were eager to protect individuals from them. Nonetheless, even negative experiences enabled individuals to familiarise themselves with their sexual likes and dislikes. Consenting sexual exploration can therefore enable understanding of sexual acts. Nevertheless, being able to refer to a support network was at times vital to allow individuals to protect themselves from relationships that they no longer experienced as positive.

In all cases of actual incidents of sexual violence that were described by respondents a significant factor was that the violator was a person in a position of trust, who had access to the individual they violated. All of the incidents took place in segregated or family environments. This confirms the claim that protection by containing individuals in such settings is ineffective (Hingsburger 1995; McCarthy and Thompson 1996), as the possibility of the presence of violators can never be removed completely. Conversely, the particular social circumstances within segregated settings increase risk, as discussed below.

All of the respondents in this study experienced segregation at some point in their lives. The daily reality within segregated environments is often characterised by a range of distinctive processes, as was indicated in Figure 6.1. For instance, individuals were given insufficient opportunities to make choices and to exercise self-determination. Instead, they were encouraged to make tokenistic selections from a pre-arranged 'menu'. Many realised that their 'choices' were restricted and they did not feel that they had any real control. Such disempowerment increases risk. In order to preserve a readiness to be self-determined a person needs to believe that change is possible and that their choices will have immediate consequences. An individual who has become accustomed to choosing from a range of pre-set options may not think that standing up for themselves when threatened with an unsought sexual approach is possible, unless this option is presented to them on their pre-arranged 'menu'.

In Figure 3.1 it was illustrated that segregated systems may prevent social intercourse with the 'outside', even if an individual is at times assisted to access resources in their locality. As long as interactions within the exosystem are managed and determined by others on the person's behalf they remain within a 'protective bubble' of known social contacts. Consequently they do not have free access to their exosystem. They remain within what could be conceptualised as an extended microsystem, as they never leave their allegedly 'safe' habitual social spaces. Figure 6.1 illustrated this through the reinforced boundaries of segregated systems. Individuals within miss out on the benefits that arise from community inclusion, such as making choices that have not been pre-selected, taking on responsibilities and control of their own lives, as well as taking on ordinary social roles, such as that of a customer in a shop, leisure facility, bar or pub. Many respondents were furthermore fearful of the outside world. They accepted that they were at a higher risk of a range of external dangers, such as road hazards, verbal assault, theft and violence. As a result they more readily conformed to the particular treatment they received within segregated settings.

In the absence of external social contacts and friendships many respondents in this study invited emotional intimacy with their support workers. Some were explicit about their eagerness to please, which can significantly impair their readiness to exercise resistance in that relationship. At times some support workers expressed their superiority by labelling individuals as 'attention seeking' or 'drama queens'. Such labels prevent individuals from being listened to, which may result in reports of sexual violence being ignored, particularly when the person who seeks to be heard uses unconventional, non-verbal means of communicating distress.

Even within segregated environments, many respondents endured bullying and impairment-specific name-calling. This indicates that the stigma associated with disability, which occurs in the wider society and which is, for example, reflected by the popular media (Mitchell and Snyder 2001), affects individuals within protective environments, too. The barriers posed by segregation will not block out all influences from the macrosystem. Nonetheless the exo- and microsystem are closer to the individual and can thus have a greater impact on shaping a person's experiences. This explains why many respondents are continually disempowered within 'home' and day service settings, despite a recent change of policy rhetoric on the macrosystem, which seeks to promote more choice.

Those individuals who lived independently had generally more control. For instance, they were able to choose with whom they wanted to live and how they would like to spend their time. They directed when and how support should be provided to them and they were more able to access community resources and networks. However, this flexibility was also present in the daily lives of a few individuals who lived with family members or within more 'traditional' service structures, because they were encouraged to lead inclusive lives. Group homes and family environments do therefore not necessarily have to be segregated systems. Younger respondents were more likely to benefit from more enabling practices within their families, which indicates that everyday life is changing for this generational cohort. This is likely to be influenced by a shift towards independent living principles. These were first put forward by disability rights advocates and they are more recently reflected in changes to social policies on the macrosystem.

Forming a positive disability identity, and with this increasing the readiness to speak up for oneself, continues to be a challenge for many people with learning difficulties who remain exposed to unequal opportunities and different social circumstances compared to non-disabled people. In the following it is explained why these processes can be seen to form a continuum.

A continuum of violence

This section explores the extent to which violence against people with learning difficulties can be understood as occurring systematically. In this context it is useful to consider Kelly's (1988) feminist conceptualisation of a continuum of violence, which was briefly introduced in Chapter 3. She asserts that: 'The manifestation of men's gender power through the routine use of aggression against women is connected to "non-routine" assaults, such as rape, which are extensions of more commonplace intrusions' (Kelly 1988, p.27). Men and women with learning difficulties are similarly affected by an imbalance of power, which is routinely exerted by non-disabled helpers, professionals and wider macro-forces. Examples of respondents' oppression and exploitation were outlined throughout this book and summarised in the previous section. In line with Kelly's (1988) suggestion these processes can be seen to be forming a continuum, as illustrated in Figure 6.2.

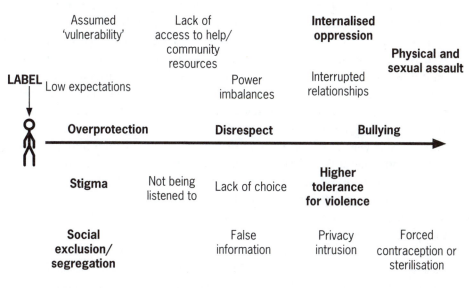

Figure 6.2 A continuum of violence

The reader should note that this continuum is not hierarchical. That means that it does not intend to indicate that, for example, not being listened to has a less damaging impact than bullying. Both can cause severe harm. The continuum merely suggests that one act is perhaps likely to be more frequently perpetrated than the other. It seeks to draw attention to the fact that boundaries between incidents of mundane intrusions, derogatory treatment and violence are blurred, which can make it difficult for an individual to distinguish that which is seen to be 'acceptable' as part of the everyday from that which crosses the line and is seen, even by others and the law, as an act of violence.

The continuum only applies to individuals who are *labelled* with learning difficulties, as the label – an acknowledgement of the individual's deviation from non-disabled norms – causes differential treatment. This became evident in the case of a woman who was labelled when she was in her early thirties. The processes on the continuum only started at that point. Beforehand she and her partner lived independently in the community. Now she is told that she requires support with a range of daily living tasks, which restricts her choices and independence (Emma, see Chapter 5). It is therefore not the impairment *per se* that determines whether individuals are subjected to specialised treatment. Instead, the cause lies with the social response to impairment labels.

Once an individual is labelled the continuum often starts with different, usually lower expectations. Individuals are assumed to be 'vulnerable' or less capable. When an individual makes a mistake, this is then often seen as caused by the impairment. For instance, if a woman with learning difficulties went on a shopping spree and purchased an item she could not afford, for instance an expensive pair of shoes, this might be accredited to her impairment. It might be assumed that she is unable to control her budget. If a non-disabled woman does the same, this may be attributed to compulsive buying or to her desire to seek or express an identity through consumption (Dittmar 2007). She may even receive positive feedback about her purchase. While there is nonetheless a wealth of help available for such women (Muller and Mitchell 2010), this would typically not result in the allocation of a support worker to accompany them on any future shopping excursion.

Moreover, many people with learning difficulties continue to be socially excluded within segregated settings. They are consequently often denied the benefits resulting from full citizen status. Their dominant identity becomes that of a person who is labelled with learning difficulties and who is 'vulnerable' and in need of special treatment. Assumed 'vulnerability' thus becomes a barrier that prevents individuals from negotiating their own risks and developing autonomy. Referring to the above cited example, they may not be given the opportunity to make mistakes in the first place.

Those living within segregated environments had difficulties accessing community resources, which also meant that they would have little opportunity to report an incident of violence externally. One respondent described that she once called 999 when she felt threatened by her ex-boyfriend. However, as soon as the police arrived they were dealt with by the staff. The woman was not given a chance to speak to the officers in private (Rachel, see Chapter 5). Lack of unsupervised access to community resources also makes it difficult to obtain contradicting evidence in the event of having received false or value-laden information about sexuality. One respondent, who had a sexual preference for the same sex, was unaware of positive approaches to homosexuality (e.g. Pride London 2010). He was led to conceptualise his desires as taboo, which impacted negatively on his sense of self and denied him his own sexual feelings (Paul, see Chapter 3).

Respondents described that staff would at times walk into a person's room without knocking, which crosses boundaries into a person's private space. Relationships with support workers were at times imbalanced and insufficient respect was given to other personal relationships that were of importance to a person. Some of those broke down due to a lack of support to facilitate contact. This furthers the socio-emotional reliance on support workers.

Some women were given contraceptives to which they had not fully consented. In some cases this meant that inadequate information on associated health risks was provided, but in two cases the women were explicit that they did not agree to this medical invasion at all. Professionals and carers controlling the fertility of women with learning difficulties must be seen as a physical intrusion into their private sphere.

Most participants understood that they were treated differently as a result of their label. The segregated environments in which a large proportion lived, worked and socialised provided few opportunities for self-realisation. As stated in the previous section, most individuals had also been bullied at school and for some the bullying continued at their day centres. Respondents reported that they have been addressed with derogatory terms by members of the general public. A significant proportion had internalised the oppression they were subjected to and understood that they were more likely to be targeted in such ways because of their impairments.

In many cases this led to a negative sense of self. Some expressed the wish to be 'normal' or to lead a 'normal' life. Others were in denial or battled against impairment effects in an attempt to pass as 'normal'. However, those who reject their impairment and struggle on without help may also deny themselves the opportunity to seek support when they are confused about or threatened with an unsought sexual approach. A reduced sense of self furthermore disables the readiness to stand up for oneself.

Some spoke about a higher tolerance for violence within segregated settings. Respondents reported that, when a person with learning difficulties perpetrated a violent offence against another user of their service, this did not lead to prosecution. Individuals were told to ignore the other person, because they 'cannot help it'. Yet, people with learning difficulties, too, have a responsibility not to physically, emotionally or sexually hurt others. Services that do not acknowledge this contradict their responsibility to protect users from harm. The way in which environments respond to reports of violence can thus further aggravate risk.

These were just a few examples of disabling, intrusive and violating processes that were described by respondents. They can indeed be envisaged as occurring systematically and as part of a continuum with boundaries that are unclear and shifting: privacy intrusions, having one's expressed wishes overruled, a lack of opportunities for self-fulfilment and being made to feel less worthy are processes that are often ingrained in disabled people's everyday lives. This makes it difficult for individuals to decide when the boundary between routine invasions and violence has been crossed, especially if they live, work and socialise in segregated environments that have a higher tolerance for violence compared to mainstream settings. Sexual violence can, as Kelly (1988) suggests, be seen as a mere extension on this continuum of habitual intrusions.

However, despite this exposure to a multitude of disabling processes, it would be false to assume that all people with learning difficulties consequently lack the skills needed to defend against sexual violence. The subsequent section summarises the sexual knowledge and assertiveness skills that were demonstrated by the research sample. It is also considered whether it is useful to conceptualise a person's particular level of risk in terms of 'vulnerability'.

'Vulnerability' amongst the research sample

Despite the absence of, or inferior levels of, sex education, the majority of respondents (over 80%) had a basic understanding of sex and sexuality. They were able to give descriptions of the mechanics of sexual behaviour. All of the respondents who answered this question could name a comprehensible term for their own sexual body parts (penis/vagina/breasts/chest − not including testicles) and three quarters could name those of the opposite sex, which implies that most would have some relevant vocabulary to describe sexual acts. Individuals who never received formal sex education had picked up information from television or from within their social environments, for example by overhearing conversations or through peer talk. Half of the respondents were aware of their right to privacy. They knew that their personal space should not be invaded; however, some were also acutely aware that this was not always respected by others. Knowledge about STIs and their prevention on the other hand was generally low, except amongst some of the younger respondents. Yet, it was argued that such knowledge is not directly relevant to enable individuals to identify or report an unsought sexual approach.

A third of respondents believed that all sex was 'rude' or 'bad'. This view had been indoctrinated by biased information about sex and sexuality. It induced guilt and shame. As a result only half of the respondents made a clear distinction between wanted and unwanted sex. This can create hazardous environments. For example, individuals who are taught that all inter-personal sexual contact is 'bad' may not distinguish between consenting sexual activity and violence, should they nonetheless seek a sexual outlet. Other users of services are the largest group of perpetrators against people with learning difficulties (Brown, Stein and Turk 1995; McCarthy and Thompson 1996). Value-laden sex education and a prohibition of positive sexual outlets will therefore increase the likelihood of violence taking place within service settings and with this affect the people who use them. While this increases situational risk, it is unlikely to aggravate the particular level of 'vulnerability' of the person who views all sexual contact as taboo. Although it has a potentially detrimental effect on their personal and sexual relationships, this mindset could help a person to identify any unsought sexual approach as unwanted.

This research also asked to what extent people with learning difficulties are able to exercise autonomy in their everyday lives. Even though this study retrieved a wealth of data on self-determination, this question is difficult to answer. Chapter 4 illustrated that choice-making by people with learning difficulties who live in protective environments is often hindered or restricted to a limited menu of options. Since these individuals are not free to make unrestricted choices in their daily lives, it is difficult to say whether they would be able to make autonomous choices if they were given the opportunity to do so. However, the seven respondents who lived independently demonstrated that they could make independent decisions and selections. This could suggest that people with learning difficulties can become competent at making choices if they are given the support and opportunities to do so.

Sometimes people who were living independently made choices that would not always be considered sensible. One young man, for instance, preferred to spend his money on video games, rather than on smart clothing, an option that was preferred by his mother (Tyler, see Chapter 5). Yet, as long as a person is aware of the consequences of their less sensible choice (e.g. they might have to wear unfashionable, faded or damaged items) they would be considered to have capacity to make this decision under the Mental Capacity Act (HMSO 2005b).

Disabled people have often been described as a 'burden' to those they live with (Dalley 1988; Finch and Groves 1980). The concept 'vulnerability' furthermore implies that they are passive and in particular need of protection. Yet, the findings from this study suggest that people with learning difficulties are anything but passive. Respondents have demonstrated that they can be proactive social actors when this is encouraged or when others require them to adopt such roles. A third of the respondents had lived or are currently living with a disabled relative or a relative over the age of 65 who requires some assistance. When their parents grew older or acquired an impairment the offspring with learning difficulties who had not moved on from the family home often played a more central role in supporting them than their non-disabled siblings. In some cases, this vital support ensured that their parents could remain living in the community. Their role as 'carer' was however hardly acknowledged.

Almost all of the respondents in this study have furthermore demonstrated the cognitive ability to stop unwanted sexual approaches. In fictitious examples they were able to identify risks and to distinguish them from social opportunities, to stop an assault and to seek help. They had a clear understanding of their right not to be violated. A third of the respondents furthermore described how they had successfully reported or prevented violent incidents in their real lives, which indicates that people with learning difficulties can play an active role in directing and regaining their own protection. This is perhaps a surprising finding. Self-referrals usually account for a mere fraction of referrals for adult protection.

In summary, findings of a good level of basic knowledge on sexuality and sexual violence, as well as the substantial presence of resistance skills, lead to the conclusion that for many of the respondents the accusation that they are inherently sexually 'vulnerable' is not accurate. This departure from existing assumptions may be caused by variations in sampling strategies. While concerns about adult protection arise from reports about severe cases of violence against individuals who are in need of protection, such as the Jenkins case (Brammer 2005; Mencap et al. 2001), this study drew on a general sample of people with learning difficulties. It did not specifically target survivors of violence. This meant that the accounts of individuals who had successfully exercised resistance as well could be included.

A further explanation for these unexpected findings could be that respondents' accounts of real-life resistance related to commonplace experiences that do not usually receive a lot of research attention. Such accounts are not acknowledged by adult protection statistics. Those only reflect severe cases of violence against individuals who were unable to protect themselves and who received professional interventions. Many of the respondents in this study never had to be referred.

Nonetheless, individuals who possess a good level of self-defence skills may at times find themselves in a 'vulnerable' situation. Inherent 'vulnerability' and situational 'vulnerability' are however two different matters. The former would only apply to selected individuals, while the latter could affect anyone. As Beckett (2006) asserts, all human beings can be 'vulnerable' at some points in their lives. People who have been labelled with learning difficulties tend to find themselves disproportionately affected by 'vulnerability'-creating situations, such as isolation and dependency relationships. 'Vulnerability' then becomes a self-fulfilling prophecy, as the assumption of inherent 'vulnerability' gives rise to the creation of situational 'vulnerability'.

It may be questioned whether 'vulnerability', as it is used in contemporary policy-writing, is at all a helpful concept. The applicability of the term is further challenged by the fact that a significant proportion of respondents were unaware of it. Those who did know what it meant mostly excluded their adult selves from the definition. 'Vulnerability' was consequently not seen as a relevant or helpful concept that enabled people to understand their situation better.

Initially the research advisors also did not understand what 'vulnerability' meant; although they were aware that professionals use the term. Yet, when I translated the term to imply 'helplessness' or 'defencelessness', individuals felt offended by it. They were adamant that they are not helpless. The group then summarised their views in the following statement: 'Using the word "vulnerability" is like talking to our backs, because we don't understand that word. No jargon! You should talk to our faces and not to our back!' The advisors felt that professionals' use of words that many people with learning difficulties find hard to comprehend will hinder individuals' understanding and with this they become unable to challenge what is being said about them.

This research therefore suggests that 'vulnerability' is not a helpful concept. It focuses on the individual, which distracts attention away from wider social processes that increase risk. It furthermore neglects an evaluation of situational risk factors. In the following section, some alternative approaches to risk prevention are outlined.

RECOMMENDATIONS ARISING FROM THE RESEARCH

Contemporary Britain is a 'risk society', in which risk is continually assessed, managed and monitored (Beck 1992). However, all activities in the social world carry an element of risk. Adult citizens thus have a right to take risks, to make mistakes and to reflect on such experiences. Nevertheless, disabled people are often excluded from full adult social status and its associated rights and responsibilities (Priestley 2003). Concern about their heightened risk is often expressed through the label 'vulnerability'. Like risk, this concept is initially a mere social construct: we believe that people with learning difficulties possess a range of characteristics that make them more likely to experience sexual violence, which prompts us to intervene, in order to prevent harm. As a consequence the various risks to which they may be exposed are often managed by family members, support staff and professionals on their behalf.

A focus on inherent 'vulnerability' can become oppressive, as the only solution to such an approach would be to protect an individual. While protection by an outside body is of importance to all of us at some points in our lives, people with learning difficulties cannot be expected to rely solely on safeguarding by others. This would be disempowering, as it increases dependency on protectors, usually support staff and family carers. It would also be less effective than supporting a person to strengthen their own self-defences, as protective relationships themselves become easily exploitable. The immediate presence of the protector can furthermore not be guaranteed at all times. For instance, even in highly supervised environments individuals will inevitably be left to spend some time alone.

Preventative work should therefore aim to seek universalistic solutions. Universalistic solutions focus on changing the environment (Westcott and Cross 1996). They are situated in the macro-, exo- and microsystems and take the pressure for change off the individual and re-focus it on the environment. Universalistic solutions would, for instance, challenge power imbalances that are allowed to exist in a given society.

This book has highlighted repeatedly that changes on the macrosystem can have notable impacts on the lives of individuals, as they will work to re-shape exo- and microsystems as well. The law, social policies and practice guidelines can therefore play an important role in shaping the experiences of people with learning difficulties. However, it is often left up to those who are supporting people with learning difficulties on a daily basis to implement these changes and to use their own initiative. The following discussion consequently highlights in what ways changes to policy and day-to-day practice can increase the sexual competence and self-determination skills of people with learning difficulties.

Making sexuality information accessible

Access to holistic information about sex and sexuality is crucial to enable individuals to make more informed choices about their participation in proposed sexual acts. People with learning difficulties are often disadvantaged in their access to information from the popular media (due to information being presented in inaccessible formats), peers and support services (due to increased surveillance and segregation). These barriers need to be broken down.

Various practitioners have developed excellent resource packs for sex education, which feature accessible information (e.g. McCarthy and Thompson 1998; The Children's Learning Disability Nursing Team 2009). As with other topics, sex education for people with learning difficulties must be broader and more concrete than that for non-disabled individuals. This may include practical support and advice, which takes account of the fact that for some young people with learning difficulties this may be the only opportunity to explore these issues. Sex education for this group must therefore be even more comprehensive than that for non-disabled children.

Sex education must be non-judgemental and give instructions about all forms of available sexual practices, including homosexuality. This will have a number of positive effects on the reduction of risk of sexual violence. First, it will enable individuals to detect a wider range of unwanted sexual approaches. Second, if they are taught to distinguish 'good' and 'bad' sex in terms of consenting and forced participation, rather than with reference to the educator's value system, this will make distinctions between consenting sex and violence clearer for individuals. However, adults who have missed out on comprehensive sex education at school will not benefit from changes in today's school curriculum. Nonetheless, they should be offered support to increase their knowledge. It must not be assumed that sexuality is only of interest to younger people. Both older and younger respondents in this study saw it as an important topic.

A positive practice example is the sexual health service that was mentioned in the introduction. This mainstream service offered sex education courses for adults with learning difficulties. In comparison to sex education that is provided within segregated contexts, for example at college or at a day centre, this had the advantage that participants came to a new environment, where they could discuss sexuality with specially trained staff, who were experienced at putting individuals at ease when discussing sexuality. Talking to an allocated reference person about sexuality bypasses the embarrassment a person may feel when talking to their daily support staff about intimate concerns. Many respondents in the group training booked additional individual sessions to talk to sexual health workers about confidential issues. The training thus introduced individuals to a vital community resource and it was hoped that they would continue to access the service should they require it after they completed the course.

Although it took place in a segregated setting, the women's group at a day centre that was described in Chapter 3 is a further positive example. Here women were able to talk about body confidence, intimate health issues and sexuality. However, such group discussions are often not enough. Individuals should also be introduced to community-based resources, in order to become more confident at accessing these by themselves. This group showed participants how they can access bra fittings in lingerie departments, for example.

To further assist sexual exploration, adults with learning difficulties should have the option to access products and services from the sex industry that are legally available to non-disabled adults, if they choose to do so. Little is known about this sensitive subject and further research that reveals how this could be facilitated would be beneficial. This should particularly address concerns about informed consent.

A final point was raised about the prescription of hormonal contraception to women who were currently not sexually active. Such decisions should be considered with great care. Not only is the use of non-essential medication an invasion into women's privacy, but it can also have the unintended effect of removing a protective factor. The perceived risk of an unwanted pregnancy could put off a potential violator and consequently act to protect a woman. If all fails an actual pregnancy will help to detect that violence has taken place and it will provide genetic evidence that can lead to the perpetrator's prosecution under the Sexual Offences Act (HMSO 2003).

Enabling social and sexual relationships

Peer talk, sexual experience and exposure to mainstream society in general can further an individual's understanding of sexuality. Consenting sexual experiences will enable individuals to learn about various aspects of sexuality, for example by trying out sexual practices. Positive sexual experiences can enable a person to understand better how to distinguish these from negative ones, while being in love and being loved has a positive impact on an individual's sense of self.

Many respondents spoke about numerous preventative interventions, designed to address a range of risks, such as instructions about the clothes they should wear to avoid sexual attention or not being allowed to leave protective environments unaccompanied. However, such risk management may lead to self-fulfilling prophecies. For instance, a woman who is free to choose clothes that some may find 'sexually provocative' may receive more sexual attention. However, this may help her to become more aware of implicit sexual messages in social interactions and to become more confident at responding to them, either affirmatively or assertively, depending on her inclination. Risk will remain a central element in such interactions and as Rogers (2009) points out, a person may require support to manage it. Yet, if an individual is systematically shielded from risks the social construct of 'vulnerability' will become a socially created reality.

This research has shown that even negative experiences within consenting sexual relationships can be important learning opportunities. Individuals should therefore be supported to lead consenting relationships. This suggestion is in line with the Human Rights Act (HMSO 1998, Article 8(1)) and the UN Convention on the Rights of Persons with Disabilities (United Nations 2006, Article 22). It is furthermore backed by *Valuing People Now* (Department of Health 2009b). However, this strategy does not stipulate how this should be done. More specific policy instructions should suggest ways in which services could deliver these aims. Some regional authorities in the UK have developed relationship policies for this purpose (e.g. NHS Lothian 2004). These policies are part of the macrosystem, but they could potentially have an immediate impact on the services that are used by individuals.

Support with sexual relationships should include practical help, like enabling an individual's contact with their partner, support to access sexual health and family planning services, as well as relationship advice. Furthermore, opportunities to be private must be created in the everyday lives of people with learning difficulties. For example, The Speakup Committee recommend that individuals who live in residential group settings should be allowed privacy with their partner in their bedrooms (Hollomotz and The Speakup Committee 2009).

Individuals who wish to meet new friends or a potential partner should be enabled to do so. For instance, they could be supported to access leisure, education and work facilities. However, mere physical presence in the community will not enable individuals to meet new people. Staff should allow individuals to interact with others, even when this seems to be casual everyday contact, like buying a drink in a bar. Individuals with speech impairments in particular should not be excluded from such vital practice at, and opportunities for, interaction with others. Another option would be to access dating services. As an alternative to mainstream agencies Stars in the Sky (2010) was set up especially for people with learning difficulties. The agency implements additional precautions, such as the chaperoning of dates. Although not all people with learning difficulties will prefer such a segregated service, this does add to the list of options.

A further topic that was only marginally addressed by this study is the community re-integration of people with learning difficulties who have sexually offended. Further research in this area could highlight examples of good practice and identify difficulties, which could inform future practice. This is an important area for exploration, as an appropriate level of support has the potential to increase individuals' quality of life. Supporting an individual to find legal sexual outlets may furthermore limit the risk of re-offence and with this reduce risk within service settings.

Towards social inclusion

In many societies (macrosystem) within which it continues to be acceptable to segregate marginalised groups who do not conform to a given social norm. Within segregated settings friendships are often not sufficiently respected and dependency on support workers is nurtured. Segregation has many negative consequences for an individual's ability to self-defend, as summarised earlier. Social inclusion, on the other hand, can make it more likely that individuals can access community resources. It has the potential to broaden their social networks, which can counteract isolated dependency relationships. Individuals who live independently are also more able to practice autonomous decision-making. These processes should therefore be encouraged to increase resistance.

A few respondents in this study conceptualised disability as a socially created condition, which led them to develop a more positive sense of self. Individuals had learned about social approaches through participation in self-advocacy groups, where they also learned to speak up for themselves. These groups can therefore be understood as potentially enabling mechanisms that can change a person's sense of self and increase their likelihood to exercise autonomy. Access to independent self-advocacy groups should therefore be supported.

Social inclusion and independent living for all disabled people are universalistic solutions. They require a major restructuring of the ways in which services, and indeed the entire macrosystem, work. These issues are much harder to resolve than attributing individual 'vulnerability' to marginalised groups and continuing to segregate them for their own 'protection'. However, they are crucial processes that have the potential to provoke genuine change, whereas segregation has been shown to be ineffective.

Enabling people to stop and report acts of violence

Self-determination is an acquired behaviour. Individuals need to feel in control before they can be expected to resist sexual violence. Accordingly, individuals must become experts at exercising self-determination in their everyday lives. Individuals must therefore be routinely allowed to choose beyond a restricted menu of pre-selected options. This will enable them to deal with unexpected and unfamiliar situations, as unsought sexual approaches also fall into this category. Choice places control with the individual. This can furthermore promote the development of a positive self-image and self-assertion, making it more likely that a person will stand up for themselves.

Many respondents in this study said that risky situations are best handled by asking others for help. However, at the point of access many encountered barriers. Some were labelled as 'drama queens' or 'challenging'. This may mean that they cannot rely on being listened to when they need to report a problem. The resources that individuals would need to enable them to direct their own protection thus become unavailable. We should therefore seek to increase the proportion of self-referrals by creating the space for individuals to report their concerns. Disabled and older adults who responded to the *No Secrets* consultation (Department of Health 2009a) are in favour of such an approach. They agreed that adults themselves should have more control in directing their own safeguarding. This book demonstrates that individuals are already aspiring towards increased levels of control in the absence of clear policy guidance that protects their right to take the lead. The introduction of more explicit guidance could create greater consistency.

This leads on to the next point. 'Challenging' behaviour, too, can simply be a way to communicate dissatisfaction (Beukelman and Mirenda 1998). Accordingly, it is worth asking why individuals have a need to express themselves in that way. Some individuals may begin to display 'challenging' behaviour as a result of violent experiences (Hingsburger

1995). Noting changes in behaviour and questioning their causes should therefore be a vital aspect of adult protection work. For instance, when Josie kicked the man who attempted to touch her breasts (see Chapter 5), this could be labelled as 'challenging behaviour'. Alternatively, it could be seen as a clumsy act of self-defence within a context where she cannot rely on being supported to find a more civilised solution. Family members and staff must be prepared to listen to such communication, whilst re-directing unacceptable behaviour and helping the person to find alternative ways of expressing themselves.

Furthermore, there needs to be zero tolerance of invasive and violent behaviour within segregated settings. This ensures that individuals are more likely to understand their right to report unsought violent or sexual intrusions and that they can rely on their concerns being taken seriously. For instance, any person in the UK who experiences sexual harassment in their workplace is entitled to seek support in line with the Employment Equality (Sex Discrimination) Regulations (HMSO 2005a). It would be unacceptable for segregated environments to have a different set of rules. Social environments must send out the unambiguous message that all forms of derogatory treatment and violence are unacceptable, in order to call a halt to processes that would otherwise lead to a continuum of violence.

Recommendations arising from the research: discussion

This book has pointed to a range of difficulties that arise from constructing people with learning difficulties as 'vulnerable'. First, 'vulnerability' is an inherent part of the human condition. It therefore makes little sense to label a particular population in that way. Second, the special status of 'vulnerable' adults leads to their differential treatment. Paradoxically this book has demonstrated that interventions that attempt to protect individuals actually reduce self-defence skills and that they often introduce further, situational risk factors. In other words, the social construction of 'vulnerability' leads to its actual creation. 'Vulnerability' has thus become a self-fulfilling prophecy. While the commitment of government bodies, professionals, individual staff and allies of disabled people to prevent and end sexual violence must be applauded, we should fundamentally re-think the way in which this support is provided, in order to plan interventions that have the potential to achieve the desired effect, instead of wasting good intentions on aggravating the problem. This book has made a range of suggestions on ways in which this can be facilitated.

References

Abbott, D. and Burns, J. (2007) 'What's love got to do with it?: Experiences of lesbian, gay, and bisexual people with intellectual disabilities in the United Kingdom and views of the staff who support them.' *Sexuality Research and Social Policy: Journal of NSRC 4*, 1, 27–39.

Abbott, D. and Howarth, J. (2007) 'Still off–limits? Staff views on supporting gay, lesbian and bisexual people with intellectual disabilities to develop sexual and intimate relationships.' *Journal of Applied Research in Intellectual Disabilities 20*, 2, 116–126.

Abery, B.H. (1999) 'Self-determination: A Roadmap to a Higher Quality of Life for Persons with Deafblindness.' In I. Assop (ed.) *A Training Curriculum for Parents and Interveners of Children and Youth who are Deafblind.* Ogden: University of Utah, Shy-Hi Institute.

Acock, A.C. and Ireland, N.K. (1983) 'Attribution of blame in rape cases: the impact of norm violation, gender, and sex-role attitude.' *Sex Roles 9*, 2, 179–193.

Adams, R.G. and Allan, G. (1998) *Placing Friendship in Context.* Cambridge: Cambridge University Press.

Adult Support and Protection (Scotland) Act (2007) UK: The Queen's Printer for Scotland.

Anderson, P. and Kitchin, R. (2000) 'Disability, space and sexuality: access to family planning services.' *Social Science and Medicine 51*, 8, 1163–1173.

Annison, J.E. (2000) 'Towards a clearer understanding of the meaning of "home".' *Journal of Intellectual and Developmental Disability 25*, 4, 251–262.

Arksey, H. and Knight, P.T. (1999) *Interviewing for Social Scientists: An Introductory Resource with Examples.* London: SAGE.

Armstrong, D. (2003) *Experiences of Special Education: Re-evaluating Policy and Practice through Life Stories.* London: Routledge Falmer.

Armstrong, F. (2002) 'The historical development of special education: humanitarian rationality or "wild profusion of entangled events"?' *History of Education: Journal of the History of Education Society 31*, 5, 437–456.

Armstrong, F. (2003) *Spaced Out: Policy, Difference and the Challenge of Inclusive Education.* Dordrecht; London: Kluwer Academic.

Association of Directors of Social Services (2005) *Safeguarding Adults – A National Framework of Standards for Good Practice and Outcomes in Adult Protection Work.* London: The Association of Directors of Social Services.

Atkinson, D. (1997) *An Auto/biographical Approach to Learning Disability Research.* Aldershot: Ashgate.

Atkinson, D. (2004) 'Research and empowerment: involving people with learning difficulties in oral and life history research.' *Disability and Society 19*, 7, 691–702.

Atkinson, D. and Williams, P. (1990) *Mental Handicap: Changing Perspectives: Workbook 2: Networks*. Milton Keynes: Open University Press.

Bankoff, G., Frerks, G. and Hilhorst, D. (2004) *Mapping Vulnerability: Disasters, Development and People*. London: Earthscan.

Barnes, C. (1990) *Cabbage Syndrome: The Social Construction of Dependence*. London: Falmer Press.

Barnes, C. and Mercer, G. (2010) *Exploring Disability (Second Edition)*. Oxford: Polity.

Barnett, O.W., Miller-Perrin, C. and Perrin, R.D. (2005) *Family Violence Across the Lifespan: An Introduction (Second Edition)*. London: SAGE.

Baron, S., Riddell, S. and Wilson, A. (1999) 'The secret of eternal youth: identity, risk and learning difficulties.' *British Journal of Sociology of Education 20*, 4, 483–499.

Bass, H. (1983) 'The development of an adult's imaginary companion.' *Psychoanalytic Review 70*, 4, 519–533.

Bauman, Z. (2000) *Liquid Modernity*. Cambridge: Polity Press.

Bayley, M. (1997) 'Empowering and Relationships.' In P. Ramcharan, G. Roberts, G. Grant and J. Borland (eds) *Empowerment in Everyday Life: Learning Disability*. London: Jessica Kingsley Publishers.

BBC News (2005) 'Stars pack Elton "wedding" party.' 22 December. Available at http://news.bbc.co.uk/go/pr/fr/–/1/hi/entertainment/4546670.stm, accessed on 1 October 2010.

Beck, U. (1992) *Risk Society: Towards a New Modernity*. London: Sage.

Becker, H., Stuifbergen, A. and Tinkle, M. (1997) 'Reproductive health care experiences of women with physical disabilities: a qualitative study.' *Archives of Physical Medicine and Rehabilitation 78*, 12, Supplement 5, S26–S33.

Beckett, A.E. (2006) *Citizenship and Vulnerability: Disability and Issues of Social and Political Engagement*. Basingstoke: Palgrave Macmillan.

Belsky, J. (1980) 'Child maltreatment: an ecological integration.' *American Psychologist 35*, 4, 320–335.

Beukelman, D.R. and Mirenda, P. (1998) *Augmentative and Alternative Communication: Management of Severe Communication Disorders in Children and Adults (Second Edition)*. Baltimore; London: P.H. Brookes Publishers.

Birch, M. and Miller, T. (2000) 'Inviting intimacy: the interview as therapeutic opportunity.' *International Journal of Social Research Methodology 3*, 3, 189–202.

Birrell, I. (2009) 'Mind your language: words can cause terrible damage.' 6 November. *The Independent*.

Blaikie, N. (2009) *Designing Social Research: The Logic of Anticipation (Second Edition)*. Cambridge: Polity.

Block, P. (2000) 'Sexuality, fertility, and danger: twentieth-century images of women with cognitive disabilities.' *Sexuality and Disability 18*, 4, 239–254.

Boeckmann, R.J. and Turpin–Petrosino, C. (2002) 'Understanding the harm of hate crime.' *Journal of Social Issues 58*, 2, 207–225.

Booth, T. and Booth, W. (1994) *Parenting under Pressure: Mothers and Fathers with Learning Difficulties*. Buckingham: Open University Press.

Booth, T., Simons, K. and Booth, W. (1990) *Outward Bound: Relocation and Community Care for People with Learning Difficulties.* Milton Keynes: Open University Press.

Boyd, D. (2007) 'Why Youth Love Social Network Sites: The Role of Networked Publics in Teenage Social Life.' *The John D. and Catherine T. MacArthur Foundation Series on Digital Media and Learning,* 119–142.

Braddock, D.L. and Parish, S.L. (2001) 'An Institutional History of Disability.' In G.L. Albrecht, K.D. Seelman and M. Bury (eds) *Handbook of Disability Studies.* London: SAGE.

Brammer, A. (2005) 'Learning Disability and the Law.' In G. Grant, P. Goward, M. Richardson and P. Ramcharan (eds) *Learning Disability: A Life Cycle Approach to Valuing People.* Maidenhead: Open University Press.

Brimblecomb, F.S.W., Tripp, J., Kun, D., Smith, R. *et al.* (1985) *The Needs of Handicapped Young Adults.* Exeter: Paediatric Research Unit, Royal Devon and Exeter Hospital.

Brisenden, S. (1989a) 'A charter for personal care.' In *Progress.* 16: Disablement Income Group.

Brisenden, S. (1989b) 'Young, gifted and disabled: entering the employment market.' *Disability and Society 4,* 3, 217–220.

Brisenden, S. (1998) 'Independent Living and the Medical Model of Disability.' In T. Shakespeare (ed.) *The Disability Reader – Social Sciences Perspectives.* London: Continuum.

Brown, H. (1994) '"An ordinary sexual life?": a review of the normalisation principle as it applies to the sexual options of people with learning disabilities.' *Disability and Society 9,* 2, 123–144.

Brown, H. and Thompson, D. (1997) 'The ethics of research with men who have learning disabilities and abusive sexual behaviour: a minefield in a vacuum.' *Disability and Society 12,* 5, 695–707.

Brown, H., Stein, J. and Turk, V. (1995) 'The sexual abuse of adults with a learning disability: report of a second two-year incidence survey.' *Mental Handicap Research 8,* 1, 3–24.

Brown, I. and Brown, R.I. (2009) 'Choice as an aspect of quality of life for people with intellectual disabilities.' *Journal of Policy and Practice in Intellectual Disabilities 6,* 1, 11–18.

Bulmer, M. (1987) *The Social Basis of Community Care.* London: Unwin Hyman.

Burton, M. and Kagan, C. (2006) 'Decoding "Valuing People".' *Disability and Society 21,* 4, 299–313.

Calderbank, R. (2000) 'Abuse and disabled people: vulnerability or social indifference?' *Disability and Society 15,* 3, 521–534.

Cambridge, P. (1996) *The Sexuality and Sexual Rights of People with Learning Disabilities: Considerations for Staff and Carers.* Plymouth: BILD Publications.

Cambridge, P. (2007) 'Editorial.' *Tizard Learning Disability Review 12,* 1, 2–3.

Central England People First (2010) 'Who are we?' Available at www.peoplefirst.org.uk/whoarewe.html, accessed on 5 June 2010.

Chamba, R., Ahmad, W., Hirst, M. and Lawton, D. (1999) *On the Edge: Minority Ethnic Families Caring for a Severely Disabled Child.* Bristol: Policy Press.

Channel 4 (2010) *The Sex Education Show.* Available at http://sexperienceuk.channel4.com/sex-education, accessed on 5 June 2010.

Chappell, A.L. (1992) 'Towards a sociological critique of the normalisation principle.' *Disability and Society 7*, 1, 35–51.

Chappell, A.L. (1994) 'A question of friendship: community care and the relationships of people with learning difficulties.' *Disability and Society 9*, 4, 419–434.

Chappell, A.L. (1998) 'Still Out in the Cold: People with Learning Difficulties and the Social Model of Disability.' In T. Shakespeare (ed.) *The Disability Reader: Social Science Perspectives.* London: Cassell.

Civjan, S.R. (2000) 'Making sexual assault and domestic violence services accessible.' *Impact 13*, 3, 10–11.

Cohen, S. (2002) *Folk Devils and Moral Panics: The Creation of the Mods and Rockers (Third Edition).* London: Routledge.

Cole, A., Williams, V. and Lloyd, A. (2007) *Having a Good Day? A Study of Community–Based Day Activities for People with Learning Disabilities.* London: Social Care Institute for Excellence.

Commission for Social Care Inspection (2007) *CSCI/SKILLS FOR CARE: Guidance on Common Induction Standards.* London: CSCI: Quality Performance and Methods Directorate.

CommuniGate (2010) *The Federation of Local Supported Living Groups.* Available at www.communigate.co.uk/lancs/spireprestonsupportedhousing/page2.phtml, accessed on 8 November 2010.

Community Care (2000) 'Support groups outraged as judge ditches consent code. 16 May. Available at www.communitycare.co.uk/Articles/2000/05/16/4697/Support-groups-outraged-as-judge-ditches-consent-code.htm, accessed on 1 October 2010.

Cooper, C., Sellwood, A. and Livingston, G. (2008) 'The prevalence of elder abuse and neglect: a systematic review.' *Age Ageing 37*, 2, 151–160.

Corteen, K. and Scraton, P. (1997) 'Prolonging "Childhood", Manufacturing "Innocence" and Regulating Sexuality.' In P. Scraton (ed.) *'Childhood' in 'Crisis'?* London: UCL Press.

Crossmaker, M. (1991) 'Behind locked doors: institutional sexual abuse.' *Sexuality and Disability 9*, 3, 201–219.

Crow, L. (1992) 'Renewing the social model of disability.' *Coalition News.* Available at www.leeds.ac.uk/disability-studies/archiveuk/Crow/Social%20model.pdf, accessed on 1 October 2010.

Dagnan, D., Look, R., Ruddick, L. and Jones, J. (1995) 'Changes in the quality of life of people with learning disabilities who moved from hospital to live in community-based homes.' *International Journal of Rehabilitation Research 18*, 115–22.

Dalley, G. (1988) *Ideologies of Caring.* Basingstoke: Macmillan.

Davies, C.A. and Jenkins, R. (1997) '"She has different fits to me": how people with learning difficulties see themselves.' *Disability and Society 12*, 1, 95–110.

DCODP (1986) *The Seven Needs Derby.* Derbyshire: Derbyshire Coalition of Disabled People.

Deakin, J. (2006) 'Dangerous people, dangerous places: the nature and location of young people's victimisation and fear.' *Children and Society 20*, 5, 376–390.

Deal, M. (2003) 'Disabled people's attitudes toward other impairment groups: a hierarchy of impairments.' *Disability and Society 18*, 7, 897–910.

Department of Health (1989) *Caring for People: Community Care in the Next Decade and Beyond.* London: HMSO.

Department of Health (2000) *No Secrets: Guidance on Developing and Implementing Multi-agency Policies and Procedures to Protect Vulnerable Adults from Abuse.* London: Department of Health.

Department of Health (2001) *Valuing People: A New Strategy for Learning Disability for the 21st Century: A White Paper.* Norwich: Stationery Office.

Department of Health (2005) *Independence, Well-being and Choice: Our Vision for the Future of Social Care for Adults in England.* Green Paper, London: Department of Health.

Department of Health (2007) *Valuing People Now: From Progress to Transformation – A Consultation on the Next Three Years of Learning Disability Policy.* London: Department of Health.

Department of Health (2008a) *Individual Budgets.* Available at www.dh.gov.uk/en/SocialCare/Socialcarereform/Personalisation/Individualbudgets/DH_4125774, accessed on 20 January 2009.

Department of Health (2008b) *Safeguarding Adults – A Consultation on the Review of the 'No Secrets' Guidance.* London: Department of Health.

Department of Health (2009a) *Safeguarding Adults – Report on the Consultation on the Review of 'No Secrets'.* London: Department of Health.

Department of Health (2009b) *Valuing People Now: A New Three-year Strategy for People with Learning Disabilities.* London: Department of Health.

Department of Health (2010a) Written Ministerial Statement. Government response to the Consultation on Safeguarding Adults: The Review of the No Secrets Guidance. Available at webarchive.nationalarchives.gov.uk/+/www.dh.gov.uk/en/Consultations/Responsestoconsultations/DH_111286, accessed on 1 October 2010.

Department of Health (2010b) *Clinical Governance and Adult Safeguarding.* London: Department of Health.

Dittmar, H. (2007) *Consumer Culture, Identity, and Well-being: The Search for the 'Good Life' and the 'Body Perfect'.* Hove: Psychology.

Douglas, M. (1986) *Risk Acceptability According to the Social Sciences.* London: Routledge and Kegan Paul.

Dowse, L. (2001) 'Contesting practices, challenging codes: self advocacy, disability politics and the social model.' *Disability and Society 16*, 1, 123–141.

Dowson, S. (1990) *Keeping it Safe: Self-advocacy by People with Learning Difficulties and the Professional Response.* London: Values into Action.

Dunn, M.C., Clare, I.C.H. and Holland, A.J. (2008) 'To empower or to protect? Constructing the 'vulnerable adult' in English law and public policy.' *Legal Studies 28*, 2, 234–253.

Edgerton, R.B. (1967) *The Cloak of Competence: Stigma in the Lives of the Mentally Retarded.* Berkeley: University of California Press.

Elley, S. (2008) *Sex and Relationship Education and Young Peoples' Lived Experiences.* Leeds: University of Leeds.

Emerson, E. and McVilly, K. (2004) 'Friendship activities of adults with intellectual disabilities in supported accommodation in Northern England.' *Journal of Applied Research in Intellectual Disabilities 17*, 3, 191–197.

Emerson, E., Robertson, J., Gregory, N., Hatton, C. *et al.* (2001) 'Quality and costs of supported living residences and group homes in the United Kingdom.' *American Journal of Mental Retardation 106*, 5, 401–415.

Everyman Campaign (2010) Information available at www.everyman-campaign.org, accessed on 1 October 2010.

Fehr, B.A. (1996) *Friendship Processes.* Thousand Oaks, California and London: Sage.

Feld, S.L. (1997) 'Structural embeddedness and stability of interpersonal relations.' *Social Networks 19*, 1, 91–95.

Finch, J. and Groves, D. (1980) 'Community care and the family: a case for equal opportunities? *Journal of Social Policy 9*, 4, 487–511.

Finkelstein, V. (1980) *Attitudes and Disabled people: Issues for Discussion.* New York: International Exchange of Information in Rehabilitation.

Finkelstein, V. (1991) 'Disability: An Administrative Challenge? (The Health and Welfare Heritage).' In M. Oliver (ed.) *Social Work: Disabled People and Disabling Environments.* London: Jessica Kingsley Publishers.

Finlay, W.M.L. and Lyons, E. (1998) 'Social identity and people with learning difficulties: implications for self-advocacy groups.' *Disability and Society 13*, 1, 37–51.

Finlay, W.M.L. and Lyons, E. (2001) 'Methodological issues in interviewing and using self-report questionnaires with people with mental retardation.' *Psychological Assessment 13*, 3, 319–335.

Finlay, W.M.L., Antaki, C. and Walton, C. (2008a) 'Saying no to the staff: an analysis of refusals in a home for people with severe communication difficulties.' *Sociology of Health and Illness 30*, 1, 55–75.

Finlay, W.M.L., Walton, C. and Antaki, C. (2008b) 'Promoting choice and control in residential services for people with learning disabilities.' *Disability and Society 23*, 4, 349–360.

Finney, A. (2006) Domestic Violence, Sexual Assault and Stalking: Findings from the 2004/05 British Crime Survey. Home Office Online Report. Available at www.homeoffice.gov.uk/rds/pdfs06/rdsolr1206.pdf, accessed on 1 October 2010.

Firth, L. (2009) *Tackling Child Abuse.* Cambridge: Independence Educational Publishers.

Fitzgerald, E. (2006) 'DNA may be key to catching rapist.' 14 September. *Manchester Evening News.*

Flatley, J., Kershaw, C., Smith, K., Chaplin, R. and Moon, D. (2010) *Crime in England and Wales 2009/10: Findings from the British Crime Survey and Police Recorded Crime.* London: Home Office.

Fleming, I. (1973) *Live and Let Die.* (Director: Guy Hamilton.)

Fleming, I. (1983) *Octopussy.* (Director: John Glen.)

Foundation for People with Learning Disabilities (2001) *Consultation on Setting the Boundaries: Reforming the Law on Sexual Offences – The Mental Health Foundation and Foundation for People with Learning Disabilities Response.* London: Foundation for People with Learning Disabilities.

Furey, E. and Niesen, J. (1994) 'Sexual abuse of adults with mental retardation by other consumers.' *Sexuality and Disability 12*, 4, 285–295.

Garbarino, J. and Eckenrode, J. (1997) *Understanding Abusive Families: An Ecological Approach to Theory and Practice (Second Edition).* San Francisco: Jossey-Bass.

Garside, R., Ayres, R., Owen, M., Pearson, V.A. and Roizen, J. (2001) '"They never tell you about the consequences": young people's awareness of sexually transmitted infections.' *International Journal of STD and AIDS 12*, 9, 582–588.

Gleeson, K. and Frith, H. (2004) 'Pretty in pink: young women presenting mature sexual identities.' In A. Harris (ed.) *All About the Girl: Culture, Power, and Identity.* London: Routledge.

Goffman, E. (1961) *Asylums: Essays on the Social Situation of Mental Patients and Other Inmates.* Garden City, NY: Doubleday.

Goffman, E. (1963) *Stigma: Notes on the Management of Spoiled Identity.* Englewood Cliffs, NJ: Prentice-Hall.

Goodley, D. (2000) *Self-advocacy in the Lives of People with Learning Difficulties: The Politics of Resilience.* Buckingham: Open University Press.

Gould, S.J. (1996) *The Mismeasure of Man (Revised and Expanded Edition).* London: Norton.

Green, K. (2008) 'EXCLUSIVE: Craig Dean returns to 'Hollyoaks'. 9 June. Available at www.digitalspy.co.uk/soaps/a98580/craig-dean-returns-to-hollyoaks.html, accessed on 1 October 2010.

Grieve, A., McClaren, S. and Lindsay, W.R. (2007) 'An evaluation of research and training resources for the sex education of people with moderate to severe learning disabilities.' *British Journal of Learning Disabilities 35*, 1, 30–37.

Guess, D., Benson, H.A. and Siegel-Causey, E. (1985) 'Concepts and issues relating to choice-making and autonomy among persons with severe disabilities.' *Journal of the Association for Persons with Severe Handicaps 10*, 79–86.

Gunn, M. (1994) 'Competency and Consent – The Importance of Decision-making.' In A. Craft (ed.) *Practice Issues in Sexuality and Learning Disabilities.* London: Routledge.

Guterman, N.B., Lee, Y., Lee, S.J., Waldfogel, J. and Rathouz, P.J. (2009) 'Fathers and maternal risk for physical child abuse.' *Child Maltreatment 14*, 3, 277–290.

Haavik, S.F. and Menninger, K. (1981) *Sexuality, Law, and the Developmentally Disabled Person: Legal Clinical Aspects of Marriage, Parenthood, and Sterilization.* Baltimore: Paul H. Brooks.

Hadrian, S. (2006) 'British Soap "Emmerdale" Takes On A Lesbian Teen Relationship.' 11 May. *After Ellen.* Available at www.afterellen.com/TV/2006/5/emmerdale. html?page=0,1, accessed on November 2010.

Hall, P. and Innes, J. (2010) 'Violent and Sexual Crime.' In J. Flatley, C. Kershaw, K. Smith, R. Chaplin and D. Moon (eds) *Crime in England and Wales 2009/10: Findings from the British Crime Survey and Police Recorded Crime.* London: Home Office.

Harris, P. (1995) 'Who am I? Concepts of disability and their implications for people with learning difficulties.' *Disability and Society 10*, 3, 341–351.

Hartnett, E., Gallagher, P., Kiernan, G., Poulsen, C., Gilligan, E. and Reynolds, M. (2008) 'Day service programmes for people with a severe intellectual disability and quality of life: parent and staff perspectives.' *Journal of Intellectual Disabilities 12*, 2, 153–172.

Health 24 (2009) 'Sex Survey 2009 – Romance blooms at the office.' Available at http://health.mweb.co.za/sex/Sex_survey/1253-4088,49634.asp, accessed on 1 October 2010.

Healthcare Commission (2006) *Joint Investigation into the Provision of Services for People with Learning Disabilities at Cornwall Partnership NHS Trust.* London: Healthcare Commission.

Healthcare Commission (2007) *Investigation into the Service for People with Learning Disabilities Provided by Sutton and Merton Primary Care Trust.* London: Healthcare Commission.

Heavy Load (2010) Stay up Late Campaign. Available at http://stayuplate.org, accessed on 1 October 2010.

Hendey, N. and Pascall, G. (1998) 'Independent living: gender, violence and the threat of violence.' *Disability and Society 13,* 3, 415–427.

Hester, M., Kelly, L. and Radford, G. (1996) *Women, Violence and Male Power: Feminist Activism, Research and Practice.* Buckingham: Open University Press.

Hevey, D. (1993) 'From self-love to the picket line: strategies for change in disability representation.' *Disability and Society 8,* 4, 423–429.

Hingsburger, D. (1995) *Just Say Know! – Understanding and Reducing the Risk of Sexual Victimisation of People with Developmental Disabilities.* Quebec, Canada: Diverse City Press.

Hirst, M. (2001) 'Trends in informal care in Great Britain during the 1990s.' *Health and Social Care in the Community 9,* 6, 348–357.

HMSO (1985) *Sexual Offences Act.* London: Her Majesty's Stationery Office.

HMSO (1989) *Children Act.* London: Her Majesty's Stationery Office.

HMSO (1998) *Human Rights Act.* London: Her Majesty's Stationery Office.

HMSO (2003) *Sexual Offences Act.* London: Her Majesty's Stationery Office.

HMSO (2004) *Children Act.* London: Her Majesty's Stationery Office.

HMSO (2005a) *Employment Equality (Sex Discrimination) Regulations.* London: Her Majesty's Stationery Office.

HMSO (2005b) *Mental Capacity Act.* London: Her Majesty's Stationery Office.

HMSO (2006) *Safeguarding Vulnerable Groups Act.* London: Her Majesty's Stationery Office.

Hoare, J. and Povey, D. (2008) 'Violent and Sexual Crime.' In C. Kershaw, S. Nicholas and A. Walker (eds) *Crime in England and Wales 2007/08 – Findings from the British Crime Survey and Police Recorded Crime.* London: Home Office Statistical Bulletin.

Holland, J., Ramazanoglu, C., Sharpe, S. and Thomson, R. (1992) *Pressured Pleasure: Young Women and the Negotiation of Sexual Boundaries.* London: The Tufnell Press.

Hollomotz, A. (2009) 'Beyond "vulnerability": an ecological model approach to conceptualizing risk of sexual violence against people with learning difficulties.' *British Journal of Social Work 39,* 1, 99–112.

Hollomotz, A. and The Speakup Committee (2009) '"May we please have sex tonight?" People with learning difficulties pursuing privacy in residential group settings.' *British Journal of Learning Disabilities 37,* 2, 91–97.

Hollway, W. and Jefferson, T. (1997) 'The risk society in an age of anxiety: situating fear of crime.' *The British Journal of Sociology 48,* 2, 255–266.

Holmbeck, G.N., Johnson, S.J., Wills, K., McKernon, W., Rolewick, S. and Skubic, T. (2002) 'Observed and perceived parental overprotection in relation to psychosocial adjustment in preadolescents with a physical disability: the mediational role of behavioral autonomy.' *Journal of Consulting and Clinical Psychology 70,* 1, 96–110.

Hughes, M. (2010) 'David Askew: a human tragedy and national scandal.' 12 March. *The Independent.*

Illich, I. (1977) 'Disabling Professions.' In I. Illich, I.K. Zola, J. McKnight, J. Caplan and H. Shaiken (eds) *Disabling Professions*. New York and London: Marion Boyars.

ITV (2010) *Emmerdale*. Available at www.itv.com/Soaps/emmerdale/default.html.

Jackson, M. (1987) '"Facts of life" or the Eroticisation of Women's Oppression? Sexology and the Social Construction of Heterosexuality.' In P. Caplan (ed.) *The Cultural Construction of Sexuality*. London: Routledge.

Jacobs, R., Samowitz, P., Levy, J.M. and Levy, P.H. (1989) 'Developing an AIDS prevention education program for persons with developmental disabilities.' *Mental Retardation 27*, 4, 233–237.

Jahoda, A. and Markova, I. (2004) 'Coping with social stigma: people with intellectual disabilities moving from institutions and family home.' *Journal of Intellectual Disability Research 48*, 8, 719–729.

Jehn, K.A. and Shah, P.P. (1997) 'Interpersonal relationships and task performance: an examination of mediating processes in friendship and acquaintance groups.' *Journal of Personality and Social Psychology 72*, 4, 775–790.

Jenkins, R., Davies, R. and Northway, R. (2008) 'Zero tolerance of abuse of people with intellectual disabilities: implications for nursing.' *Journal of Clinical Nursing 17*, 22, 3041–3049.

Jenkinson, J.C. (1993) 'Who shall decide? The relevance of theory and research to decision-making by people with an intellectual disability.' *Disability and Society 8*, 4, 361–375.

Jónasdóttir, A.G. (1988) 'Sex/gender, power and politics: towards a theory of the foundations of male authority in the formally equal society.' *Acta Sociologica 31*, 2, 157–174.

Jones, C. *et al.* (2004) *People with Learning Disabilities and Same Sex Relationships: Results of a Study Undertaken in Edinburgh in 2004*. Edinburgh: Partners in Advocacy.

Kaeser, F. (1992) 'Can people with severe mental retardation consent to mutual sex?' *Sexuality and Disability 10*, 1, 33–42.

Keilty, J. and Connelly, G. (2001) 'Making a statement: an exploratory study of barriers facing women with an intellectual disability when making a statement about sexual assault to police.' *Disability and Society 16*, 2, 273–291.

Kelly, L. (1988) *Surviving Sexual Violence*. Cambridge: Polity.

Kennedy, C. (2003) 'Legal and psychological implications in the assessment of sexual consent in the cognitively impaired population.' *Assessment 10*, 4, 352–358.

Kent, A., Massie, B. and Tuckey, L. (1984) *Day Centres for Young Disabled People*. London: RADAR.

Kidder, L.H., Boell, J. and Moyer, M. (1983) 'Rights consciousness and victimisation prevention: personal defence and assertiveness training.' *Journal of Social Issues 39*, 155–170.

Kinsey, A.C., Pomeroy, W.R. and Martin, C.E. (2003) 'Sexual behavior in the human male.' *American Journal of Public Health 93*, 6, 894–898.

Kishi, G., Teelucksingh, B., Zollers, N., Park-Lee, S. and Meyer, L. (1988) 'Daily decision-making in community residences: a social comparison of adults with and without mental retardation.' *American Journal of Mental Retardation 92*, 5, 430–435.

Kitzinger, C. and Frith, H. (1999) 'Just say no? the use of conversation analysis in developing a feminist perspective on sexual refusal.' *Discourse Society 10*, 3, 293–316.

Koller, R. (2000) 'Sexuality and adolescents with autism.' *Sexuality and Disability 18*, 2, 125–135.

Koskela, H. (1997) '"Bold Walk and Breakings": women's spatial confidence versus fear of violence.' *Gender, Place and Culture – A Journal of Feminist Geography 4*, 3, 301–320.

Levy, D.M. (1943) *Maternal Overprotection.* New York: Columbia University Press.

Lim, M., Hellard, M., Aitken, C. and Hocking, J. (2005) *Young People's Knowledge and Self Perceived Risk of Sexually Transmissible Infections.* Melbourne: Centre for Epidemiology and Population Health Research, Macfarlane Burnet Institute for Medical Research and Public Health.

Lindsey, L.L. (2005) *Gender Roles: A Sociological Perspective (Fourth Edition).* Upper Saddle River: Pearson Prentice Hall.

Lingsom, S. (2008) 'Invisible impairments: dilemmas of concealment and disclosure.' *Scandinavian Journal of Disability Research 10*, 1, 2–16.

Lloyd, V., Gatherer, A. and Kalsy, S. (2006) 'Conducting qualitative interview research with people with expressive language difficulties.' *Qualitative Health Research 16*, 10, 1386–1404.

Lord Chancellor's Department (1997) *Who Decides? Making Decisions on Behalf of Mentally Incapacitated Adults.* London: Stationery Office.

Lyden, M. (2007) 'Assessment of sexual consent capacity.' *Sexuality and Disability 25*, 1, 3–20.

Mansell, J. (2006) 'Deinstitutionalisation and community living: progress, problems and priorities.' *Journal of Intellectual and Developmental Disability 31*, 2, 65–76.

Mansell, J., Beadle-Brown, J., Cambridge, P., Milne, A. and Whelton, B. (2009) 'Adult protection: incidence of referrals, nature and risk factors in two English local authorities.' *Journal of Social Work 9*, 1, 23–38.

Marquis, R. and Jackson, R. (2000) 'Quality of life and quality of service relationships: experiences of people with disabilities.' *Disability and Society 15*, 3, 411–425.

McCain, M.N. (2006) 'Foreword.' In C. Vine and R. Alaggia (eds) *Cruel but not Unusual: Violence in Canadian Families.* Waterloo: Wilfrid Laurier University Press.

McCarthy, M. (1998) 'Whose body is it anyway? Pressures and control for women with learning disabilities.' *Disability and Society 13*, 4, 557–574.

McCarthy, M. (1999) *Sexuality and Women with Learning Disabilities.* London: Jessica Kingsley Publishers.

McCarthy, M. (2000) 'Consent, Abuse and Choices – Women with Intellectual Disabilities and Sexuality.' In T. Rannveig and K. Johnson (eds) *Women with Intellectual Disabilities: Finding a Place in the World.* London: Jessica Kingsley Publishers.

McCarthy, M. and Thompson, D. (1996) 'Sexual abuse by design: an examination of the issues in learning disability services.' *Disability and Society 11*, 2, 205–217.

McCarthy, M. and Thompson, D. (1997) 'A prevalence study of sexual abuse of adults with intellectual disabilities referred for sex education.' *Journal of Applied Research in Intellectual Disabilities 10*, 2, 105–124.

McCarthy, M. and Thompson, D. (1998) *Sex and the 3Rs: Rights, Responsibilities and Risks. A Sex Education Package for Working with People with Learning Difficulties.* Brighton: Pavilion Publishing.

McRobbie, A. (1978) 'Working Class Girls and the Culture of Femininity.' In Women's Studies Group (ed.) *Women Take Issue: Aspects of Women's Subordination.* London: Hutchinson.

McVilly, K.R., Stancliffe, R.J., Parmenter, T.R. and Burton-Smith, R.M. (2006a) '"I get by with a little help from my friends": adults with intellectual disability discuss loneliness.' *Journal of Applied Research in Intellectual Disabilities 19,* 2, 191–203.

McVilly, K.R., Stancliffe, R.J., Parmenter, T.R. and Burton-Smith, R.M. (2006b) 'Self-advocates have the last say on friendship.' *Disability and Society 21,* 7, 693–708.

Mencap (2001) *Behind Closed Doors – Preventing Sexual Abuse Against Adults with a Learning Disability.* London: Mencap.

Mencap (2007) *Bullying Wrecks Lives.* London: Mencap.

Mencap (2009a) *Independent living.* Accessed at www.mencap.org.uk/page.asp?id=1519. Link no longer active.

Mencap (2009b) *Mencap Response to Safeguarding Adults: A Consultation on the Review of the 'No Secrets' Guidance.* London: Mencap.

Milligan, M.S. and Neufeldt, A.H. (2001) 'The myth of asexuality: a survey of social and empirical evidence.' *Sexuality and Disability 19,* 2, 91–109.

Mitchell, D.T. and Snyder, S.L. (2001) 'Representations and its discontents – the uneasy home of disability in literature and film.' In G.L. Albrecht, K.D. Seelman and M. Bury (eds) *Handbook of Disability Studies.* London: SAGE.

Morin-Papunen, L.C., Martikainen, H., McCarthy, M.I., Franks, S., Javelin, M. and Pouta, A. (2006) 'O–33: should long-term hormonal contraception be reconsidered? Metabolic and inflammatory outcomes in women using oral contraceptives and the levonorgestrel–releasing intrauterine device in a general population.' *Fertility and Sterility 86,* 3, Supplement 1, S15–S15.

Morris, J. (1991) *Pride against Prejudice: Personal Politics of Disability.* London: Women's Press.

Morris, J. (1993) *Independent lives?: Community Care and Disabled People.* Basingstoke: Macmillan.

Morris, J. and Keith, L. (1995) 'Easy targets: a disability rights perspective on the "children as carers" debate.' *Critical Social Policy 15,* 44–45, 36–57.

Mullender, A. (1996) *Rethinking Domestic Violence: The Social Work and Probation Response.* London: Routledge.

Muller, A. and Mitchell, J.E. (2010) *Compulsive Buying: Clinical Foundations and Treatment.* London: Routledge.

Murphy, G.H. and O'Callaghan, A.L.I. (2004) 'Capacity of adults with intellectual disabilities to consent to sexual relationships.' *Psychological Medicine 34,* 7, 1347–1357.

Myhill, A. and Allen, J. (2002) *Findings 159: Rape and Sexual Assault of Women: Findings from the British Crime Survey.* London: Crown Copyright.

National Statistics (2008) 'Living arrangements.' Available at www.statistics.gov.uk/cci/nugget.asp?id=1652, accessed on 8 November 2010.

NHS Employers (2006) *NHS Employers Guidance – Bullying and Harassment.* Leeds: The NHS Confederation (Employers) Company Ltd.

NHS Lothian (2004) *Making Choices Keeping Safe – Policy and Practice Guidelines on Relationships and Sexual Wellbeing when Working with People with Learning Disabilities.* Edinburgh: NHS Lothian

Nirje, B. (1994 [1969]) 'The normalization principle and its human management implications.' (Classic article from 1969) *SRV–VRS: The International Social Role Valorization Journal 1,* 2, 19–23.

North Country Gazette (2007) 'DNA evidence links aide to rape of disabled woman.' 10 May. *North Country Gazette.*

O'Brien, J. (1994) 'Down stairs that are never your own: supporting people with developmental disabilities in their own homes.' *Mental Retardation 32,* 1–6.

O'Brien, J. (2005) 'Out of the institution trap.' In K. Johnson and R. Traustadóttir (eds) *Deinstitutionalization and People with Intellectual Disabilities: In and Out of Institutions.* London: Jessica Kingsley Publishers.

O'Brien, P., Thesing, A., Tuck, B. and Capie, A. (2001) 'Perceptions of change, advantage and quality of life for people with intellectual disability who left a long stay institution to live in the community.' *Journal of Intellectual and Developmental Disability 26,* 1, 67–82.

Office for Disability Issues (2007) 'Factsheet – Employment.' Available at www.officefordisability.gov.uk/docs/res/factsheets/Factsheet_Employment.pdf, accessed on 1 October 2010.

Office for Disability Issues (2008) *Independent Living: A Cross-government Strategy about Independent Living for Disabled People.* London: Office for Disability Issues.

Office for National Statistics (2009) *Labour Force Survey – Quarter 2.* University of Essex, Colchester: UK Data Archive.

Oliver, M. (1983) *Social Work with Disabled People.* London: Macmillan.

Oliver, M. (1989) 'Disability and Dependency: A Creation of Industrial Societies.' In L. Barton (ed.) *Disability and Dependency.* London: Falmer.

Oliver, M. (1992) 'Changing the social relations of research production?' *Disability, Handicap and Society 7,* 2, 101–114.

Oliver, M. (1996) *Understanding Disability: From Theory to Practice.* Basingstoke: Macmillan.

Oliver, M. (1997) 'Emancipatory Research: Realistic Goal of Impossible Dream?' In C. Barnes and G. Mercer (eds) *Doing Disability Research.* Leeds: The Disability Press.

Oliver, M. (2009) *Understanding Disability: From Theory to Practice (Second Edition).* Basingstoke: Palgrave Macmillan.

Oliver, M. and Barnes, C. (1998) *Disabled People and Social Policy: From Exclusion to Inclusion.* London: Longman.

Pain, R. (2000) 'Place, social relations and the fear of crime: a review.' *Progress in Human Geography 24,* 3, 365–387.

Parmenter, T.R. (2001) 'Intellectual Disability – Quo Vadis?' In G.L. Albrecht, K. Seelman, D. and M. Bury (eds) *Handbook of Disability Studies.* London: Sage Publications.

Patient UK (2009) 'Implanon® – The Contraceptive Implant.' Available at www.patient. co.uk/health/Implanon-The-Contraceptive-Implant.htm, accessed on 1 October 2010.

Pearson, D., Rouse, H., Doswell, S., Ainsworth, C. *et al.* (2001) 'Prevalence of imaginary companions in a normal child population.' *Child: Care, Health and Development 27*, 1, 13–22.

People First (2010) 'Why learning difficulty and not learning disability?' Available at www.peoplefirstltd.com/why-learning-difficulty.php, accessed on 29 June 2010.

People First Workers (1996) *Speaking Out for Equal Rights Workbook 2.* Buckingham: Open University Press, People First and Mencap.

Perkin, H.J. (1989) *The Rise of Professional Society: England since 1880.* London: Routledge.

Pitkeathley, J. (1989) *It's My Duty, Isn't It? The Plight of Carers in Our Society.* London: Souvenir Press.

Pound, C. and Hewitt, A. (2003) 'Communication Barriers: Building Access and Identity.' In J. Swain, S. French and C. Cameron (eds) *Controversial Issues in a Disabling Society.* Buckingham: Open University Press.

Powers, L., Wilson, R., Matuszewski, J., Phillips, A. *et al.* (1996) 'Facilitating Adolescent Self-determination: What Does it Take? In D.J. Sands and M.L. Wehmeyer (eds) *Self-determination Across the Lifespan: Independence and Choice for People with Disabilities.* London: Paul H. Brookes.

Pride London (2010) Pride London Home Page. Available at www.pridelondon.org, accessed on 27 August 2010.

Priestley, M. (1998) 'Constructions and creations: idealism, materialism and disability theory.' *Disability and Society 13*, 1, 75–94.

Priestley, M. (2003) *Disability: A Life Course Approach.* Oxford: Polity.

Priestley, M., Riddell, S., Jolly, D., Pearson, C. *et al.* (2010) 'Cultures of welfare at the front line: implementing direct payments for disabled people in the UK.' *Policy and Politics 38*, 2, 307–324.

Prime Minister's Strategy Unit (2005) *Improving the Life Chances of Disabled People.* London: Prime Minister's Strategy Unit.

Proctor, G. (2001) 'Listening to older women with dementia: relationships, voices and power.' *Disability and Society 16*, 3, 361–376.

Qualifications and Curriculum Authority (1999) 'About the Primary Curriculum – Statutory Requirements.' Available at http://curriculum.qcda.gov.uk/key-stages-1-and-2/Values-aims-and-purposes/about-the-primary-curriculum/index.aspx, accessed on 8 November 2010.

Rapley, M., Keirnan, P. and Antaki, C. (1998) 'Invisible to themselves or negotiating identity? The interactional management of "being intellectually disabled".' *Disability and Society 13*, 5, 807–827.

Rodgers, J. (1999) 'Trying to get it right: undertaking research involving people with learning difficulties.' *Disability and Society 14*, 4, 421–433.

Rogers, C. (2009) '(S)excerpts from a life told: sex, gender and learning disability.' *Sexualities 12*, 3, 270–288.

Rogers, C. (2010) 'But it's not all about the sex: mothering, normalisation and young learning disabled people.' *Disability and Society 25*, 1, 63–74.

Rousso, H. (1982) 'Special considerations in counselling clients with cerebral palsy.' *Sexuality and Disability 5*, 2, 78–88.

Ryan, J. and Thomas, F. (1987) *The Politics of Mental Handicap (Revised Edition)*. London: Free Association.

Sable, M.R., Danis, F., Mauzy, D.L. and Gallagher, S.K. (2006) 'Barriers to reporting sexual assault for women and men: perspectives of college students.' *Journal of American College Health 55*, 3, 157–162.

Sanders, K.Y. (2006) 'Overprotection and lowered expectations of persons with disabilities: the unforeseen consequences.' *Work: A Journal of Prevention, Assessment and Rehabilitation 27*, 2, 181–188.

Sanders, T. (2007) 'The politics of sexual citizenship: commercial sex and disability.' *Disability and Society 22*, 5, 439–455.

Saxton, M., Curry, M.A. and Gross, J. (2001) '"Bring my scooter so I can leave you" – a study of disabled women handling abuse by personal assistance providers.' *Violence against Women 7*, 4, 393–417.

Saxton, M., McNeff, E., Powers, L., Curry, M.A., Limont, M. and Benson, J. (2006) 'We're all little John Waynes: a study of disabled men's experience of abuse by personal assistants.' *Journal of Rehabilitation 72*, 4, 3–13.

Scambler, G. (1989) *Epilepsy*. London: Tavistock.

Shah, S. and Priestley, M. (2009) 'Home and away: the changing impact of educational policies on disabled children's experiences of family and friendship.' *Research Papers in Education, 25*, 2, 155–174.

Shakespeare, T. (1993) 'Disabled people's self–organisation: a new social movement?' *Disability and Society 8*, 249–264.

Shakespeare, T. (1994) 'Cultural representation of disabled people: dustbins for disavowal?' *Disability and Society 9*, 3, 283–299.

Shakespeare, T. (2000) 'The Social Relations of Care.' In G. Lewis, S. Gewirtz and J. Clarke (eds) *Rethinking Social Policy*. London: SAGE.

Shakespeare, T. (2006) *Disability Rights and Wrongs*. London: Routledge.

Shakespeare, T. and Watson, N. (2002) 'The social model of disability: an outdated Ideology?' *Research in Social Science and Disability 2*, 9–28.

Shakespeare, T., Gillespie-Sells, K. and Davies, D. (1996) *The Sexual Politics of Disability: Untold Desires*. London: Cassell.

Sheard, L. (2010) *Women's Use of Public Spaces and their Feelings of Personal Safety*. Leeds: University of Leeds.

Shevin, M. and Klein, N.K. (1984) 'The importance of choice-making for students with severe disabilities.' *Journal of the Association for Persons with Severe Handicaps 9*, 159–166.

Slater, C.J. (2004) 'Out of the Closet, into the Classroom – Gay Students, Teachers and Research Action.' In F. Armstrong and M. Moore (eds) *Action Research for Inclusive Education: Changing Places, Changing Practice, Changing Minds*. London: RoutledgeFalmer.

Smith, P.K. and Sharp, S. (1994) *School Bullying: Insights and Perspectives*. London: Routledge.

Sobsey, D. (1994) 'Sexual Abuse of Individuals with Intellectual Disability.' In A. Craft (ed.) *Practice Issues in Sexuality and Learning Disabilities*. London: Routledge.

Soukup, C. (2006) 'Hitching a ride on a star: celebrity, fandom, and identification on the world wide web.' *Southern Communication Journal 71*, 4, 319–337.

Spethmann, K. (2009) 'Friends with benefits: sex survey reveals success of meeting partners through friends.' Available at www.examiner.com/x-2856-Chicago-Singles-Guide-Examiner~y2009m3d19-Friends-with-benefits-Sex-survey-reveals-success-of-meeting-partners-through-friends, accessed on 1 October 2010.

Stancliffe, R.J. (2001) 'Living with support in the community: predictors of choice and self-determination.' *Mental Retardation and Developmental Disabilities Research Reviews 7*, 2, 91–98.

Stancliffe, R.J., Abery, B. and Smith, J. (2000) 'Personal control and the ecology of community living settings: beyond living-unit size and type.' *American Journal on Mental Retardation 105*, 6, 431–454.

Stars in the Sky (2010) Stars in the Sky: Dating and friendship service for adults with learning difficulties. Available at www.starsinthesky.co.uk, accessed 28 May 2010.

Stevens, S.E. (1996) 'Adolescents with physical disabilities: some psychosocial aspects of health.' *Journal of Adolescent Health 19*, 157–164.

Stevenson, C.J., Pharoah, P.E.D. and Stevenson, R. (1997) 'Cerebral palsy – the transition from youth to adulthood.' *Developmental Medicine and Child Neurology 39*, 336–42.

Stone, E. and Priestley, M. (1996) 'Parasites, pawns and partners: disability research and the role of non-disabled researchers.' *British Journal of Sociology 47*, 4, 699–716.

Strand, M., Benzein, E. and Saveman, B.-I. (2004) 'Violence in the care of adult persons with intellectual disabilities.' *Journal of Clinical Nursing 13*, 4, 506–514.

Swain, J. and French, S. (2000) 'Towards an affirmation model of disability.' *Disability and Society 15*, 4, 569–582.

Swain, P.A. and Cameron, N. (2003) '"Good Enough Parenting": parental disability and child protection.' *Disability and Society 18*, 2, 165–177.

Swango-Wilson, A. (2009) 'Caregiver perception of sexual behaviors of individuals with intellectual disabilities.' *Sexuality and Disability 26*, 2, 75–81.

The Children's Learning Disability Nursing Team (2009) *Puberty and Sexuality for Children and Young People with a Learning Disability (a supportive document for National Curriculum objectives)*. Leeds: NHS Leeds.

The National Autistic Society (2006) *B is for Bullied: The Experiences of Children with Autism and their Families*. London: The National Autistic Society.

The Royal College of Psychiatrists (2009) 'Specific learning disabilities: information for parents, carers and anyone who works with young people.' Available from www.rcpsych.ac.uk/mentalhealthinfo/mentalhealthand growingup/specificlearningdifficulties.aspx, accessed on 8 November 2010.

Thomas, C. (1999) *Female Forms: Experiencing and Understanding Disability*. Philadelphia: Open University Press.

Thompson, D. (1994) 'Sexual experience and sexual identity for men with learning disabilities who have sex with men.' *Changes 12*, 254–263.

Thompson, N. (2006) *Anti-discriminatory Practice (Fourth Edition)*. Basingstoke: Palgrave Macmillan.

Tolman, D.L. (2001) *Dilemmas of Desire: Teenage Girls talk about Sexuality*. London: Harvard University Press.

Turk, V. and Brown, H. (1993) 'The sexual abuse of adults with learning disabilities: results of a two year incidence survey.' *Mental Handicap Research 6*, 3, 193–216.

Union of the Physically Impaired Against Segregation (1976) *Fundamental Principles of Disability*. London: Union of the Physically Impaired Against Segregation.

United Nations (2006) *United Nations Convention on the Rights of Persons with Disabilities*. New York: United Nations General Assembly.

Walby, S. and Allen, J. (2004) *Home Office Research Study 276: Domestic Violence, Sexual Assault and Stalking: Findings from the British Crime Survey*. London: Home Office Research, Development and Statistics Directorate.

Walker, A., Maher, J., Coulthard, M., Goddard, E. and Thomas, M. (2001) *Living in Britain – Results from the 2001 General Household Survey*. Norwich: HMSO.

Walker, P. (2009) 'Police errors contributed to suicide of tormented mother Fiona Pilkington.' 28 September. *The Guardian*.

Wallis, N. (2007) 'My lifelong desire.' 15 January. *The Guardian*.

Walmsley, J. (1996) 'Doing what mum wants me to do: looking at family relationships from the point of view of people with intellectual disabilities.' *Journal of Applied Research in Intellectual Disabilities 9*, 4, 324–341.

Walmsley, J. (2005) 'Institutionalization: A Historical Perspective.' In K. Johnson and R. Traustadóttir (eds) *Deinstitutionalization and People with Intellectual Disabilities: In and Out of Institutions*. London: Jessica Kingsley Publishers.

Watson, N. (2002) 'Well, I know this is going to sound very strange to you, but I don't see myself as a disabled person: identity and disability. *Disability and Society 17*, 5, 509–527.

Weber, M. (1978 [1922]) *Economy and Society: An Outline of Interpretive Sociology* (trans. Ephraim Fischoff *et al.*). Berkeley: University of California.

Weeks, J. (1989) *Sex, Politics and Society: The Regulation of Sexuality since 1800 (Second Edition)*. London: Longman.

Wegner, L. and Flisher, A.J. (2009) 'Leisure boredom and adolescent risk behaviour: a systematic literature review.' *Journal of Child and Adolescent Mental Health 21*, 1, 1–28.

Wehmeyer, M.L. and Bolding, N. (2001) 'Enhanced self-determination of adults with intellectual disability as an outcome of moving to community-based work or living environments.' *Journal of Intellectual Disability Research 45*, 5, 371–383.

Wehmeyer, M.L., Sands, D.J., Doll, B. and Palmer, S. (1997) 'The development of self-determination and implications for educational interventions with students with disabilities.' *International Journal of Disability, Development and Education 44*, 4, 305–328.

Westcott, H. (1993) *Abuse of Children and Adults with Disabilities*. London: NSPCC.

Westcott, H. and Cross, M. (1996) *This Far and no Further: Towards Ending the Abuse of Disabled Children*. Birmingham: Venture Press.

Whelan, E. and Sparke, B. (1979) *Learning to Cope*. London: Souvenir Press.

Wiegerink, D.J.H.G., Roebroeck, M.E., Donkervoort, M., Stam, H.J. and Cohen-Kettenis, P.T. (2006) 'Social and sexual relationships of adolescents and young adults with cerebral palsy: a review.' *Clinical Rehabilitation 20*, 12, 1023–1031.

Wiley Adult Day Care Services (2009) 'Wiley Adult Day Care Services – An Introduction.' Available at www.youtube.com/watch?v=MKJ5sYveES4, accessed on 1 October 2010.

Williams, V. and Robinson, C. (2001) '"He will finish up caring for me": people with learning disabilities and mutual care.' *British Journal of Learning Disabilities 29*, 2, 56–62.

Windahl, S., Signitzer, B. and Olson, J.T. (2009) *Using Communication Theory: An Introduction to Planned Communication (Second Edition).* London: SAGE.

Wolfensberger, W. (1972) *The Principle of Normalization in Human Services.* Toronto: National Institute on Mental Retardation.

Wolfensberger, W. (2004 [1983]) 'Social Role Valorisation – A Proposed New Term for the Principle of Normalization.' In D.R. Mitchell (ed.) *Special Educational Needs and Inclusive Education: Major Themes in Education.* London: Routledge.

Women's Health Information (2009) 'Health Risks of Hormonal Birth Control.' Available at www.womens–health.co.uk/risks.html, accessed on 1 October 2010.

Wood, K. and Jewkes, R. (1998) *'Love is a Dangerous Thing': Micro-dynamics of Violence in Sexual Relationships of Young People in Umtata.* Cape Town: CERSA-Women's Health – Medical Research Council.

Woodin, S. (2006) *Social Relationships and Disabled People: The Impact of Direct Payments.* Leeds: University of Leeds.

World Health Organization (1996) *ICD–10 Guide for Mental Retardation.* Geneva: Division of Mental Health and Prevention of Substance Abuse.

World Health Organization (2001) *International Classification of Functioning, Disability and Health: ICF.* Geneva: World Health Organization.

Yamaki, C. and Yamazaki, Y. (2004) '"Instruments", "employees", "companions", "social assets": understanding relationships between persons with disabilities and their assistants in Japan.' *Disability and Society 19*, 1, 31–46.

Yeandle, S., Bennett, C., Buckner, L., Shipton, L. and Suokas, A. (2006) *Who Cares Wins: The Social and Business Benefits of Supporting Working Carers.* Sheffield: The University of Sheffield Hallam's Social Inclusion Centre.

Yool, L., Langdon, P.E. and Garner, K. (2003) 'The attitudes of medium-secure unit staff toward the sexuality of adults with learning disabilities.' *Sexuality and Disability 21*, 2, 137–150.

Zarb, G. (1992) 'On the road to Damascus: first steps towards changing the relations of disability research production.' *Disability and Society 7*, 2, 125–138.

Zola, I.K. (1982) *Missing Pieces: A Chronicle of Living with a Disability.* Philadelphia: Temple University Press.

Subject Index

Author Index